FALCON FREEWAY

FALCON FREEWAY

A BIG YEAR OF BIRDING ON A BUDGET

CHRISTIAN HAGENLOCHER

Illustrated by
ANDREW GUTTENBERG

THE BIRDING PROJECT

Dedicated to my mom, Liz.
Her unconditional love and support has blessed me and my family beyond measure.

CONTENTS

Preface   ix

1. The New Year   1
2. Lost   12
3. The Beginning   21
4. An Early Start   35
5. An 'EPIC' Big Year   47
6. Island Life   55
7. Learning   67
8. Spring Chickens   75
9. Florida   86
10. Come Back with New Birds   105
11. The Biggest Week   114
12. North by Northwest   122
13. Birding Attu   135
14. Weathered Out   150
15. Journey to Hog Island   155
16. Return to Alaska   167
17. Heat and Adversity   175
18. California   182
19. Rocky Mountain High   189
20. Heading Offshore   208
21. A Gambell   219
22. On Top of the World   246
23. Rails and Rice   280
24. Christmas Geese   286
25. The Year's End   299

Afterword	309
Acknowledgments	311
Big Year Numbers	315
Birding "Green" and Big Years	317
Tips for Living on the Road	321
Bird List	325
About the Author	349
About the Illustrator	351

PREFACE

Over the last 100 years the activity of watching birds has changed dramatically. In recent decades birdwatching, or "birding," has evolved speedily and grown both in popularity and practice. Improvements to technology have changed how we find and share birds, allowing us to learn more about their amazing and complex lives.

In the spring of 1953 Roger Tory Peterson, a celebrated naturalist and artist, traversed the continent with British friend James Fisher. Their 100-day cross-country trip targeted many premier birding destinations, which appear in many modern Big Year itineraries. This duo of natural historians wrote a fascinating book that incorporated their observations, interactions, and thoughts from this journey into an educational book titled *Wild America*. After reading this marvelous story, I was hooked.

There are many published books on Big Year birding adventures, but two classic stories stand above the rest. Kenn Kaufman's travels chronicled in *Kingbird Highway* epitomized budget-friendly birding. For Kenn, sacrificing the comfort of reliable transportation and knowing where his next meal was coming from was the price of admission for living out a year-long dream of birding across the continent. His story inspired my own journey, and my title is a tribute to not only this wonderful man's remarkable storytelling ability, but the example he has set for others. I owe him a debt of gratitude.

Times have changed, as has the fabric of our continent's biodiversity. Humans have impacted nearly every corner of the landscape, with increased carbon emissions, noise pollution, urban and agricultural developments, and careless disposal of waste. I quickly realized that while on my travels, I needed to be making observations and writing them down, to chronicle this point in our history. It is a rare intersection of human impact, changing landscapes, and an ecological conscience—trying to understand the landscape and lessen my own impact on it—while doing a very intensive carbon-hungry activity: birding.

This book is an imperfect attempt to share my story: what I've learned as well as what I saw, and the mindset I embraced to undertake such an adventure. Inspired by the journeys of Kenn Kaufman and Roger Tory Peterson, I have called my story *Falcon Freeway* to reflect what doing a Big Year on a budget means now in the 21st century. Hitchhiking is not as safe or culturally acceptable, highways are now multi-lane free-ways, and yet the spontaneous adventure and freedom of Big Year birding remains unchanged. Rather than using my photographs, I asked rising artist Andrew Guttenberg to create pen and ink illustrations, as a nod to the amazing artwork of Roger Tory Peterson and Kenn Kaufman, continuing a tradi-tional approach to a modern work.

With hope, I share this story with the intention to do for others what *Kingbird Highway* did for me: inspire, illuminate, and pave the way for the grand adventure ahead.

1

THE NEW YEAR

THE NEW YEAR came and went passing quietly just like any other night. There were no fireworks and no parties—no dressing up and getting down on the dance floor. In what had become the "new normal" for me—at 26, I swapped friends for family, carbonated beverages for water, and opted out of watching the televised ball drop in Times Square to go to bed early. I had a big day ahead—I was going birding.

Ever since I was young, I always slept well at my grandparents house, and this time was no exception. Although my 4am alarm came much earlier than I would have liked, I went upstairs to find that Papa and Nana (my mom's dad and stepmom) were already awake and more excited than I was for my birding trip into Canada. I took a sleepy sip of pomegranate juice that was set out on the counter, and was quite surprised to realize it had been spiked with ginger ale to wake up my taste buds. My sandwiches and snacks were already made and packed for a day on the road. I realized how lucky I was to have a supportive family.

A delicate layer of ice crystals covered the mossy boulders

and prehistoric-looking sword ferns that lined the steep drive-way. Thin shafts of moonlight shined down through dense boughs of cedars and firs, illuminating my bursts of warm breath in the frigid night air. Slightly winded from the walk, I examined the fragile crystals glistening in the moonlight, waiting for my body to catch up to my mind.

Perhaps only a minute passed, but the cold made it seem like an eternity. The audible thumping of my heartbeat soon slowed, and my ears could take in the stillness of the surrounding forest. I played the call of a Northern Saw-whet Owl. Silence answered each series of toots, my mind using the blank canvas of silence to paint images of what it wanted to hear. My pulse quickened as I imagined what creatures were out there in the woods.

Years ago, my uncle had walked up this same driveway to his car at night, and startled a mountain lion sitting atop a freshly-killed deer. As my imagination ran wild, the silence was broken by an unidentifiable noise, an eerie, unfamiliar sound. Was this the alternate call of a Northern Saw-whet Owl? Perplexed, I listened to the stillness for another long moment, and walked back down the hill to my car.

The first day of each new year is a special day for bird enthusiasts who identify as "listers"—people who keep a list of all the birds they see. On January 1st, the 'year list' resets to zero, and every new bird seen shares equal weight. I wondered what my first bird of the New Year was going to be.

As if conjured by a magician's spell, a Barn Owl appeared in my headlights, floating across the road like a floppy mari-onette suspended by invisible wires. The heart-shaped face glowed in the flood lights of my car—and then was gone. My year list increased from 0 to 1.

The year's first lesson in economical-birding presented itself as I surveyed the parking near the ferry terminal in Port

Angeles. Daily parking was $20 which was way too much—
maybe I could find a hotel? I found a Red Lion hotel, and
decided to ask if I could leave my car in their lot. After
explaining my planned foray into Canada, I flashed a wide
smile and was rewarded with a free parking slip for hotel
guests. With a "Happy New Year!" I was out the door with free
parking for the day.

The muffled chirps of House Sparrows came from somewhere near the edge of the parking lot as I unloaded my dad's
bike from the back of my car. It was almost $50 cheaper to walk
on the ferry than it was to take a vehicle into Canada. I took my
dad's mountain bike, which would allow me to cover more
ground in Canada—and see more birds.

I packed and double-checked my bags to be sure I had all
the necessities: my passport, extra batteries, GoPro mounts, and
directions to the last report of a Redwing—a rare thrush from
Asia that had been recently spotted in Victoria, and was the
"target bird" of my trip. After grabbing some extra snacks from
my car, I double-checked it was locked and pedaled off towards
the ferry terminal.

The sidewalk was slick with frost, making riding the bike a
bit too risky. As I dismounted and looked down, I noticed a
piece of driftwood on the pavement which had a message
penned on it in black sharpie: WE DID NOT INHERIT THE
EARTH, WE BORROWED IT FROM OUR GRANDCHILDREN. Next
to the driftwood was a round rock painted to look like the earth,
covered by a peace sign. I thought about this message and what
it meant.

I boarded the *M/V Coho*, on the Black Ball Line, which
sailed nonstop from Port Angeles to Victoria. I didn't really
have a plan, other than heading straight for the location where
the Redwing had been seen. I had a printout from Google
maps of "walking directions" and a backpack packed with

anything I might need if I ran into trouble—or didn't see the bird today.

Five months earlier, I left my teaching job in St. Louis and moved to Montana to pursue a project with a wildlife cameraman who had a long resume and a great deal of experience. We worked together for several months, advancing his current film into the final stages of completion and generating support through an extensive social media campaign. Together, we dreamed about doing bigger things, telling stories about birds that would inspire people and lead to tangible conservation of bird habitat. I was eager to learn everything I could about wildlife cinematography, video editing, and the production process.

As Christmas approached, the remaining work to be done on this film was well beyond my skill set. Before returning home to spend Christmas with my Seattle family, I was given an assignment to film rare birds—filling in the holes of his vast film library. I graciously accepted the small amount of money to fund my travel, which was to begin after the New Year. I had hoped to continue learning on-site with him in Montana, but figured I would only be gone a couple of weeks and then return to Montana to continue working together.

On the ferry, I stood outside in the brisk wind, hopeful that I might spot an unusual bird or a whale. The sun barely peeked over the eastern horizon, where the silhouette of Mt. Baker stood above the surrounding snow-covered peaks of the north Cascades.

A curious passenger came out and asked me what birds I had seen, and my long list I rattled off took her by surprise. She was a beginning birder, and had brought binoculars with her on the boat, so I spent some of the time pointing out the many birds I was seeing. We spotted rafts of scoters bobbing in the swells, and scores of gulls following the ferry. Before sailing into Canadian waters, I switched my phone on Airplane Mode, thinking nothing in the world could stop me from having a great day. I was dead wrong.

As the Canadian Border Patrol agent glanced from my passport to my face, his piercing eyes seemed to look right through me to the next person in line. He filled the whole booth, and his wide neck and short haircut made him look like an elite military operative. After thoroughly examining my documents, he peppered me with strategic questions, intending to trip me up. After the fifth question, he sensed my hesitation and I knew I had failed.

"We're going to need to ask you a few more questions, if you could go down that hallway right there someone will be with you shortly," he said. In Canada, "shortly" actually meant *after everyone else disembarks the vessel and we have time to talk with you.* I waited in a walled-off area, filled with posters full of useless information that nobody reads, like the signs in restaurant bathrooms with all of the rules for employee hand washing policies.

After waiting a while, a different agent called me into a windowless room. He took my passport, wallet, backpack, and cell phone, asking that I write down the phone passcode on a piece of paper. From my prior international travels, I knew that handing my passport to anybody who then walked away with it was a bad thing. I felt helpless. I stared hard at the two-sided glass window, wondering if someone was watching me through the other side. Was I worried? Not really. The worst that could happen was that I would miss the bird, or be sent back to the U.S. No big deal. It was just a bird. I wondered if that kind of attitude was acceptable were I ever to do a Big Year. The bird would either be there when I arrived, or it wouldn't be. Stressing out about Immigration was not something I'd ever do. So I just sat there, entertained by my own thoughts about the situation. Eventually my bag was returned, and the agent I had spoken with called me into a room, where I brought everything except my bike.

"Is there anything sharp that could hurt me inside your bag?" he asked.

"Yes," I replied. "I have a small knife in the top pocket of my backpack."

"Any needles, or other sharp objects?"

"No, just my knife." I watched him unpack my bag, carefully inspecting the items inside. He handed my items back one by one. As he handed me my spotting scope he asked, "What's the purpose of your visit to Canada?"

"Personal. I'm birdwatching."

"What are you trying to see?" I held back the first comment that came to me—*birds, obviously...*

"A Redwing. It's a rare thrush from Asia."

This particular thrush is typically found across Europe and Asia, yet some individuals can get off-course and end up in North America by mistake. According to reports from the American Birding Association's (ABA) Rare Bird Alert, one was being seen in a neighborhood in Victoria almost daily.

His stoic look didn't change, amidst my skepticism that he even knew what a Redwing was. "And it's been seen in Canada?" I detected a hint of curiosity in his voice. "What does it look like?"

"It has..." I paused before describing the bird in technical terms, using jargon like '*supercilium.*' "Here, let me show you the picture on my phone." I wasn't going to impress or confuse him more by listing off the bird's field marks, or comparing it to any similar bird like an American Robin. I pulled my phone back towards me across the counter and in a few taps, flashed an image I had screen captured of the bird. The Redwing wasn't in my bird guide on my iPhone since it wasn't normally found in North America. I had taken screen-shots to be sure I could reference the field marks, or character-istics to look for. I went on to explain to him how I'd heard of the bird, how I knew where it was, and what my plan was for finding it.

"Here's my situation," I explained. "I don't know how long I'll be in Canada. If I see the bird today, I'll be on the 4pm boat back to the US. If I don't, I'll spend the night somewhere and find the bird tomorrow. I don't know anybody in Canada, or the person whose yard the bird is in. I just have these printed direc-tions." The uncertainty in my voice was palpable.

Seemingly satisfied with my responses, he handed my wallet back to me after going through all of the contents. I knew immediately when they took my wallet where this conversation would eventually lead.

"Do you carry a firearm? Why don't you have it with you today? Are you aware of Canada's laws about firearms?" The questions were endless. They clearly had found my CCW (Carrying a Concealed Weapons) card in my wallet. The barrage of questions continued. I responded as politely as I could. I wasn't carrying a weapon with me. I knew Canada's laws, and could have brought a handgun with me. The rules state that I can bring in a firearm, I just didn't want the hassle of the extra paperwork or questions. Obviously that came free of charge anyways. I made a conscious choice to leave it locked at home because I didn't need it to go birding in Canada.

At this point, all of the other passengers had disembarked and a crowd of agents had gathered around us, intrigued by my birding quest (or gun knowledge?). After a final barrage of ques-tions, they cautioned me about staying in the country too long. I had been determined to be a passable immigrant, at least for the day—I was free to go.

Despite having printed Google Maps directions to follow, the instructions gave me a pedestrian route, and I was on a bike. Naturally, I improvised, determining the route that I should take based on the map and what I was seeing. I could ride in the road like a car, and if I was careful, make up for lost time. This didn't work, and soon I was lost. Instinctively, I opened my phone, forgetting I'd put it on airplane mode. A quick detour to Starbucks solved that issue; I connected to their wifi, downloaded a barrage of texts, notifications, and an email saying the Redwing had been spotted earlier in the morning. *Great,* I thought, *of course it would be seen while I was held up.* I got my bearings, and headed out, biking as swiftly as I could. I stuck to sidewalks, not wanting my ignorance of Canadian traffic laws to land me another interview with Canadian authorities. I hopped curbs, cut across parking lots, and wove through trails until I reached the neighborhood where the Redwing had been reported.

I spent the next three hours and forty-five minutes searching for the Redwing. A small nearly-black falcon streaked overhead—surely Merlin of the *suckleyi* subspecies. I also noted that crows here were slightly smaller than the American Crows I was used to seeing; these birds were surely "pure" Northwestern Crows.

Five hours passed since the latest morning Redwing report, despite the presence of many other birders searching. Then, without warning—it appeared. Alongside a small group of birders, I got great looks at this beautiful bird. Just as suddenly as it had materialized, it flew around the corner of some condominiums and disappeared into the maze of houses. I glanced at my phone—the ferry was to leave in 59 minutes. Rather than risk spending the night in Canada, I jumped on the bike and raced toward the ferry, sacrificing my intent to film the bird in hopes I could do better the next time.

⬤

Back home in Washington, I gathered all of my film equipment and packed the car for the road trip ahead. My plan was simple: chase as many rare birds as possible and film them, awaiting further instructions from my employer. I would drive all day, sleep in my car, and eat as much food as my parents would let me take from home. I would only have to spend money on gas, and could travel thousands of miles on a relatively small budget.

I packed an assortment of camping gear, my Yeti cooler, and cleaned out my parent's pantry of dry goods. I had a two-week supply of canned fruit, applesauce, granola bars, pasta, and crackers. My parents' Costco membership came in handy for picking up bulk quantities of a few last-minute snacks for the road.

Much of the drive passed uneventfully. My girlfriend Teresa called. We had been dating long-distance for less than a year, and regular phone conversations allowed us both to keep learning more about each other and talk about our plans for the future.

We made some small talk as I drove along, trying to explain what exactly I was doing. It didn't really make sense to me, so explaining it to someone else wasn't easy. Essentially, I had been given some money to drive around and film birds, so I went with it. I couldn't answer all of her questions about when I would make it to St. Louis next, and where I thought things were going with any relationship.

I had a lot to think about as I drove south along Interstate 5 towards California. The radio dial sat untouched, and the hours passed in silence. For a while, this silence was uncomfortable—painful even. I was afraid of my own thoughts. The *what if's, you can't,* and other negative suggestions began to creep in. I realized that fear lay at the root of many of these uncomfortable thoughts. I tried to tease out these thoughts. *What was I afraid of?* My mind wandered, as I looked out the window. I thought about Montana, my family, my future, and Teresa.

Slow down. The thought came to me quietly at first, but louder the second time. SLOW DOWN! I listened. I hadn't thought much about the cars behind me on the two-lane highway. It seemed like everyone else wanted to go faster than me—already I was driving just over the speed limit, so I obediently followed this feeling and slowed down, allowing the cars to pass. Several cars zoomed ahead, jockeying for position and passing one another as they flew down the road and out of sight.

Minutes later, I came up and over a rise and stepped on my brakes hard. Black skid marks arced across both lanes and a trail of broken tail lights and bumper pieces littered the road, leading to a cluster of cars blocking both southbound lanes in a multi-car accident. Many of the cars that had passed me earlier now sat motionless in the road, some facing the wrong direction. I reacted quickly, steering around the debris and exiting on the off-ramp which was fortuitously located before the jumble of cars. I got back on the highway immediately after the accident. Nobody appeared hurt, and I noticed someone on their phone in the car; I was sure emergency services had already been called.

My heart began to beat out of my chest as I considered what may have transpired, had I not listened to the voice within. I tried to silence the voice in the back of my head. *If I hadn't slowed down, maybe I would have been in that pileup...* Shaken but grateful, I put hundreds of miles more behind me before calling it a night. This early experience provided an immediate lesson in for me to see the benefits of listening to my inner voice. I had plenty of times to exercise the muscle of humble listening, which would become a foundation for my decision making in the months ahead.

2

LOST

I LEANED up against the old, six-drawer metal desk, left to rust atop a rocky hillside outside the town of Alpine, Texas. Nearly 35 years ago, students from Sul Ross University hauled the huge desk up a mountain, and dubbed it the Writing Desk. An online travel blog stated that it was a nice hike up to the top of the hill where the abandoned desk sat—a place for "reflection and contemplation." The same website claimed a notebook to be hidden in one of the drawers, where only those who knew to look could find. The basic online instructions regarding its location went something like this: "Hike up the hill to a pile of rocks. Keep following the obvious trail to The Desk." Instead, I'd found the desk after wandering away from the less-than-obvious trail, across the scrubby terrain of rocks, cacti, and other pointy plants, and past a dead tree decorated with rusted bicycles.

I sat awkwardly behind the desk in a plastic blue chair, quasi-alone on the hill as the setting sun bathed the flat landscape in front of me in warm light. This was a spot for contemplation, so reluctantly I imbibed. I pondered the harsh contrast within the beautiful desert landscape, until the irony was lost, blown away by the swirling dust storm of my thoughts which had been brewing all day. Confusion, guilt, doubt, and fear crept back into my thoughts. I leaned back in the chair as I closed my eyes and winced, in preparation to mentally relive the events of the day that led me here to the desk.

The morning began rather unceremoniously, when I woke up in a Walmart parking lot in El Paso, nearly 220 miles away from the uncomfortable plastic chair I sat in. I had neglected to set an alarm on my iPhone, knowing that the crescendo of activity outside would be enough to get me going. I'd parked my Subaru Outback away from the front entrance, yet in a well-lit area pointed toward the exit, if I needed to make a hasty departure. I'd learned a thing or two about car camping in Walmart parking lots, having slept in the back of my car for the previous nine nights. After changing clothes and eating a package of S'mores Pop Tarts, I pulled straight into Monday-morning traffic on Interstate 10.

As I drove back into cell service, my phone buzzed--interrupting my thoughts and tempting me with new notifications. A voicemail from the Montana producer was among the missed calls. I was relieved; I hadn't heard from him in a couple of days, and was hoping he'd called to say we had some funding available to keep me on the road. The voicemail rambled, lamenting an unsigned contract, and quite unprofessionally severed our mutually agreed upon understanding of our partnership. This seemed to me like a conversation that needed to be had over the phone, so I called him back—no answer. I knew he was home; he just called me from the landline! *Seriously?* I was upset—this wasn't how things were supposed to go! I considered making a couple of phone calls to people who had pledged additional financial support to our project he wasn't aware of, but decided to wait—maybe he would change his mind. In stunned silence I continued down the highway, wondering what I would do. Despite knowing exactly where I was on the map, I was lost.

I waited all afternoon for a him to call me, so I could clarify my intentions and get this straightened out. The call never came, and slowly it dawned on me that it never would. I silently analyzed my situation for hours, alone with my thoughts for hundreds of miles until I eventually broke the silence to call my girlfriend Teresa. As a registered nurse, Teresa was very good at patiently listening, then offering calm and reassuring words of support. I explained how I was now unemployed in the middle of nowhere in Texas, using my hard-earned money to affordably reach the next rare bird to film for a guy who no longer wanted my help. After I blurted out my frustrations and concerns, Teresa mentioned her roommate Amanda was also in Texas on a road trip to Big Bend National Park. Coincidentally, Amanda was in Alpine, the next large town on the road I was on. Teresa knew I could benefit from some interaction with others, and after a quick exchange of texts, I was on my way to meet Amanda and her boyfriend Andrew for lunch at a local restaurant.

The steaming plate of food was a welcome distraction for the five minutes it took me to inhale it. In between bites I explained what had just happened. I was showered with sympathy, which made it that much worse. I hated sympathy, and it definitely didn't make me feel better by talking about how much this situation sucked. After picking at the leftover carnage from the plate following the great breakfast burrito massacre, I didn't know what I wanted to do next. I was still hungry, but didn't want to order more food, as this meal had cost more than I'd spent on any meal on the road so far. I had cheaper food in the car I could always eat later.

Finishing my meal so quickly allowed me to tell some

stories. I recounted some details about my road trip and everything that had happened since the beginning of the year. I told the story of carrying my dad's bicycle onto a ferry and being detained by Canadian border authorities. I recounted the marathon-drive from Washington to southern California while narrowly escaping a multi-car pileup on the freeway.

I had learned the hard way how to sleep in the back of my car, in rest areas and shopping mall parking lots. I'd gained entry onto an active military base, survived a southern Arizona snowstorm, and hiked into steep mountain canyons, carefully checking every rock crevice for rattlesnakes. In the past two weeks, I'd covered more ground and seen over 200 species of birds, including rarities such as the Sinaloa Wren, Rufous-capped Warbler, Streak-backed Oriole, Rufous-backed Robin, and Redwing.

When they finished eating, Amanda and Andrew paid for my lunch—a gesture of kindness that neither knew how much it meant to me at the time. Before my unplanned stop in Alpine I intended on driving until well after dark—Laredo was another six hours away, and somehow the afternoon had slipped away unnoticed. Amanda and Andrew convinced me to join them for this weird-sounding hike to a desk on a hill they had read about online. I wasn't quite ready to leave their company and return to hours of sitting in solitude, trapped with my own thoughts about a now-uncertain future—so I agreed.

Flirty giggles floated through the scrubby landscape, and I opened my eyes returning to the present moment. The warm light of the setting sun painted the hills in vivid colors, bathing the desert in beauty and light. The blue chair creaked as I leaned forward, placing all four chrome legs in the dusty soil. Amanda and Andrew returned to the desk, walking hand in hand, and their contagious laughter helped dissolve the haze of my own thoughts.

Hidden deep in the dented drawers was a tattered notebook and a Sharpie. As many had done before us, we took turns
adding our inscriptions to this unique piece of local folklore,
before making our way down the trail as the sun dipped below
the mountaintops in the distance.

Amanda and Andrew had rented a cozy small apartment
near the main street in downtown Alpine, before their trip into
Big Bend National Park the following day. I knew I should hit
the road, but not before cleaning up. I saw an opportunity to
shower for free before I left town. It had been several days since
I stood under running water, and I tried to wash away the self-
pity, doubt, and fear along with the caked dust and sunscreen
smudges. It was hard to let go of my personal feelings, but
surrendering the fear I had about the unknown provided a brief
moment of clarity. Without the fear, I realized, all that was left
was my love for birds and adventure. There were plenty more
birds to be found, and it was time to hit the road.

⸺

Silently the hours passed, until the town of Alpine was nearly
500 miles in my rearview mirror. I considered turning on the
radio as a distraction, but I wasn't yet ready to escape the
purgatory of my own thoughts. The clarity I had experienced
earlier had vanished, replaced by an incoming tide of upsetting
thoughts.

Like a tempestuous sea, waves of anger and frustration
washed over me. I thought about everything all at once, then
nothing at all. I was hurt, then afraid, then numb. Hours
passed, the angry thoughts subsided, and like the shifting
currents I was confronted with confusion and blame. I sat
stoically behind the wheel, enduring my emotions over
hundreds of miles. *Why do I feel this way?* I confronted each

thought, rather than ignoring it. As I unpacked each feeling and concern, I realized again that fear was the culprit behind every grievance. Every. Single. One. With this truth exposed, I began to settle down, and started to notice things beyond my windshield.

The highway was lined with a vertical forest of undead trees. Every 300 feet stood the skeleton of a pine trunk, commissioned to hold a string of suspended wires in the air. Like a drunken musical staff, these wires dipped at the lowest point in between each pole, then rose back up into the outstretched arms of the next. In the distance, these poles merged together in an optical illusion, a crowded army rising from a shimmering sheet of water that never grew closer.

At 60 miles per hour, the wood and wire transformed into a three-dimensional piece of music. I assigned notes to each power line, and envisioned the music unfold as each span between the telephone poles became a measure, separated by wooden bar lines. As the wires rose and fell, perched birds became notes on this living piece of music. Two doves sitting side by side were eighth notes, a single kestrel was a whole note, and a kingbird sprinkled in a staccato note unexpectedly. A trio of doves on the top wire, followed by a mockingbird on the bottom wire composed the introductory notes to the first movement of Beethoven's Fifth Symphony.

I could identify many of the avian silhouettes with relative ease against the bright morning light. It was second nature for my brain to automatically put an ID on most of the shapes, though doing so was an acquired skill that came with lots of practice. The medium-sized raptor with a long tail was a Harris's Hawk. All of the recurring kingbird clones were surely Western Kingbirds. In high school, while my friends were having fun going to movies and concerts, I was watching weather reports, and trying to go birding at migrant traps when the warbler diversity peaked. My iPod had more bird calls than regular songs. Years of studying field guides and range maps was finally being put to the test.

I composed music with birds on the wires for as long as the birds lasted, and then tried to identify the roadkill I passed. Left to my own thoughts, I made a list of things I was grateful for. When I ran out of ideas, my mind wandered and tolerate the silence. Like a new shoe that's uncomfortable at first but breaks in with time, the silence began to feel more comfortable the further south I traveled.

Noisy flocks of Red-crowned Parrots flew over the suburban streets of Harlingen to roost for the night as I passed by. The Rio Grande Valley in south Texas is an ecological paradise for birders. With a nearly tropical climate, many of the plants and animals spread across the towns of McAllen, Weslaco, and Brownsville reminded me of my past trips to the tropics.

This region is made up of a patchwork of native thornscrub habitat—Tamaulipan tentacles that extend northwards from Central America and Mexico to grip the southern tip of Texas. Home to many unique tropical species of flora and fauna, entering southern Texas is almost like traveling further south to the tropics.

The resulting bird life of the Rio Grande Valley is incredible; cryptically-patterned Common Pauraques rest next to trails—nearly invisible to the passerby. Through the scrub, calls from the vibrant Green Jay and Plain Chachalacas can often be heard before they are seen. Great Kiskadees and other tropical birds will remind any birder why the Rio Grande Valley is such an amazing place to see birds.

During my childhood I lived only a couple of hours up the

coastline from this ecological paradise. My Dad was a pilot for the US Navy, and flew in a squadron based in Corpus Christi. Despite only being three years old, I have distinct memories from this time.

My earliest recollections from living in Texas help to explain my fascination with the natural world. I remember being carried around the Museum of Natural History in Corpus Christi. I vividly remember searching each zoological exhibit for a small mouse, hidden among the taxidermy wildlife dioramas. Sometimes the mouse was concealed among oak leaves and acorns on the forest floor, or nearly underfoot a lion or giraffe in the African savanna. It was a scavenger hunt—a search for an animal within the surrounding environment. I loved the search just as much as the thrill of finding it (often with the help from my parents). I believe this early experience, together with reading numerous *iSpy* and *Where's Waldo?* books, prepared me for a life of seeking and finding.

The cryptic camouflage of a roosting Common Pauraque can make spotting this species quite difficult

South Texas was rich in birding sites, with many dedicated wildlife preserves and refuges available for me to explore. Amid sprawling farmland, housing developments, and urban sprawl, these remnants of native habitat were well-marked and many were publicly accessible. Laguna Atascosa National Wildlife Refuge, together with the Lower Rio Grande Valley National Wildlife Refuge, protects over 100,000 acres of habitat across South Texas. The endangered Ocelot roams free through the tangled undergrowth, virtually undetected by the thousands of people who cross the refuge to South Padre Island for a day at the beach.

While living in Corpus, we'd often visit the beaches of South Padre Island. My parents knew this was the perfect spot to run all of the boundless energy out of a toddler. I played in the sand, splashed in the surf, and chased seagulls along the beach. My fascination with birds began at this time, yet it wasn't exclusive. I still loved fire trucks, dinosaurs, and chasing birds. However, chasing birds along the beach was a futile, yet at a young age marked the beginning of my never-ending pursuit of birds.

3

THE BEGINNING

I ARRIVED at the Frontera Audubon Center just after sunrise. This 15-acre oasis in urban Weslaco, Texas would be my first introduction to birding the Lower Rio Grande Valley. This thicket of native habitat had attracted rare birds in the past, including a White-throated thrush and a skulking Blue Mockingbird, both normally found in Mexico.

The only car in the empty parking lot, my Subaru Outback looked as out of place and lost as I felt. I wasn't even sure how to get inside, or even when the center opened. I'd never been here before, and realized that perhaps I'd been too hasty with this chase. Picking up my iPhone, I searched recent eBird reports for any helpful information about the bird I had come here to see—the Crimson-collared Grosbeak.

In 2002, the Cornell Lab of Ornithology created eBird, an online database of bird sightings submitted by users around the world. This was a revolutionary new tool for bird-finding while in the field, and was free to anyone who created an account. With eBird, I could easily log in and check to see recent reports at any birding location I visited anywhere in the world.

Scrolling through other birders' submitted checklists, I found photos of the grosbeak. Like other cardinal-like birds in its family, the Crimson-collared Grosbeak has a thick-set triangular bill, used for crushing seeds and fruits. This particular bird was a female, and sported a dull greenish plumage and a dark hood, covering her face and throat.

Some eBird checklists included comments, which I hoped would be helpful to me in searching for this bird. People's descriptions from the day prior- "perched high in thickets opposing main feeding station," didn't mean anything to me as an out-of-town birder. Older comments like 'continuing bird' and 'seen by large group' were just as unhelpful.

I got out and began walking around the parking lot, noticing the closed gate and a sign that read "CLOSED MONDAYS" made me grateful that I didn't come on a Monday. According to the hours it wasn't open yet, but I noticed a man inside the building, and politely knocked on the window and he walked over and opened the door.

"Good morning!" I tried to make my greeting sound cheerful, hoping to mask the frustration I felt for not doing the proper research and showing up early at a place I couldn't get into yet. "Can I go birding here?"

He tried his best in broken English to say they weren't open yet, and he was just a groundskeeper. Switching to Spanish, I politely asked if I could pay him and go in early. He smiled, and told me to wait; he would make a phone call.

While he was talking on the phone, I remembered the years of high school Spanish I suffered through—doing my best at the time but earning less than average grades. Outside the classroom, the language clicked for me. Two of my soccer teammates from Guatemala and Ecuador spoke Spanish with me on the field, which eventually translated into the classroom. In college, I tested out of the minimum Spanish requirement by using enough slang words in my interview that the professor thought I had lived in Guatemala! I still elected to take Spanish in college, with a desire to continue traveling to Spanish-speaking countries in search of tropical birds.

The gardener hung up the phone and agreed to let me in, but it would cost me five dollars. This was the last bill in my wallet, representing the end of the funds I'd been given to film birds on this road trip. I'd worked so diligently over the last two weeks to manage money, cut corners, and just "keep on going." I knew that this moment would come, and in my mind, this was the end of my birding funds and conclusion to my adventure. *At least I would go out doing something I enjoy* I thought to myself as I handed over a $10 bill for the $5 admission. He told me to return later when the Audubon staff could give me the correct change.

I wandered around the maze of winding trails through a seemingly impenetrable thicket of plants I couldn't name. I had the entire place to myself. Greeted by unfamiliar birdsong, I moved at a snail's pace, standing still until movement caught my eye. Standing motionless, I waited until the feathered blur paused in an opening among the brush, long enough to catch a glimpse of any field mark I could use to identify it.

Plain Chachalacas ran dinosaur-like through the undergrowth, climbing up in bushes and feeding on insects. The haunting calls of White-tipped doves floated from the dense bushes. Green Jays flashed as they crossed the opening on the trail in front of me. A mouse-like scurrying of leaves in the undergrowth turned into a Clay-colored Thrush after I crouched down to peer through the undergrowth at the robin-like bird.

Now I understood why this place was so special to birders. This park was an island of remnant native sabal palms and thorn scrub habitat—the surrounding neighborhoods and subdivisions were ignorantly landscaped—full of introduced plant species. In this thorn-scrub habitat came the birds native to this habitat further south: Olive Sparrow, Buff-bellied Hummingbirds, and Great Kiskadees were plentiful. A Painted Bunting and other migrants materialized and disappeared before I could get a photo. My list of "lifers"—birds that I'd never seen before—began to grow.

The number of people on the trails also began to increase, as the Audubon Center opened and other birders arrived. Most were residents of the area, and some were obviously visiting birders like me. Some of these birders were "chasers" who had come with one goal in mind: finding the Crimson-collared Grosbeak. These birders briskly walked past me to the main feeding station, their floppy-brimmed hats cinched tightly to their heads. In their eyes, I wasn't worth stopping for, since I stood between them and their goal.

I hadn't yet found the feeding station on my own, figuring I was just as likely to find the grosbeak along the trails. As I walked past birders perched on benches they asked me if I'd seen the bird. No elaboration was necessary—as everyone seemed to have the same target in their sights. I think many of the older birders were waiting for the grosbeak to come out into the open, or for me to find it. Nobody had seen the bird so far. I didn't think a "sit and wait" strategy was best, so I decided to keep walking around, doing so until I'd walked every trail in the place.

On yet another lap of the trails, I noticed a younger birder who may have been in his twenties. He wore a gray knit cap topped with a bright ball of red yarn, pulled over a mop of unruly straight brown hair. An overgrown beard cloaked his face, nearly covering the neckline of a worn Alaska Maritime Supply sweatshirt. He sported a pair of ripped jeans that hung loosely over a dirty pair of New Balance tennis shoes. *He looks like he just got off a fishing boat in Alaska,* I thought to myself. My curiosity got the best of me, and I walked over to him and began a conversation.

"Are you looking for the grosbeak?" I asked.

"Yeah, but it's not around right now—there are lots of other good birds though," he replied. Puzzled at how he could so casually state that the bird wasn't around, I changed the subject. "What else have you been seeing?"

"I re-found the Tropical Parula, and also saw a Black-headed Grosbeak and a female Painted Bunting." The last bird he said with a hint of pride as if it wasn't typical to find it here. "And the usual stuff," he added. These were good birds, and this guy knew them—maybe better than I did.

His name was Andy, and he had come here to chase the Crimson-collared Grosbeak, "and find other good birds too." Andy was a dedicated birder, and I soon realized his level of experience and knowledge of Texas birds exceeded mine. Our conversation turned to the rarities we both had seen so far. A shared love for birds and bird-finding formed the foundation of this new friendship.

By noon, it became apparent that the Crimson-collared Grosbeak had not yet been seen by anyone. Many birders had left for work one by one, and others were now departing in groups. As I had suspected, the sitting-on-the-bench strategy was not paying off.

Still hopeful, Andy and I continued our search. Though it had warmed up to 65 degrees, the sky was overcast and bird activity had died down. We decided to continue walking around, actively searching out this bird, which had to be feeding on something in the vicinity.

We began a systematic search for fruiting trees and shrubs; starting in the orchard, we combed the preserve, putting eyes on every bird, and identifying any shrub that had fruit on it.

Suddenly, from a thicket just off the trail, we heard a rising and falling high-pitched slurry 'swEEEeee' call. We looked at each other, recognizing it immediately as a Crimson-collared Grosbeak. Behind a shed, the bird called again. We both ran toward the sound, until the bird called again from in front of where we stood. We looked up into a tangle of bushes and both spotted the bird at the same exact moment. Andy shouted some joyful expletives and ran to get other birders who he knew were here to see this bird. I watched the female grosbeak as it nonchalantly destroyed some rounded fruits with its massive bill, and I tried to take some photos, holding my phone up to the eyepiece of my binoculars. I managed some shaky shots.

Andy returned, out of breath from running along the trails and alerting everyone that we had found the bird. The joy of finding, and sharing, a bird got Andy excited, which in turn got me excited. Within minutes, the Crimson-collared Grosbeak disappeared back into the thick foliage, only occasionally calling every few minutes, before finally going silent.

Satisfied with our incredible up-close views of this species, which was new for both of us in the American Birding Association (ABA) area, we stopped by the visitor's center to update the sightings board and I collected my $5 in change for my entrance fee. With 46 species of birds seen, including some nice rarities, I'd certainly got my money's worth.

"What's next?" I asked Andy, as I handed him a packet of fruit snacks from my car. We had just completed our eBird checklist in the parking lot, so others who left early could know the bird was still present. There were several other rare birds around the area, and I knew he would have an idea of how to best approach finding them all.

"Let's go for the Jacana," Andy replied. He was referring to the Northern Jacana, a chicken-like marsh bird with freakishlylong toes, perfectly suited to walk on water lilies and swampy grasses. Normally found across Mexico and Central America, this particular individual had spent the last several months at Santa Ana National Wildlife Refuge, much to the delight of birders.

Twenty minutes later we arrived at Santa Ana and followed the trails into the wetlands. In a flash of yellow wings the Jacana appeared out of the reeds, as if to welcome us to the refuge. A variety of other birds showed themselves, making a pleasant afternoon of birding until it was time for dinner.

Andy's friend Tiffany met us for dinner at a local Mexican restaurant, where I shared my birding stories from the previous week. I described being detained at the Canadian border, enduring a marathon drive from Seattle to San Diego, filming rare birds in the mountains of Arizona, and then having the carpet pulled out on my professional endeavors, being left high and dry in Texas. I'd seen a plethora of rare birds, and according to Andy, I was already ahead of pace to have a record-setting Big Year.

As I continued to talk both Andy and Tiffany finished eating—and I realized how much had happened to me in such a short amount of time. As I finished my food, they generously split the bill—treating me to dinner. Neither were unaware I had only five dollars cash left in my wallet.

We returned to Tiffany's house, where we stayed up for a while and talked about all things birding.

"Have you heard of 'Humans of New York'?" Tiffany asked.

"Of course" I answered. "That's the blog with street portraits and interviews of random strangers in New York City." I'd seen these interviews posted on Facebook, and always enjoyed reading the blog posts.

"It would be cool if you did that with birders" she

suggested. I thought about it for a moment. Since I left Seattle, I'd already met a dozen interesting people, all of whom were searching for birds like I was. "That's actually a great idea," I said. "I'll be sure to give you credit for that idea when I make it famous" I joked. That night as I lay in the back of my Subaru falling asleep, I mulled over her idea. *That would be a unique approach to doing a Big Year— focusing on birders as well as finding birds*. I knew that with technology, I could share birders' stories across social media, connecting a network of people across the country. I fell asleep before I could develop the idea any further.

The loud barking of dogs woke me up the next morning. As I rolled over in the back of my car, I realized that it was light out, and the cool night air was being replaced with a warm Texas breeze, flooding in through my open car windows. The dogs continued barking; not one, or two, but dozens of dogs. I vaguely remembered the night before, when Tiffany said something about living on the property of an animal shelter.

I went inside and found Andy on the couch, while Tiffany had begun making breakfast for us—fresh eggs, grapefruit jelly, and some kind of delicious homemade fruit spread served with toast. Since Tiffany had a meeting for work, Andy and I decided to bird Bentsen Rio Grande State Park and look for the Hook-billed Kite. At the park's entrance, I took portraits of both Tiffany and Andy and following Tiffany's suggestion—interviewed them in my first birder interviews for the year.

I had the chance to talk with Andy as we stood out on the levee scanning the sky for Hook-billed Kites leaving their morning roosts. I had no idea that, about a short three years later, this area would become Ground Zero for a reinforced border wall, shining the national spotlight on the National Butterfly Center and Bentsen Rio Grande Valley State Park.

I tried to feel out his plans for the day, which I didn't want to derail or latch onto if he wanted to bird on his own. We talked about continuing the hunt for rare birds together. I was finding birds faster with him, and enjoying the camaraderie.

A string of recent rarities discovered at Lions Shelley Park included a Flame-colored Tanager and Golden-crowned Warbler, a diminutive bird that breeds in northeast Mexico. This non-migratory species doesn't show up north of the border very often and made a perfect "target bird" for the afternoon. The park was only three hours away, and Andy had made plans for us to meet up with Clay, an experienced Texas birder. Clay was skilled in digiscoping- using his Swarovski spotting scope paired with a digital camera or phone to make incredible images.

Within the first 10 minutes in the park, Andy had spotted the Golden-crowned Warbler, furtively lurking nowhere near the ground, but 15 feet high in a tangle of leaves. Not long afterward, Clay spotted the Flame-colored Tanager, and we picked up a Greater Pewee as well. The afternoon hours flew by as we birded intently, continuing on from Lions Park to find shorebirds across Nueces County. The day's species list (and consequently, my year list) continued to grow.

As I listened from the back seat to Andy and Clay discuss the recent changes in bird distribution across Texas, it became clear that I was out of my league. Andy had competed in the Great Texas Birding Classic, a statewide birding tournament that I wasn't aware existed. My mind began to wander down the road ahead of us, to the next bird on our list: the endangered Whooping Crane.

When I was young, my aunt took me to see Whooping Cranes near Port Aransas along the Gulf coast of Texas. Too young to remember this particular excursion myself, I've asked her to tell me the story in times since. She recalls loading me in my dad's regatta blue Ford Bronco II. I sat up front in the "monkey seat"—the middle seat hidden by the fold-down center console. She insists I wanted to be where the action was, and have an unlimited view to be the first one to see everything. According to Aunt Holly, I was careful with the binoculars, and stayed quiet and sat still. I was a very good listener, and credit my good behavior to the way my parents were raising me. Aunt Holly recalls my mom was always expectant of good. She decided I would have "terrific twos" instead of the "terrible twos" most parents might experience. That particular day near Port Aransas was terrific—we easily spotted a flock of Whooping Cranes close to the road.

In repeat fashion, we found a Whooping Crane close to the road, providing an excellent study of this endangered species. Before, I hadn't added this species to my life list, since I don't remember seeing it and couldn't identify it on my own when I was young. We continued birding, losing track of time until darkness fell and it was time to eat dinner.

Clay had graciously invited me to join Andy at his house for dinner. A talented chef, he made spare ribs, beans, and pasta, which were a welcome change from my more budget-friendly quick-and-dirty meals.

So far, my meals consisted mostly of dried goods, canned soups from home, fruit snacks, and Top Ramen, which only required a cup of hot water, which I got from McDonald's for free. Although I hadn't been on the road for very long, I had began to figure out some "travel hacks" for saving money, like filling out the customer surveys on receipts to earn free food, and clipping coupons from discarded local papers.

After fuel, food was my largest expense for birding by car. It was tempting to eat fast food but as cheap as McDonald's food is, it's not great to eat long-term—as plenty of documentaries can attest. I only bought groceries twice the entire month

—since I stocked up on free food from home, and only needed to resupply on milk, juice, and ramen while on the road so far.

Following dinner, we drove to a local park Clay was familiar with and we heard the *"hip-hip hip-hip hip-hip-hooray"* call of Common Pauraques as if they were celebrating the day's birding accomplishments. We had seen 5 birds which were classified as a Code 3 or higher, and I had added an additional 30 species to my year list. Leaving the park, I caught a glimpse of a pauraque as it caught a flying nsect in the glow of the headlights, then swooped low back to its perch in the inky darkness.

Absorbed in the magic of immersion in a new and stimulating environment searching for birds, I hadn't thought all day about my life's troubles. I remembered that I was so caught up in birding, hadn't thought about Teresa all day.

Like a slowly-sinking ship, it occurred to me that instead of trying to salvage the pieces of our relationship, it was best to make a clean break. She deserved someone who could care about her more than himself. Someone who had a job and a clear direction in life. I didn't want to take the uncertainty, fear, and doubt that I felt and share that burden with anybody else. I wanted to forget about it. In that moment I knew that for her sake and mine, our relationship had to end.

Instead of waiting until our paths crossed in the uncertain future, I made the hardest phone call of my life. I couldn't argue with the feeling of peace and calm that came afterward, which confirmed that breaking up with her was the right thing to do.

January was half way over, and I had seen and heard nearly 300 species of birds, including 23 new species I'd never seen before. Although I had plans to drive to Houston next, to visit my brother Kevin, Andy pressured me to first drive to Illinois where a rare Black-tailed Gull had been spotted. He was right; I knew that if this evolved into a true Big Year effort, then I couldn't pass up a rarer bird like this; I also understood that there would be some birds I would have to miss. It would be impossible to get them all, but that's what made doing a Big Year the ultimate challenge in birdwatching. *Family first,* I told myself, as I pointed my hood in the direction of Houston.

Blue Jay perched atop an ornamental tree in Houston

Jay! Jay! I opened my eyes before quickly closing them again, blinded by the thin shafts of sunlight that snuck through the wooden blinds of my brother's apartment in suburban Houston. I heard it again, outside. JAY! JAY! JAY! The unmistakable call of the Blue Jay. Sprawled across an expensive, over-sized sofa that felt wrong to put my feet up on—I was finally able to relax. The non-stop birding had been physically and mentally exerting, although I thrived on it. *JAY! JAY!*

Months had passed since I moved from St. Louis, Missouri leaving behind Blue Jays, Teresa, and my job as a high school Biology teacher. In fairness, I hadn't completely moved out of the range of Blue Jays, and I kept dating Teresa long-distance. However, after four years of teaching Science at the same private school I attended growing up, I recognized it was time for a change. I chased my dream job of being a wildlife film-maker all the way to Montana.

JAY! JAY! JAY! This bird just won't shut up, I thought to myself, as I grabbed my binoculars and went outside onto the balcony. Below, the sleepy neighborhood street consisted of single-story homes shaded by towering oaks planted decades ago. The modern high-rise apartment building stood in stark contrast to these older neighborhoods, which quickly were being developed to accommodate Houston's growing population.

I stared into the sprawling branches at eye-level, where a brilliant blue and white bird sat in protest, clearly upset by something. Perhaps a Cooper's Hawk was lurking nearby. Through my binoculars I could see the familiar bold black bars on the vibrant blue bird, whose crisp pattern could have been painted on with a fine-tipped brush. This bird transported me back in time to a snowy morning of my childhood, spent pressed up against the cold glass of my grandmother's kitchen window, eager to get as close as I could to the Blue Jays outside on her bird feeder.

Kevin and I sat at a donut shop in The Heights, a suburb of Houston. Eager to support my search for birds, he asked what new species we could find around Houston. On my iPhone, I opened BirdsEye, a bird-finding app that uses data from Cornell's eBird database to The weather forecast looked bleak, but several nearby birding hotspots looked promising before the forecasted rains arrived. After finishing our donuts, we headed towards Houston's Arboretum.

If asked, Kevin wouldn't consider himself a birder. Having me as a brother has trained him to always be on the lookout. His sharp eyes and local familiarity with Houston's parks came in handy. We explored the Houston Arboretum, finding a well-camouflaged American Woodcock near the boardwalk, and spotted Fulvous Whistling-Ducks among the domestic Mallards at a local park.

We laughed as we reminisced about our childhood together, and he provided some sound advice about how to proceed with my life from this point of uncertainty. This was the first time in a while that Kevin and I had spent time together, just the two of us. Kevin has always been my best friend; growing up we did everything together. When I'd moved to Missouri to go to boarding school, the world we shared was split and began our separate but parallel experiences.

As Monday approached, Kevin returned to his desk job, and I realized I should move on before I got too comfortable sleeping on his couch. I had seen ten new birds for the year with Kevin—but only nine of them counted. The introduced Red-vented Bulbul, despite breeding down the street from my brother's apartment—was not "officially" countable.

Kevin reinforced that I was much more capable than I believed I was, and could do anything I set my mind to. With this boost of confidence, I needed time and space to develop this Big Year idea further. I had a supportive network of friends and colleagues in Missouri, and St. Louis was the perfect place to incubate these ideas, and hatch a plan for a purposeful, mission-driven Big Year.

4

AN EARLY START

THERE's something therapeutic about highway driving. The hum of rubber on road as the miles fly past, combined with the low soothing vibration of the engine and a rhythmic string of eighth notes as the tires glide over breaks in the highway pavement. I felt in tune with the road—grounded, which allowed my thoughts to wander beyond the road ahead into the mental realm of time and memory.

My exposure to birds began before I can remember, as told to me by family and friends. Ever since I could stand up on my own two legs unassisted, I ran. Most toddlers take their first wobbly steps, and then graduate to the awkward duck-like phase of taking a few uneasy steps, then waddling across the room before landing on their butt. I wobbled, toddled, then ran. My mom would take me to open fields and beaches to let me run until I couldn't run any longer. Apparently chasing seagulls was good exercise—who knew?

My dad's mom Suzanne loved birds. She was a regular participant in the annual Audubon Christmas Bird Count, and diligently maintained a bird feeder throughout the winter when birds needed it the most. Nothing impeded "Grammie" from keeping her feeder full—not even her first grandchild. She carried me, only four months old, in one arm and a bucket of birdseed in the other.

I was lucky to spend some of my childhood living in Vermont, living over a river and through the woods from her house. Many snowy days were spent looking out the window watching the arrival and departures of Northern Cardinals, Blue Jays, and Black-capped Chickadees. An old Peterson field guide, worn from years of reverent use, sat on the windowsill nearby a pair of binoculars. Birds were just as special to her as her grandkids; I remember her calling me and my brother "her little chickadees." Framed artwork from esteemed bird artist John James Audubon hung on walls in her Vermont country estate.

Before I would embark into the woods, Grammie would pack a snack bag for me—a small ziplock bag full of treats, that I could use to bring home treasures from the woods after the snacks were gone. Sometimes the bags held feathers from a Wild Turkey, or an arrowhead-shaped rock, or if I was lucky— an owl pellet. The years I spent living in Vermont were the happiest and most carefree days of my youth, spent exploring nature as far as I could roam until summoned for dinner. These were the formative years of my childhood.

I took my first cross-country road trip at the age of six years old. I can remember the smell of the stiff leather bench seat of the U-Haul truck my dad drove from Washington to Indiana. Throughout my childhood, time spent with my dad was partic- ularly memorable, since he was often deployed overseas. The times he was home were special, and I remember them all.

I recall the long stretches of highway across the Badlands, stopping for a mini-biology lesson when we passed an inter- esting road-killed animal or bird. As a six-year-old, I was fascinated by the rough scales of a rattlesnake, and the wind-blown feathers of a Golden Eagle, grounded from its home in the sky by power pole. We stopped at Wall Drug in South Dakota to see the cowboys, and picked strawberries outside our Indiana hotel at night under a sky of fireflies. My dad taught me more about nature than any school teacher in my youth.

For most eight-year-olds, visiting their grandmother at work wasn't very exciting. I however, couldn't wait to visit my mom's mother Libby at her skyscraper office in downtown Seattle. She worked in the Washington Mutual Tower—home of my "spark bird"—the bird that got me interested in birds once and for all.

Forty-eight floors above the busy city streets, on a railing outside the Perkins Coie law firm sat a male Peregrine Falcon. Stuart was named after the Seattle street, as was his mate Bell. This pair of falcons had selected a ledge on the top floors of the building as a nest site—delighting many Seattleites.

I remember visiting her one day, stopping briefly to greet her and then running to look for the falcons. Stuart had caught a pigeon and was plucking it on an office ledge outside a conference room window on her floor. I watched in amazement as the sleek bird sat feet away, disregarding the excited kid pressed against the glass, unknowingly making the window washer's job much more difficult.

With a motion reminiscent of a wind-up toy, Stuart plucked the pigeon—pinned firmly beneath crossed front talons in typical falcon fashion. Breezy updrafts whisked clumps of feathers away over the urban canyons far below. Minutes later, the pigeon resembled a partially-feathered thanksgiving turkey with legs. Satisfied with his handiwork, Stuart opened his wings and was lifted off the ledge by the invisible updrafts, spiraling over the city streets up and out of sight.

I knew exactly where he was headed. In a flash, I ran past my grandmother's reception desk back to the elevators and down to the lobby where a TV screen showed a live-feed of the nest box. (This is before online bird cams) I had missed the prey exchange, but there was Stuart sitting dutifully on the scrape while Bell fed somewhere off-screen. At the time, this was the coolest birding experience of my life, sparking an insatiable interest in raptors.

In the years following I read every book in the public library—fiction and non-fiction—about the Peregrine Falcon. *My Side of the Mountain* was a favorite that planted the seed in my head to one day become a licensed falconer. I made good on that promise years later, capturing my first Red-tailed Hawk from the wild and training her to hunt by my side through Missouri's squirrel-filled woods. It would be the first of many partnerships between myself and a wild raptor.

Since medieval times, the Peregrine Falcon's speed and agility has been admired by falconers. Unable to climb the steep cliffs to capture young falcons, they resorted to capturing young birds on their migratory routes. In Latin *peregrinus* means 'pilgrim' or 'wanderer'. A Peregrine's migratory journey in a year's time can cover over 15,000 miles.

Growing up with a Navy pilot for a father our family wandered around a lot, following orders from the U.S. Government. I was born when my Dad was stationed in Maine, before we were transferred to Texas, followed by Vermont. Our second move to Maine was short-lived; when my dad found out that Alaska Airlines needed pilots, our family relocated to Seattle.

I became well-versed in packing boxes, making and leaving friends, and starting again at a new school. Although I left friends behind, there were always birds wherever I lived; I never was outside the range of the Peregrine Falcon.

*Seattle's celebrity Peregrine Falcon pair Stuart and Bell sparked my
interest in raptors—a gateway to my interest in birding*

In 1870, St. Louis was a burgeoning town of immigrants,
with nearly half of them of German descent. Carl Daenzer was
German newspaper owner who responded to the complaints of
residents who missed the birds of their homeland and found
the local bird diversity rather dull. In cooperation with a newspaper colleague, Daenzer purchased a crate of nearly 20
Eurasian Tree Sparrows and released them in Lafayette Park,
located in the heart of German neighborhoods.

The released birds mysteriously disappeared for an entire
year, and then on April 24, 1871 one was spotted and reported
nearby. From then on, Eurasian Tree Sparrows were wildly
successful, due in part to the plentiful food sources (including
spilled grain from Anheuser-Busch and other German brew-
eries) and no direct competition until the later arrival of
English House Sparrows.

The species quickly spread around the St. Louis area and beyond, crossing the river to Alton and Grafton, Illinois. Some made it as far downstream as Paducah, Kentucky—undoubtedly assisted by steamboats!

The Eurasian Tree Sparrow has been steadily expanding its range—the advent of eBird makes analyzing trends like this much easier

Like the Eurasian Tree Sparrow, I was also a transplant to the city of St. Louis. Near the end of my 8th grade year I came to the conclusion that my Washington public high school wasn't going to provide the education I wanted. I had plenty of friends, played on a competitive traveling soccer team, and was ready to take on the challenges of high school. Something didn't feel right.

I sat down with my parents and asked them if I had any other options; going to my local high school didn't seem that appealing or challenging. I knew they both had met at a private school in St. Louis, and had dated through college and built a nice life together. Perhaps, if I went to this school I could followed in their footsteps of success.

I visited the school during my 8th-grade year, spending a weekend on campus living in the boy's dormitory, participating in track practice and making new friends. Deciding that it was worth starting over and leaving my old friends and teams behind, I headed to private school in St. Louis for my freshman year of high school.

As a teenager, I had amassed quite the collection of bird books. I frequently flipped through my many field guides, not looking at the birds but at the range maps. I was fascinated by the broad swaths of color for some species, and the strange lumps, lines, bars, and splotches for others. I had to closely examine some range maps, nearly squinting to see a small dot representing the small range of a particular species.

I noticed the Yellow-billed Magpie could only be found across California's Central Valley, while the Colima Warbler's range barely cross the Mexican border into the Chisos mountains of southwestern Texas. I wondered what these places were like and why the birds only occurred there. Someday I would find out.

My freshman year at a new school started by taking on more than I could reliably handle. I made the JV soccer team, and a full load of classes took up much of my time, especially Honors English. I lived in the boy's dormitory only a one-minute walk away from school, which worsened the claustrophobia of being immersed in this new experience. My escape was the 300 acres of fields, forest, streams, and lakes. I dreamed of running away; each day I spent longer and longer straying further from school, but I always came back.

High School is an unusually awkward time for most teenagers, and my experience was no exception. I was determined to try everything: jazz band, soccer, wrestling, tennis, pep band, international club, and choir. I switched from a woodwind instrument to the brass section as I learned the valve trombone and euphonium. Failing to qualify for state in my athletic endeavors didn't dissuade me, and my musical interests waned as athletics took over my life. Never "great" at any one thing, but "good" in many areas, I enjoyed trying new things and taking advantage of the many opportunities a liberal arts college-prep school offered.

At the time, nobody on campus supported my passion for birds. When I asked, my friends seemed to never want to venture into the fields (*too many ticks...*) or take a walk in the forest (*full poison ivy*) or try to catch largemouth bass in the ponds (*and get bitten by mosquitoes and snapping turtles? No way!*).

I struggled academically in my Biology class which focused more on life's micro-processes like photosynthesis and cellular respiration than it did on birds and ecology. I spent some weekends hanging out with my Biology teacher, but mostly because I had a crush on her daughter—who also loved animals.

Preston, the other Science teacher taught higher-level Science classes including Marine Biology and Ecology. Years ago, he studied birds under great ornithologists and was an avid birder, but now other things occupied his time and interests. Through my eyes as an underclassman, he seemed unapproachable, and he openly doubted many of my local bird sightings which was discouraging. It would take years to move past our early interactions, before we became friends.

All of this changed the day our school hired Mr. Warrick as the new Athletic Director. This type of personnel change would have happened without me caring, except the incoming A.D. must have mentioned on his resume that he was a birder. Word travels fast at a small school, and as the only self-professed birder on campus, *everyone* made sure I knew of the new hire before he even arrived on campus.

Preston confirmed Mr. Warrick was also a *lister*—which meant he didn't just watch birds, but he kept detailed records of every bird he saw on his life list. He even traveled the world to see unusual birds, many found in obscure and dangerous countries. I heard he had been even been shot at by natives in New Guinea while looking for birds. With each new rumor I heard, the more excited I was to meet this intrepid birder.

I didn't have to wait long before I had my first Athletic Director sighting. Dressed in sharply-pressed khakis, brown dress shoes, and a blue button-down collared shirt, Mr. Warrick looked all business. His dark hair was buzzed with military precision, framing a serious expression on his face I discovered was constant. He definitely doesn't look like a birdwatcher.

Where was the floppy hat and vest? As a teenager I clung to birding stereotypes, which were reinforced by the khaki-clad wardrobe of nearly every member of the single St. Louis Audubon Society bird walk I attended. What *did* a "serious" birder look like? I largely ignored that question for a long time.

Mr. Warrick looked me straight in the eye, shook my hand firmly, and invited me into his office to talk. After I sat down, I couldn't help feeling as if I was in trouble. As I looked around his office, my eye was first drawn to a set of bird books on the shelf, and then to a pair of Swarovski binoculars on his desk near the window. I began to relax—we had a lot to discuss.

Over the next few years, Mr. Warrick and I began learning about the birds of Missouri together. We were both transplants; I'd moved from Seattle, and he relocated from Florida for his job. I had already subscribed to the statewide birding Listserv (a website where group members can post bird sightings that are simultaneously emailed out to all subscribers of the group) yet he taught me how to sort through the reports of the more common birds and pay close attention to the rare bird sightings. I'd seen many of Missouri's common birds, yet the Missouri Rare Bird Alert was pretty much a digest of birds I'd never seen in the state. Several of these rare birds were missing from Brad's list too, and that began a new chapter in my birding experience: chasing.

In my eyes, January 1, 2006 marked the beginning of my development as a "real" birder. I stood in a church parking lot nearby my school—our designated meeting point, waiting for Mr. Warrick to pick me up. Several days earlier, a Townsend's Solitaire was reported nearby, and we were going to go chase this rare bird—if it was still around. The gray thrush was far from its normal range in the Rocky Mountains, and despite having previously spotted this species in the West, both of us wanted to start the year off with a rare bird for our newly-minted Missouri state lists.

Mr. Warrick rolled up in his Porsche Cayenne, which looked like it had driven straight off the new car lot. I sat down into the heated leather seat, and we zoomed off towards the community college where the bird had been seen. Using my *Sibley Guide to Birds of North America*, I reviewed the field marks out loud as we accelerated onto the highway, hitting the speed limit in seconds. Driving with Brad was exhilarating, and greatly enhanced the experience of chasing a rare bird.

Finding the out-of-place Townsend's Solitaire at a college campus on a Sunday wasn't a difficult task—the bird perched in a tree at eye level, allowing me to practice using binoculars to see it well. I'd never really used binoculars. My past attempts had been futile; I found most optics fuzzy and the focus knob hard to operate. Growing up, most pairs of binoculars I had attempted to use were either constructed cheaply, or got dirty, fuzzy, or wet—and stopped working.

Mr. Warrick had brought his extra pair of Zeiss binoculars for me to try out. Looking through them was a whole different experience! The amount of light this pair of binoculars let in was incredible, and the image was crystal clear. I could see individual feathers of the bird's eye ring and subtle pale edges to the feathers along the wing. Even better, Mr. Warrick let me borrow his backup pair of binoculars and take them home.

When spring arrived, I could now look into the canopy and spot warblers, which before had only been recognizable to me by their songs. Having a quality pair of binoculars at my disposal elevated my birding skills to the next level, and sparked a genuine interest in seeing birds that before had been too difficult to see without quality optics. Before long, my interest in broadening my own understanding of Missouri's local birds turned into a desire to travel and see birds elsewhere.

My first chance to travel abroad came during my junior year of high school. I registered for Preston's marine biology course, knowing this class was a prerequisite for the spring break trip to Belize. Many of my peers were eager to spend their vacation on tropical beaches, where they would get tan and have awesome pictures to share on their Myspace accounts. I just wanted to go to see tropical birds.

Leading up to our departure, we spent much of the day in group seminars learning methodologies for coral reef surveys, and practicing with our snorkeling gear in the pool. We reviewed slideshows covering Belize's incredible biodiversity. Preston definitely included some information about birds for me. He didn't nudge me back on task when I stopped listening during other lesson topics, as I was too absorbed studying a field guide to the birds of Belize.

Preston became quite supportive of my interest in birds and accompanied me on morning bird walks with a local guide. We stayed out late at night, walking the entrance road to Cockscomb Basin, shining our headlamps into the glowing ruby-red eyeshine of Common Pauraques. Together we spotted birds near ancient Mayan ruins hidden in dense jungles, and identified the Yellow "Mangrove" Warbler in the pungent muck of coastal mangrove swamps. He even came to my aid after I was bit by an octopus on a dive. Our relationship which had gotten off on the wrong foot years before was re-written as we traveled across the country of Belize together.

I saw over 100 species of birds on that first trip to Belize, which only whet my appetite for tropical birding. I had no idea that six years later I would be leading this same trip to Belize as a newly-minted Science teacher, fresh out of college and teaching Marine Biology in Preston's stead. Of course, I invited Preston to come along on the trip and show me the ropes, which he gladly accepted.

Throughout high school, I was embraced by the local St. Louis birding community. Members of the Webster Groves Nature Study Society and St. Louis Audubon gave me rides before I had my driver's license, and showed me Eurasian Tree Sparrows, Mississippi Kites, and countless other birds I'd only read about in bird books.

During my senior year, I put my skills to the test and did a "Big Month" inside a 50-mile circle encompassing the St. Louis area. This was my first attempt at merging travel logistics and birding, and indicated an inkling to do a Big Year of my own someday.

My high school years were crucial to my development as a young birder. Traveling internationally, learning to use binoculars, and finding mentors who supported and challenged me were all crucial to accelerating my learning about the birds of North America and beyond.

5

AN 'EPIC' BIG YEAR

I FIRST LEARNED what a Big Year was when I was in high school. I had no idea that people spent an entire year—from January 1st through the final day in December—searching for birds across a certain geographic area. Many birders focused their Big Year efforts within the American Birding Association (ABA) area, comprised of the United States and Canada. I still had much to learn.

Our school librarian knew I was interested in birds, and bought Mark Obmascik's book *The Big Year: A Tale of Man, Nature, and Fowl Obsession*. She was excited to share this book for me, which introduced me to Greg Miller, a computer programmer who was one of three Big Year competitors in 1998. Greg's dogged determination through countless obstacles while doing a Big Year set his journey apart in my eyes from the other competitors.

I read other Big Year books too. *Wild America* described James Fisher and Roger Tory Peterson's incredible journey across the continent in 1953. I loved the descriptions of the places they visited and the birds that they saw. After finishing the book, my travel bucket list nearly doubled. I knew I would have to travel to Alaska's Pribilof Islands someday. The most impactful Big Year book for me was *Kingbird Highway*. Kenn Kaufman's stories of hitchhiking across North America on the cheap didn't just recount an amazing birding adventure, but it captured his journey—finding birds and persisting through adversity as he grew older and developed both as a birder and a teenager. Both stories resonated with me because they captured what life was like at that time. I always wished I had been born in an earlier time—when flowing flocks of Passenger Pigeons streamed over the eastern forests, and the magnificent Ivory-billed Woodpecker still haunted the southern swamps. Even 50 years ago, the biogeography of North America was vastly different than it is today.

I spent hours of thoughtful contemplation on the road from Houston to St. Louis. Andy's contagious enthusiasm had me convinced I could actually attempt a Big Year. He assured me I already had an amazing start; with some strategy, he predicted, I could break the coveted barrier of 700 birds. It was a lofty goal, but realistically I knew that more birds required more money. I knew that 700 was doable in a single year, but at what cost?

Doing a Big Year did not sound like a cheap venture. It required constant travel (flights, rental cars, ferries, and pelagic boat trips) which can cost big money. Factoring in the cost of lodging, food, gas, and other smaller expenses (entrance fees, tolls, ferries, etc.) I knew the cost could add up quickly.

I didn't have a steady job like Greg Miller, and I couldn't safely thumb rides like Kenn. However the previous two weeks had proved that I could travel on a budget. I'd spent under $300 in gas and food, and no money on hotels or guides. This was surely less than what other birders were spending on their Big Years.

Extrapolating my expenses over the remaining 10 months, I figured I could see over 600 birds and spend under $10,000. If I pushed for 700 species, the cost per bird would begin to increase exponentially. I shuddered at the math, but figured I would cross that bridge later.

I was young and I had a car. These were both advantages that were in my favor—I had a cost-effective mode of transportation with a built-in hotel. As far as I knew, nobody had done a driving Big Year affordably and spotted over 700 birds. This idea intrigued me. *If I continue doing this for a few dollars a day plus gas for the whole year, how many birds could I see?* To be honest, I didn't know—and that was ok.

I quickly realized there was a steep learning curve to doing a Big Year. After spending time around much better birders like Andy and Clay, it was clear I still had much to learn. Despite possessing keen observational skills, I lacked the knowledge of bird status and distribution on a continental level.

What I lacked in age and experience, I made up for with passion and grit. If I had to spend three days searching for a bird—sleeping on the ground alongside a trail, I'd do it. I was fit, willing to learn, and willing to make sacrifices to achieve my goals.

I was also willing to work. I knew that I didn't have enough saved to spend $10,000 on birding. I already had bills: college loans, car payments, and graduate school tuition to pay. If I wanted to bird, it was clear I needed to find a way to develop an income.

A Big Year would be the perfect opportunity to learn and become a better birder. Ultimately, how many birds I saw didn't matter. At the end of the year, I'd know more about

North America's birds and be better in the field than when I began. That alone was worth the journey.

⬛

I sat cross-legged on my college professors' couch in St. Louis. Scott and Karen both had been valuable mentors during my final year of college, and had continued advising me on some major life decisions following graduation. Their house in St. Louis was the perfect place for me to turn my ideas into a reality.

Scott encouraged me to review my assets. Financially, I was barely in the black. Most of my savings I had spent moving to Montana and supporting myself while I worked in a job that provided very little compensation. I had some money saved—earmarked for graduate school—which I planned to continue in the coming months regardless of where I was living or what my job was.

I owned Swarovski optics—a pair of binoculars and a spotting scope, which I had worked hard and saved for following college in my first job. Maybe Swarovski would sponsor me? If not, I could always sell these optics and use something less expensive. I also owned professional camera equipment, including a 500mm f4.0 Canon lens. If I got in a pinch, I could always sell that.

I owned all my own camping gear, and had a knowledge base of survival skills from a phase I went through in high school when I wanted to live off the land. For lodging, a vast network of friends and family around the country might come in handy too—providing a bed to sleep in and a home-cooked meal.

Perhaps my greatest asset was my willingness to work. I spent some time searching online for jobs near Florida, where ideally, I would spend the month of February. Strategically, rare birds could show up at a moment's notice, and Florida and Texas both were key places to be.

I contacted The Lodge at Little St. Simons Island, where I had visited as a guest the previous fall. I took away many amazing memories, and I felt indebted for the experience this special place had given me. I inquired about being a naturalist, but no openings were available.

There was a Kitchen Assistant position available; the responsibilities included cleaning the kitchen and dining areas, serving food to guests, and helping the chefs with food preparation. It wasn't exactly what I wanted to be doing, but it was paid work—and living on an island sounded fun! I applied and was accepted—work would begin in February.

On a pad of paper, I brainstormed what I wanted my Big Year to be. It helped to first outline what I wanted it *not* to be. I didn't want to do a Big Year exactly like any others that had come before. I admired some approaches and elements to prior Big Years. Dorian Anderson had biked around the country—I wasn't going to trade in my car for a bike, but I could integrate an environmentally-conscious approach to my travels. Kenn Kaufman proved one didn't need to be wealthy, yet I wasn't going to live for only dollars a day by eating cat food and hitchhiking.

I felt strongly that this Big Year shouldn't be about *me*. Past Big Years had revolved around the person/personality branded as "So-and-So's Big Year" I wanted to avoid that if I could, and redirect the attention towards the people I met along my journey, or conservation, and of course—the birds. Naturally, these stories would be shared through my lens and my experiences, and I was happy to be a conduit for teaching and learning.

After spending hours indoors staring at my computer, the ideas spilled out onto my notepad. What I wanted my Big Year to look like centered around four major ideas. Whether or not I could accomplish these four objectives—I wasn't sure. Putting them out there publicly would help to hold me accountable, and provide direction if I happened to get lost or lose motivation.

ENGAGE

I wanted to *Engage* with the birding community on a continent-wide scale. While the birding community undoubtedly has contributed to the success of every Big Year, not every Big Year has contributed back to the birding community—I wanted to change that. Instead of blogging only about what birds I saw each day, and telling my story, I wanted to focus more on the people I met and interview over 365 people about their passion for birds and birding. So far, I'd observed that the birding community is full of many passionate, unique, and inspiring people—each pursues birds for a slightly different reason and has a different story. I hoped that by sharing these stories, people could connect with one another and realize that they're not the only one who likes birds—many are out there.

PRESERVE

I wanted to *Preserve* bird habitat in urban and rural areas. If I could take part in tangible conservation activities in areas that were heavily impacted by people, while making sure wild places stayed wild. This would be difficult to do while traveling, but I hoped to create opportunities to achieve this in some degree. I also began research into a carbon offset program that would plant trees or limit the destruction of native habitats.

INSPIRE

I hoped that my actions would *Inspire* and motivate others, much like those before me had set an example I wanted to follow. Hopefully, sharing nature with others through social media posts and my blog would inspire others to get outside and see some of these places for themselves.

CONNECT

I wanted to Connect people, not only with one another but also foster a connection to birds—using technology in a responsible way. As people venture afield in search of birds, technology accompanies them into the field, bringing new challenges about how to use technology ethically. I wanted to promote technology that made enjoying birds easier and promoted learning. Anyone can now record bird songs on their phones, or play a recording, which might influence a bird's behavior. Armed with more information than ever, technology can help bring closer to birds, if done responsibly.

Together, these four ideas formed the pillars of my EPIC Big Year. I named my effort The Birding Project and chose a hummingbird—the most widely-recognized type of bird, as a logo. Over several days I created multiple social media accounts, built a website, and branded my Big Year ambitions the best I could, before returning to the road.

To break up the hours spent staring at my laptop, I took birding breaks to explore my favorite winter birding locations around the St. Louis area. One memorable outing was with my mentor Brad and Garrett, a sharp student who knew much more than I did about birds at his age, and had a keen eye for photographing birds. I tried to include Garrett in as many of my local birding adventures as possible. He had supportive parents, was an incredibly sharp young birder, who I knew had a bright future ahead.

The three of us stood together upstream of the confluence of the Mississippi and Missouri rivers, scanning the ice. During the winter time, the river floodplain attracts a diverse group of waterfowl, including hundreds of wintering Trumpeter Swans.

Hidden among the large white birds were several smaller Tundra Swans, their rounder heads and shorter bills were subtle features that needed careful study to make an accurate identification.

Birding with Brad and Garrett gave me the opportunity to interview people I already knew well, and explain my vision for what The Birding Project would include. I photographed their hands holding their binoculars, which would become a signature part of my interviews throughout the year.

6

ISLAND LIFE

LOCATED an hour or so north of the Florida-Georgia line, Little St. Simons Island lies only a few miles off the coast of the larger, more developed St. Simons Island. I parked my Subaru at a private marina and loaded everything I needed for the next month into a cart. I was met on the dock by a willing boat crew, who graciously helped me load my bags onto the boat.

The sea air swirled in the boat's wake, spraying a fine mist of salty droplets onto my sun-bleached arm hairs, which glistened like dew on spider silk. Long curtains of Spanish moss swung pendulum-like in the breeze, draped over the sprawling limbs of gnarled oak trees. A light wind carried the smell of newly exposed mud as the tide receded from the surrounding salt marsh—which would barely have time to dry out before the tide returned. From somewhere across the sea of cordgrass the raspy chuckle of a Clapper Rail sounded.

As I stepped off the boat and walked beneath the canopy of live oaks, I thought about the people who had also pondered this magical place for the first time. A wave of emotions washed over me—relief for finally being off the road, mixed with uncertainty about my upcoming job responsibilities.

With a long history of being privately owned, the 11,000-acre Little St. Simons Island remains one of the most pristine ecosystems in Georgia's Golden Isles. Georgia has nearly 15 barrier islands along its 110 miles of Atlantic coastline, and car accessibility to many of these islands has rapidly turned them into tourist destinations. Contrarily, this island has maintained a wildness that must be experienced to be fully understood. Covered in a patchwork of habitats ranging from sandy beaches to tidal estuaries to oak and pine forests, this island is a hotspot for coastal biodiversity.

Year-round, Little St. Simons hosts over 300 species of birds and is an important stopover point for many migratory birds. The shell-covered beaches are home to nesting American Oystercatchers and Piping Plovers. Old marine hardwood forests that were once logged for lumber and turned into pencils now stand protected.

As a young child, it was one of my dreams to live on an island. There's something innately appealing about being inaccessible, surrounded by water, sun, and sky, and forced to be content with only the things available from the surrounding landscape. I wanted to visit island ecosystems all over the world. The Galápagos, Madagascar, New Zealand, and Hawaii —all of these islands had one thing in common: unique birds. This aspect of island biodiversity is what really grabbed my attention. Although this temperate island lacked the isolation to drive unique evolutionary adaptations, it was along the Atlantic Flyway and was covered end-to-end in critical habitat for migratory birds. As far as birds were concerned, I couldn't have picked a better spot to spend a month earning money as a kitchen assistant.

My love affair with Little St. Simons Island started four

months prior when I had visited this island for the first time. I had been invited as a guest for a weekend retreat of island exploration and networking with a global network of forward-thinking individuals, all driven by a passion for conservation and birds.

I felt like a fly on the wall among a group of conservation leaders, consisting of a professional wildlife photographer, representatives from BirdLife International, The Nature Conservancy, Manomet, and the World Wildlife Fund.

In between meetings and meals was downtime to relax and enjoy the endless natural encounters to be had on the island. We caught snakes with Georgia's state herpetologist, birded with experts from Cornell's Laboratory of Ornithology, and learned about conservation issues from a variety of experts. It was a dream—learning from these incredible people and hearing the ideas generated from deep, meaningful discussion.

I left with a renewed hope for our planet and the wild creatures that depend on people doing bold initiatives for global conservation. This visit left a lasting impression on me. I knew that if there was any way I could return, even for a brief time, it would be time well spent.

I followed one of the staff along a wooden boardwalk, past the main lodge and an old ice house, until we reached my home for the next month. The simple two-story house was painted mustard-yellow with green trim and came complete with a screened-in porch with two matching rocking chairs. It looked picturesque, like a page from a *Southern Living* magazine.

After living in a car for a month, I hardly knew what to do with all of the free space in my room. I wasn't needed in the lodge until the evening when my kitchen training began, so I was free for several hours to explore the island's 11,000 acres of untouched habitat. A network of roads and trails crossed the island, connecting people with place in the most meandering way imaginable.

I grabbed a bicycle from the wooden racks. Here bikes were the main form of transportation. I inspected my bike to ensure the tires were in working order and didn't make any squeaking noises. It's hard to see wildlife when you can be heard coming from a long way off.

Biking down the road, I meandered my way through the maritime forest, dominated by live oaks, southern magnolia trees, and groves of cedars. The winding road passed through the coastal forest until the trees melted away, opening up into expanses of salt marsh, broken by stands of cabbage palms. I stopped and listened to the Northern Cardinal, singing proudly from a nearby bush. The friendly chips of Yellow-rumped Warblers greeted me at the forest edge, where an armadillo rushed across the path in front of me, stopping only to pry his nose deep into the leaf litter to sniff around before disappearing into the dense wall of palmetto fronds lining the road.

I pedaled through a puddle and up the ramp onto a wooden boardwalk, crossing a line of sand dunes before finally reaching the Atlantic Ocean. As I rode along the beach, I passed many interesting things that normally I'd stop to inspect—a Logger-head sea turtle, washed up on shore. This was the first dead sea turtle I'd ever found. Further down the beach, I came across a raft crafted by Cuban refugees, complete with an old Mercedes car engine jerry-rigged to power the makeshift boat.

I'd heard once that John Fitzpatrick, Executive Director of Cornell University's Laboratory of Ornithology, had said this island was one of his favorite places in the world to watch shorebirds. I could believe that, standing on Sancho Panza beach on the northeastern edge of the island, looking out at the expansive beach covered in shorebirds. A diversity of plovers, sandpipers, and godwits all engaged in a frantic feeding feast as the tide retreated towards the sea, exposing extensive mudflats: a shorebird buffet.

After I'd completed my assigned shifts, I was free to explore the island. By the light of the moon I walked the roads on my own, enchanted by sounds both familiar and foreign. The soothing hum of insects was the soundtrack for my nighttime exploration, and sometimes the low melodic trill of Eastern Screech-Owl would join the chorus of frogs and insects. I sometimes found the owl in the beam of my headlamp as it flew across the road, or perched nearby the lodge.

During one of my solo island adventures, I found myself staring up high into the pine trees, hearing nuthatches somewhere among the treetops. I noticed the dead skeleton of an ancient tree that probably has been standing for over a hundred years. Near the top was an exceptionally large oval hole, excavated long ago by a large woodpecker. I wondered if possibly this was the work of an Ivory-billed Woodpecker? This island held so many mysteries—I needed more time to explore.

The days passed, one after the other, like scenes from a movie. Wake up, go through the routine, and fall asleep grateful and tired at the end of each long day. The beautiful sunsets and wildness of the island made me feel like I was living in a remote paradise, virtually untouched by humans.

It was always fascinating to see who might turn up on the island as a guest. There were business executives, artists, musicians, families on vacations, and scientists. The revolving door of visitors kept my job interesting. I enjoyed meeting people and taking care of them.

One day a state shorebird biologist visited the island. Together with a small team of observers, we conducted a midwinter shorebird survey. We counted exactly 1,105 Semipalmated Plovers, 3,197 Dunlin, nearly 200 Short-billed Dowitcher, and 6 Long-billed Curlews. We had a total of 15 shorebird species for the day—none of them were new for my year list, but it was incredible to see in these numbers.

One morning, as I made my way into the staff quarters on my day off, the staff were buzzing with excitement. A fire crew would be out on the island doing a controlled burn in the slash pine forest. Fire is an important ecological tool for maintaining a healthy and balanced ecosystem. It helps clear dense woody undergrowth, returns nutrients to the soils, and helps seeds that require high temperatures to germinate.

This event was noteworthy, as it attracted more than a few guests to the island. Accompanying the fire crew, artist Philip Juras also arrived on the morning boat. A master landscape painter, Philip was already well-known on the island. He has a gift for conveying a sense of place in his paintings. The scheduled burn merged his interests of painting untouched southern landscapes and painting fire.

I spent the afternoon following the fire crews, as they set up their equipment and grabbed tools necessary to control the blaze. Hours passed as I stood mesmerized, watching the fire dance around this natural landscape in the way it has for centuries.

During my free time, I wrote grant requests and sponsorship proposals to a variety of organizations and companies to ask for support for my Big Year. Toyota and Subaru both had budgeted their charitable giving for the year, and my requests were denied. I heard a sequence of "no's" again and again, but I didn't give up. Respected optics companies had people already in place representing their brands, and I got rejection letters or no response from the ones I contacted.

While flipping through the pages of a magazine I saw an ad for Maven Optics, which I'd never heard of. They boldly claimed to be high-performance top-shelf optics, and the reviews I read seemed to corroborate their claims. I was puzzled as to why I had never heard of this brand, or seen them in the hands of birders. I found their number and gave them a call. One of the owners answered the phone, and we had a good conversation. They offered to send a demo box of different optics to me, to test out and see for myself. This was intriguing! Within a week, a box showed up on the afternoon boat with my name on it.

Like a kid on Christmas morning, I savored opening up each set of binoculars, which looked and felt brand-new. I took them into the field right away and used them side-by-side with my Swarovski SLC's. The differences were virtually unnoticeable under normal viewing conditions. They were waterproof, shockproof (I didn't test this), and felt good in my hands. Satisfied with the performance of these binoculars, I put together a sponsorship request to ask them for their support of my newly-minted Big Year.

The routine of life on the island was interrupted in the middle of February when I had just wrapped up a long eight-hour shift of working in the kitchen. I had 48 hours off before my next scheduled day of work and was honestly unsure what to do with this large block of time. I left the lodge and turned my phone off airplane mode. Instantly my phone blew up with Facebook notifications, making the decision easy for me: A Zenaida Dove had just been found in Florida, on Long Key. This bird was a Code 5, meaning that it had been seen only a handful of times before in the ABA Area.

I'd never seen a Zenaida Dove before. Native to the Bahamas, this was a super-rare bird to be found in the U.S. I mapped the driving time at 8.5 hours, from my location in Georgia to Long Key in Florida. The wheels began to turn in my head. *I could also add several other birds to my year list, attempt to find the Zenaida Dove, and interview other birders who will surely be chasing this bird...* The value added up, and after checking the boat schedule off the island, my plan was in motion.

Six hours later, I was in Miami to pick up a character named Olaf Danielson to join me on the drive south to the Keys. Olaf was doing a Big Year and was off to a fantastic start. I figured he may have been skeptical of my great start to the year, sniffing out a potential Big Year competitor. I had put up an impressive tally of birds since January 1st, but nobody else knew my resources were limited and would be lucky to see over 600 species.

I sent Olaf a Facebook message and offered to save him the rental car cost and drive down to the Keys together in my car. He accepted my invitation and adjusted his plans so he could be in Miami that night. I was eager to interview some big-name birders for The Birding Project, and a Big Year birder could be a great start. Perhaps he might even break the record!

I picked up Olaf late that same night from the airport in Miami. We continued driving south, crossing into the Keys. That is where I had my first experience with Florida's Highway Patrol. I learned about Florida's "move over" law when I failed to merge into the left lane while passing a stopped police car on the shoulder. With multiple units on the scene, one eagerly gave chase.

I explained to the officer that this was my first time getting pulled over, and I wasn't sure how to deal with the fact that I had a handgun in my glove box—a normal thing in Montana. I had all the proper permits and a concealed carry license, but I asked the officer how he'd like me to proceed to retrieve my documents. I think it was a tense experience for my passenger, but everything ended up just fine. The officer patiently explained Florida's "move over" law, and after receiving the proper documents, sent us on our way with a respectful salute.

One of the challenges to traveling in Florida's Keys is the lack of campsites. After driving all day, I was tired and so we pulled off Highway 1 into a gravel parking area and rolled down the windows and fell asleep. With all of Olaf's stuff in the back, I couldn't sleep in the back of my car as usual, so I reclined in the driver's seat and suffered through a pretty uncomfortable night's sleep. The warm sea breeze was nice, but it was hard to get comfortable. At first light, the next morning, a Florida Highway Patrol car pulled into the gravel lot, and I figured that was a sign that we better get moving. I didn't need any more run-ins with the law.

We arrived at Long Key State Park, and searched for the dove along with several other birders. We got amazing looks as the bird walked into the trail, pecking at seeds, oblivious to the cameras and big lenses. Superficially, the Zenaida (pronounced *zen-EYE-duh*) Dove looks like a larger, stocky Mourning Dove. Upon closer inspection, the square tail and white wing patch are diagnostic field marks.

The remainder of the day we searched for other birds, adding more species to both our year lists. We heard the secretive Black Rail, and I re-found the Smooth-billed Ani at Loxahatchee National Wildlife Refuge. Many of these birds were new for his year list; I'd spent some time birding Florida intently at the end of January, knowing I'd have to endure a month of not seeing many new year birds in February. This trip was a bonus—sharing costs made it cheaper for us both to see some new birds, and I could prove to Olaf that I was living out of my car and wasn't a serious competitor to his goal of beating the old Big Year record of 749 species.

Olaf was a born storyteller. He entertained me for hours with facts about Florida's history and geology, and provided a running commentary on anything and everything we passed by. He wasn't exactly garrulous, but as things came to mind he shared them. We had both visited many of the same places so far in our individual quests for birds, yet by his stories I could tell our approaches were quite different. He lamented missing birds I only wished I had the resources to chase.

On our way back to the Miami airport, I realized I had nearly forgotten to interview him for The Birding Project. I conducted a hasty interview while driving, and took his portrait outside the Southwest baggage drop, which was fitting for a jet-setting Big Year birder. I wished him luck, knowing without a doubt we would cross paths again.

I learned of the Georgia Audubon Society (GOS) field trip several days before their arrival by boat to Little St. Simons. Eager to continue interviewing birders for The Birding Project, I couldn't wait for them to arrive. I had a breakfast and dinner shift that day, leaving the main part of the day free to go birding with the group, and do some interviews.

That morning, I served breakfast to the overnight guests, cleared the tables and washed dishes, and then set tables and prepared the dining room for lunch. I was grateful for the other kitchen staff who helped streamline these jobs to facilitate my finishing on time. The birding group had already arrived by boat and loaded into the two naturalist pickup trucks, which were fitted with padded benches across the open bed. I quickly threw on some layers, grabbed my binoculars, and jumped on a bike in an attempt to catch up.

The trucks full of birders hadn't made it very far down the road, stopping frequently to check if any other migrants were mixed in with the throngs of Yellow-rumped Warblers. When I reached the truck, I tucked my bike in the bushes off the main road and jumped in with them. Immediately I was greeted by warm smiles and enthusiastic participants, many of whom had read the eBird reports I had been submitting from the island in the previous weeks. We enjoyed birding the road out to Sancho Panza beach, where thousands of shorebirds delighted everyone.

I felt particularly embraced by a woman named Krista, who wouldn't stop smiling the entire day. She was obviously thrilled to be birding, and each new bird we found earned an enthusiastic remark. It was clear that she loved birds and birding, and I loved her enthusiasm and wanted to learn her secret. In an interview, she shared her story with me. After a battle with cancer, Krista received word from her doctor that they found cancer again, and this time there was nothing they could do. Her doctor's advice was to spend time with people she likes and doing the things that make her happy. She quit her job, spent more time with her family, and unleashed her passion for birding.

"Last year I went to both ends of the world. I did Antarctica and the Arctic in one year. I went to Alaska, and Brazil, and the Tortugas... I'm birding like crazy!" she told me, with a big smile on her face. Her doctor had given her this advice: "Don't be a slave to your chemo." Wow. We talked about not being a slave to your circumstances. Here was an inspiring example of a woman who relentlessly pursued her passion, spreading joy to others while she savored each moment and every bird.

We stood quietly together, beneath the giant oak trees. She was so inspiring, and full of love. I gave her a hug and told her I hoped to bird with her again later in the year. I never had that chance, as she passed away three months later, just after her birthday. I thought about what she shared with me in her interview, the enjoyment that birding brought her. The blog post I published on The Birding Project of our interview was shared far and wide following her passing—a testament to Krista's legacy and ties within the Georgia birding community. I was grateful to overlap with her for several short smile-filled hours.

All in all, I spent 25 days on Little St. Simons Island. These days were full of hard work, love, humble service, and healing. My strategy to stay close to Florida and chase rarities if time permitted had paid off with spotting the Zenaida Dove. Even more fulfilling to me, however, was the opportunity I had to pause and reflect, giving my Big Year purpose and a more deliberate direction moving forward. I had the chance to give back to a special place that is Little St. Simons. I met wonderful people in the form of birders, artists, ecologists, gardeners, and successful business people. I made friends with the hardworking and dedicated staff. After leaving Little St. Simons Island I wrote:

Back on the road. Walmart parking lot in Alabama. Left LSSI today after a morning of work. Hard to leave the familiar, but eager to embrace the unknown. I'll always have a home on LSSI and will go back. The road is now my home.

$$7$$

LEARNING

THE BEGINNING of March brought subtle hints of spring across the South—small green buds bursting open on trees and male Northern Cardinals singing their cheerful song from atop a prominent perch. In a stark contrast, only a twelve hour drive to the northwest, the icy clutches of winter still had a firm grasp on the Rocky Mountains.

Descending into Colorado's Arkansas Valley, I was reminded by the wall of snow-covered Collegiate Peaks to the west that winter was far from over. This valley has been my home nearly every summer since the age of nine, when I first attended summer camp away from home, in the shadow of these stunning mountains. Despite being able to name all the surrounding mountains in this valley, I had never been here in March to see them blanketed in snow.

The hillsides were familiar to me—wrapped with aspens and firs in summer's leafy embrace. Winter highlighted the intimate topography of this range in a new way. Exposed ridges and avalanche chutes normally disguised by seasonal vegetation stood out, making the mountains appear smaller, yet grander at the same time.

Bobby was the director of the summer camp I attended near Buena Vista, and over the years became a dear friend and mentor to me in the summers of my youth. After moving on from that position, Bobby founded an alternative high school called The Link School, located nearby.

When Bobby invited me to come to Colorado and spend a few days teaching at Link, I couldn't say no. This was no ordinary high school; it would be what many would consider a *dream* high school. The school helps students grow into engaged learners, giving them opportunities to serve their community, explore spirituality, while learning to live in a healthy, balanced way.

At The Link School, students take unique classes like Mountain Ecology and Ornithology and embark on expeditions into the surrounding intermountain West. Whitewater kayaking, rock climbing, mountain biking, and skiing were fundamental pieces of the experiential curriculum, set in some of the roughest and most beautiful terrain the country has to offer.

The school's annual international expeditions took students to countries including Peru, Mexico, Colombia, and Ecuador—all fantastic birding destinations!

Anticipating my arrival, I thought about which new birds I could see in Colorado in March. Along with Lewis' Woodpeckers, Pinyon Jays, and multiple species of rosy-finches, Northern Goshawk immediately came to mind as a slam-dunk.

My history with Northern Goshawks in Colorado dates back to when I was 10 years old. With a cheap disposable camera, I photographed an adult male Northern Goshawk perched on a fence at the summer camp corral at eye-level. Taking flight, he launched his attack using horses as cover, flying close to the ground until his prey was in sight. The

Wyoming Ground Squirrel never stood a chance. Nearly every hunt I witnessed ended successfully, to my delight in his hunting prowess. Since then, I have been fascinated by this species of bird and wished to someday have a personalized Colorado license plate that reads: GOSHAWK

Northern Goshawk

Miles off of a Colorado county road was a Northern Goshawk territory I had spent hours searching for years ago. Not having added a Northern Goshawk to my year list, I smiled as I thought about the privilege of visiting the territory of the nest I'd found years ago, high in the mountains of Colorado. With a smile on my face, and warm layers covering my exposed skin, I began the climb up the hillsides of stunted pinyon pines up to the ridges and gullies filled with aspens and firs. The cool air stung my cheeks as I navigated through the impenetrable wall of pine branches up into the foothills—just a blip on the map compared to the magnificent backdrop of the snow-capped 14,000-foot mountains.

The forest floor was blanketed in knee-high crusty snow, interrupted now and again by a meandering string of elk tracks. Judging by the depth of these tracks, I surmised the elk had as much difficulty crossing the snowpack as I did. I would take several steps on top of the hard crust before plunging through, sinking up to my knees in the first snow of my Big Year. After a long slog, I reached the edge of a small clearing and, gazing skyward, I spotted the round platform of sticks through the sprawling branches. I felt the same sense of excitement and wonder as when I first discovered the nest. The birds were not in the immediate vicinity, but were surely in the area—I could be patient.

The air was thinner than I remembered. I sat down and leaned against a fallen log to catch my breath. I looked around at my surroundings, different from every plant community I'd seen so far this year. The tall trees swayed in the wind and tickled the low clouds, sprinkling small snowflakes with each passing gust of wind. Staring at the aspen's ivory fingers grasping at the patches of blue sky, my eyelids began to close— until I heard the familiar rising alarm call. The sound of wing- beats punctuated the silence, and the female appeared over- head and landed in front of me on a branch, partially obscured by the aspen grove. I didn't dare move a muscle. Minutes passed, maybe longer. She continued her harsh scolding; I was in her woods interrupting her affairs. Soon the smaller male appeared, his breast so finely vermiculated it seemed like a talented painter had tested his finest brush on a feathered gray canvas. I admired each move of the male as he inspected the area. His head bobbed up and down, judging my character as he could clearly see through me with his piercing red gaze. He seemed approving of my presence by preening after moving to a branch with a clear line of sight to my sprawled-out form on the forest floor. I remained still until both birds disappeared ghost-like into the forest.

The next morning nearly the entire school departed for Utah, packed into two Suburbans. Having only 12 high school students provides the freedom to travel and hold classes in the field while developing technical skills in a variety of outdoor activities.

We set up camp outside Moab and enjoyed an afternoon of rock climbing and rappelling at some well-known crags. The next morning we caravanned to the trailhead of Grand Gulch, where we unloaded and prepared for the multi-day backpacking excursion ahead of us.

Crossing a mesa dotted with scrubby pinyon and juniper, we hiked along serpentine cattle trails, weaving across the landscape. As the trails crossed onto rock and disappeared, we ambled down slickrock, descending into the canyons below. Most sections of the gulch were navigable with full packs, while others were steep. With packs off, we climbed down steep drops on all fours, passing our packs down one at a time afterward.

Two, maybe three miles passed before we took a packs-off break at a grove of cottonwoods in the canyon. Jon, the science teacher seized the moment to hold an impromptu class— describing the history of the Ancestral Puebloans, an ancient culture who lived in these canyons about 1,400 years ago. He enthusiastically described their agrarian lifestyle and explained how irrigation techniques and cultivation of crops in this landscape led to bountiful harvests of corn, beans, and squash. These crops were stored in cliff-side granaries, hidden under outcroppings of rocks or hidden on seemingly inaccessible cliff ledges. Some of the best-known examples of these structures come from Mesa Verde.

I listened carefully as Jon described the architectural and artistic skills of this culture. The Ancestral Puebloans were expert basketmakers and created fine pottery also to help store their crops. This ancient civilization is still shrouded in mystery —the entire region was abruptly abandoned. One theory suggests a drought triggered the mass migration of these people to other regions.

I could see the thoughtful contemplation on many students' faces as they listened intently. Jon ended with an open-ended question, giving the group time to reflect and write about their predictions of what might have ended this prosperous culture.

During this silent period of journaling, the musical song of a Canyon Wren tumbled down from the cliffs above. Turning my gaze upwards in the direction of the song I spotted it: a perfectly-square window high in the rocks. Raising my binoculars, an adobe wall appeared, and then another as I scanned the cliffs. This entire time we had been sitting beneath an ancient granary built by the Ancestral Puebloans.

The thrill of exploration took over. In the following days, we wandered miles through the canyons, stopping to examine each archaeological site that emerged from the landscape. Surely we passed dozens of others that went unnoticed. I helped fill in the gaps as my knowledge allowed; Jon knew much more about the Puebloan culture, and I knew more about the birds. We found bones from domestic turkeys and pictograph panels of human stick-figures with bird heads, and many winged creatures. We talked about the cultural significance of birds, and their place in religious beliefs of many groups of Native Americans.

Standing on a rock outcropping above the valley floor, I looked inside the round kiva—a ceremonial structure sunk into the shelf-like cliff. Dimly lit, smoky shafts of light reached down from the square opening above me, at the top of the ladder. Everything was remarkably well-preserved—the cedar logs looked as if they had been cut only yesterday. Bare footprints left in the fine dirt made me wonder if ancient people's spirits walked these ruins in the dark—but as I carefully left the kiva I noticed one of my students wasn't wearing any shoes.

The ancient rhythm of community life resonated deep among the canyon walls. Each night the students set up camp, cooked, and washed dishes in accord with the "Leave No Trace" principles. A student trip-leader (usually a senior) also planned the meals and led a debrief at the end of each day. I was impressed at the skills they were developing, not just in their academics, but general life skills. *If only the school had been around when I was in high school.*

Well after dark, I lay awake, listening for owls. Distant giggles echoed off the canyon walls, coming from the direction of the girls' campsite. Engulfed in my sleeping bag, I stared upwards at a wide ceiling of stars. *I can't believe I'm getting paid to do this!*

I traced the Milky Way in silent reflection. I habitually went through a mental list of everything I was grateful for from the day. An "attitude of gratitude" helped me fall asleep and focus on the good in my life, instead of worrying about everything else that seemed to be challenging.

I was grateful to be earning money for the road ahead. It was rare to be paid to share birds with others (and I loved that I was doing something I loved, with the chance to make an impact on others). I was grateful to be taking young people to a place like this. If the next generation doesn't experience these wild places, then they won't value the land or its history, and won't fight to protect it. I was grateful to be around teenagers who were kind, curious, and open-minded. I wondered if perhaps someday, I could envision myself teaching at a school like this. Just like countless nights before, I fell asleep before I could finish my list.

Teaching classes at The Link School wasn't the only schooling I was involved with. For the previous two years I'd been steadily chipping away at a master's degree in St. Louis. My interests in education and innovation aligned with a program offered by Webster University, providing a focus on Education for Global Sustainability. This program included both online courses in addition to classes on campus. I took advantage of both, completing many of the in-person classes necessary for my degree.

When I moved to Montana, I took a semester off, to focus full-time on fundraising and helping to produce the documentary for PBS. With that chapter behind me, I felt it was important to not lose my momentum, and continue the online component of my degree. I didn't want my Big Year to slow down my education, so I took a risk and registered for online courses for the quickly-approaching spring semester.

Continuing my degree came with the financial burden of paying for classes. My savings from my teaching job was dwindling, but I afford at least another semester. My paychecks from working the last month in Georgia had added a comfortable cushion, and the money I made teaching at Link was going right back into my Big Year. I wasn't sure how it was going to work out, but I trusted that it would.

8

SPRING CHICKENS

I REMAINED contemplative as I drove northwards along Interstate 25, passing the city of Ft. Collins as I made my way towards Wyoming. I thought about the many positive interactions that had taken place the week prior, with students at The Link School. It was amazing to see them embrace learning about birds. Despite our short time together, we had learned all about birds. We did a avian physiology lab, examining bird anatomy and structure. We dissected owl pellets I had collected in my travels and reconstructed the rodent skeletons. Students examined the soft edges of an owl feather, and we discussed adaptations and evolution—all prior to our canyoneering trip in Utah!

My time at Link had stretched me outside my comfort zone a little. I wasn't used to being on a schedule, but I understood the need for planning and coordinating so many moving pieces. The Link School staff had accommodated my birding needs on our expedition, allowing me to search for Gunnison Sage-Grouse near Monticello, Utah.

Until the late 1990s the slight differences in plumage and

voice of the population of sage-grouse in the Gunnison Basin had been overlooked by biologists. Only after careful study did this new species emerge, presenting birders with an exciting range-restricted bird to add to their life list.

Despite making a solid effort searching for Gunnison Sage-Grouse in Utah, the birds evaded me. Perhaps the Golden Eagle perched atop the rusted farmhouse roof nearby had something to do with it. I thought back to the steep canyon walls of Utah that I had hiked through with students, climbing to ancient cliff dwellings.

Looking forward, I thought about the upcoming birds I could see in Wyoming—most notably, the Greater Sage-Grouse. I froze my butt off spending a brutal night sleeping in the car at a Colorado lek that wasn't yet active—missing this charismatic bird in the state of Colorado. Right when I thought I knew what birds to expect and when to see them, the birding gods reminded me I wasn't in charge—and both patience and humility were necessary parts to becoming a better birder.

The pungent scent of sagebrush wafted through the open car windows, as my eyes adjusted to the night's inky darkness. I shut off my car and listened to the cooling engine as it produced a random series of metallic sounds that sounded like large raindrops falling on a tin roof.

I had obediently followed my GPS, off the Wyoming highway and down a deeply rutted dirt road until the voice matter-of-factly informed me I had arrived. This spot looked no different than everywhere else I had passed on the bumpy drive in, and for a moment I doubted I was there. Hopefully I was close enough to an open clearing in the sea of sagebrush where the following morning, I could watch a group of Greater Sage-Grouse perform their ancient mating ritual.

It was still dark several hours later, when I was roused from a deep sleep by a foreign sound. Opening an eye to check my phone, I blinded myself, having forgotten to adjust the brightness. It was 3:59 a.m. I lay still, straining my ears—silence. The warm Wyoming wind that blew yesterday had turned to a cold chill during the night, and the weather forecast soon called for snow. The silence was broken by the low hoots of a distant Great-horned Owl. I closed my eyes, reveling in the wild place I was in.

Then, a mysterious popping sound began, reminiscent of my childhood mischief inside racquetball courts, where I ran around kicking balls off every wall, ceiling, and door. I knew this sound from a bird app I listened to while waiting to see this bird in Colorado. Though I would have to wait until daylight to see the birds, I had heard my first-ever Greater Sage-Grouse. I stretched out on the folded back seat of my car and slid deep into my warm sleeping bag, and with a smile on my face, I drifted off into a light sleep.

Throughout the rest of the night, I awoke periodically as the hollow popping sounds continued outside my window. It seemed like an eternity had passed, but finally, a faint glow appeared low on the horizon in the eastern sky. Near my car, dark shapes floated around the short grass, dancing around an open stage amidst the taller sagebrush.

As the sky grew lighter, the grouse activity increased, and the drama unfolded in front of me. Dozens of Sage-Grouse danced across the lek—a name given to the display and breeding area that many of North America's chicken and grouse species use in the springtime. These "leks" are often located on flat areas with good visibility and acoustics, which allow the males to produce their low-pitched call notes as they advertise for females.

Male Greater Sage-Grouse display for females in Wyoming's sagebrush country

In the birding world, March heralds the start of "chicken season" when organized tour groups travel across the intermountain west in search of this unique family of birds. March and April are prime months to see chickens and grouse because it is mating season. A seat on a chicken tour isn't cheap, but it is a surefire way to see nearly a dozen species of North American grouse and chickens within a week. Joining a tour seemed like a lucrative idea, but I rather wanted to learn more about the birds by finding and experiencing them on my own. Armed with eBird data for nearly all the species, I figured it would be doable.

This wasn't just a scavenger hunt; it was a game of strategy. Although my knowledge of every bird was limited, I was willing and eager to learn. I'd learned a lot by interviewing birders so far, and wanted to extend my reach to biologists and conservationists who worked with grouse species. Interviewing some sage-grouse biologists in Wyoming would be the perfect place to start.

Lander, Wyoming, sits in the shadow of the southern Wind River mountain range and has the quintessential feel of a small mountain town. I'd come to visit the world headquarters of

Maven Optics, which was located along a side street in a nondescript building. If I hadn't been paying close attention, I would have missed it.

What I didn't want to miss was the opportunity to meet the guys behind the company. Brendon, Cade, Mike, and Craig comprised an experienced team of guys who were building an optics company in a very unique way—selling directly to consumers.

They welcomed me with open arms and warm Wyoming hospitality. We went out to a delicious dinner with their families and shared some good food and many laughs. They loved what I was doing with The Birding Project and wanted to help promote my cause in any way they could. I was humbled by their support and encouragement.

They told me about a new product—a spotting scope that hadn't been released yet and was in the final stages of productions. I trusted them—after all, they were the experts. Still, I had to test it out myself.

Early the next morning, I went back to a sage-grouse lek—I couldn't get enough of these charismatic birds. Just before dawn, I set up Maven's scope side by side with my modular Swarovski ATX 90, which was larger and slightly heavier overall. Both scopes were tack-sharp and offered a clear image in low light. I spent an hour watching the birds from a quarter-mile away, and savored every minute. Maven had done a great job with their design and built a top-of-the-line optic, which I hoped to add to my arsenal, replacing my Swarovski scope.

Wyoming felt like a fresh start for me, after missing some target species in Colorado had dampened my spirits. I left my birding blues at the border, optimistic for the next few days of birding. Wyoming had much of the same habitat as Colorado, giving me a second chance at birds I thought would be easy to find in Colorado. I spotted the American Dipper, North America's only aquatic songbird. The robin-sized bird fearlessly plunged into the tumultuous mountain streams, somehow emerging every time no worse for the wear, occasionally belting his song.

The American Dipper loves feeding in turbulent water

Like the dipper, I sang my song. Craig and I went birding, and he interviewed me and produced a short film, telling my story of starting The Birding Project. Although my story was far from over, this film helped generate awareness of what I had done and was hoping to do in the future with The Birding Project.

During my stay, I attended a Rotary Club meeting with Mike, where I had the chance to share what I was doing with The Birding Project with those in attendance. I'd never been to a Rotary Club function before and was surprised by how embraced and at home I felt. The kind and genuine members shook my hand, welcoming me into their community. Each person I met had a story to share or a connection to suggest.

One suggested contact was a local eBirder named Del, who accompanied me on my quest to find more birds. Together we added Black Rosy-finch, Ring-necked Pheasant, and Chukar to my year list.

I returned to the lek at sunrise, with a sage-grouse biologist from the Wyoming Department of Fish and Game. Learning about a bird species from someone who has spent their career studying them was a unique opportunity. I also visited a different lek with a team of researchers from California, who were using robotic sage-grouse to study the movements and behavior of the wild birds. I felt afterward that I didn't just add this species to my list, but I better understood this species as a whole—and the challenges facing the continued survival in an imperiled ecosystem.

Five days of cold in Wyoming had been long enough to make meaningful connections, see some new birds, and have an amazing experience with Greater Sage-Grouse, which became a highlight of my year so far. April was coming, and it was a long road ahead to get to the Gulf Coast for the start of spring migration.

Before leaving the mountain west, I still had a few more "winter" birds to check off. I drove back to Colorado, spotting many Brown-capped Rosy-Finches among a mixed flock near a ski resort. Late at night, a drive up and over Grand Mesa allowed me to hear two different Boreal Owls, which were both quite close but remained hidden in dense conifers. Driving through the Gunnison Basin, I finally spotted a distant Gunnison Sage-Grouse displaying in front of the sunrise at the well-known Waunita Hot Springs lek. My persistence had paid off.

In the town of Roswell, New Mexico, I searched for free wifi. I knew that for the next few days I would be out of cell signal, and needed to submit the week's assignments for my online classes. As I pulled into the McDonald's parking lot, I noticed there was something strange about this particular restaurant, which didn't look like any of the others I'd ever seen —it was UFO-themed!

The restaurant itself was saucer-shaped, and inside kids ran around the intergalactic playland, climbing through tunnels with french fry spaceships and planet orbs. I worked diligently for hours, and after Powerade refill number three, I figured I should head out and make it an early night since I had an early morning planned.

After dumping the fourth and fifth cups of blue Powerade into my personal water bottle, I returned to my car and turned the back into "sleep mode" for the night, under the well-lit lights of the parking lot. With my sleeping pad unrolled, sleeping bag spread out, and all the food and cooler on one side, with extra gear loaded in the passenger's seat beside me, I headed east.

Somewhere in eastern New Mexico, at the end of a dusty oil road lives a small group of Lesser Prairie-Chickens. After crossing over cattle guards and traversing ancient sand dunes, the road dead-ends in a patch of sandy rangeland covered in stubby clumps of shinnery oaks and sand sagebrush. This specific habitat type has shrunk dramatically over the past 150 years, shrinking more than 90% in size from its original range. It is widely believed that conversion to agriculture, grazing, oil and gas development, and other energy projects (such as wind farms) also significantly affect prairie-chickens. Now, fewer than 50,000 individual birds remained, scattered across eastern New Mexico, the panhandle of Texas, Oklahoma, Kansas, and the southeastern corner of Colorado.

A male prairie-chicken walked towards my car, which I'd parked along the road in the darkness the night before. The bird disappeared beneath my front wheel and then reappeared on the other side. He cocked his head sideways before jumping up onto a thick clump of bluestem, which doubled over as he struggled—flapping his wings and climbing up into the clump as high as he could go, before letting out a loud call outside my window at eye-level. I couldn't believe how bold these birds were!

Suddenly, the birds scattered as a white diesel pickup came over the hill, and pulled up right behind me. I shot the driver a disbelieving look in my mirror as he shut off the truck and talked loudly with his passenger with the windows down for a minute. It wasn't even a quarter past six, and my solo show had now turned into a group affair. No sooner than the wind had carried away the lingering diesel fumes, the birds returned.

The male's elongated brown neck feathers, called *pinnae*, stood straight up on end, as if they were electrified, revealing a wrinkly patch of bright red neck skin on their neck. Within moments this shriveled patch of skin inflated with air into a bulging red balloon! I loved it! The females seemed less enamored by this incredible display and cautiously walked around pecking at the ground. Also unimpressed were the impatient occupants of the white truck behind me, which noisily departed in a cloud of black smoke.

I quietly observed the drama that unfolded. Male birds courted several females in an elaborate jumping display, followed by doggedly chasing other males around. Two males faced off, standing opposite each other, but each bird appeared hesitant to make the first move. One flinched, and a brutal battle ensued. Both birds flapped violently and contorted their bodies in a wrestling match I didn't understand. The violence that ensued pulled feathers that drifted away with the dust, snagging on the leafless skeleton of a bush. I lost track of time, fully immersed in studying the interactions and behaviors of these incredible birds.

The wind picked up as the sun moved higher into the sky, and one by one the prairie-chickens melted back into the landscape, making their exit as if on cue. After the last bird departed, I got out of my car and picked up a single windblown feather that had landed near my car. Satisfied with this incredible morning, I retraced my tracks down the dusty oil road, where the wind had covered my tracks, leaving only shallow ruts in the sand.

Driving down the highway at 75 miles per hour, I almost didn't notice the flash of silvery-gray feathers on the side of the road. It took me almost half a mile to make sense of what I'd seen just off the shoulder of the highway, in the middle of New Mexico, far from the Pacific Ocean. *That was a Brown Pelican!* I thought to myself. I turned around, thinking that if I was right, this was a good record this far inland. Sure enough, as I pulled over on the opposite shoulder, I realized my split-second identification had been right. Sadly, it wasn't alive. I wondered if it had been hit at this spot, or perhaps it had been stuck to the front of a semi truck for the previous several hundred miles. I could only speculate about how such a bizarre occurrence happened.

Cars kill birds. In a year's time, I passed thousands of dead birds on the shoulder of our nation's roadways. It didn't matter if it was a freeway, exit ramp, or back road, the piles of feathers were there, a wing flapping in the breeze of a passing car. I saw hundreds of dead birds in Florida, and even more in Texas. If a road cut through quality habitat, there was roadkill.

I noticed more dead raptors than any other group of birds, perhaps because they're large and easy for me to identify at highway speeds. Red-tailed and Swainson's Hawks were most common in Texas, as were Barn and Great Horned Owls. Along one stretch of Texas highway, I counted at least one dead owl per mile for 15 miles. Strangely, almost every one was adjacent to an overpass. There's got to be some correlation—maybe the owls hunt along the perpendicular road, flying low over the ground where they are blindsided by oncoming traffic? Perhaps it's an acoustic dead-spot, or they are hunting pigeons underneath the overpass? I pondered the possibilities for miles.

Birds weren't the only victims; I spotted flattened alligators in Florida, dead deer in Delaware, and smashed skunks in South Carolina. In spring, the soil near the highway warms faster than the frozen ground farther out, allowing vegetation to grow through the thawed soil. Deer, elk, and pronghorn all feed dangerously close to the road. I probably saw a dead deer in every state. I also noticed that deer crossing signs differ regionally—in the east the antler shape was different than signs across the west. To me, it appeared the shapes reflect the differences in the symmetrical shape of White-tailed Deer antlers versus the branching/forking pattern of Mule Deer.

On the second to last day of March, the odometer of my Subaru rolled over to 100,000 miles on the highway in west Texas. There was something fulfilling about seeing so many zeroes on the dashboard all at once. It signaled a new start, a fresh beginning. I had saved some money after working February and March and was now ready to take on spring migration. I was seeing the continent through new eyes, and writing my own story as I chose what to do each day, over and over again. It was liberating.

9

FLORIDA

As SPRING APPROACHES, millions of tropical birds across Central and South America are driven north by the urge to breed. They feed constantly, moving north until they reach the end of Mexico's Yucatan Peninsula. With fat reserves to fuel the long journey ahead, they wait for ideal winds to set out across the Gulf of Mexico after sunset. The 600-mile crossing will take many of these birds 18 hours to reach the Texas coast, where patches of habitat provide food, fresh water, and cover from predators while they rest and replenish for their next push onwards toward their breeding grounds further north.

Many of these neotropical migrants make this journey twice a year, flying deep into the heart of North America's temperate forests to breed and raise young, before returning to the warm tropics to spend the winter months.

Birders also are drawn to these areas where tired birds seek refuge—places like High Island along the Texas Gulf Coast. People from all over the country visit in hopes of getting close-up views of colorful neotropical warblers, vireos, tanagers, and flycatchers as they make their way north to breed.

I had underestimated how early some of the spring migrants would return to the Upper Texas coast, and decided to only spend a single day birding High Island before heading to Florida. It was hard to imagine I had been in Wyoming only twelve days prior. Since then, I birded through Colorado and Arizona, across New Mexico and nearly all of Texas. My goal was to get to the Florida Keys as spring migration picked up.

I stopped at a Florida Welcome Center along the interstate. I knew from experience that it provided a clean bathroom and free orange juice. Life's simple pleasures can be found in the small things, like a free glass of freshly-squeezed orange juice.

Prior to 2016, there were only a handful of places I knew about and wanted to go that I knew doing a Big Year would take me. The Dry Tortugas in Florida was on this short list. I'd first learned about the Dry Tortugas in my high school marine biology class. I was lured in by photos of aquamarine waters, colorful reef fish, and dozens of Magnificent Frigatebirds floating lazily overhead the old fort. Ecologically, the Florida Keys belong to the tropics and are full of tropical species found throughout the Caribbean. The Dry Tortugas is one of the most geographically isolated National Parks, located nearly 70 miles west of Key West. Getting there required taking a boat, or chartering a seaplane for a stunning $600 for a full day trip. I definitely wasn't going to fly there.

At the end of January, I birded across southern Florida in search of the American Flamingo that had been hanging out around Bunche Beach near Fort Myers. That chase gave me the opportunity to be interviewed by the local news and help educate people on how special birding is!

At Bunche Beach I met Greg Miller, one of the three real-life 1998 Big Year birders portrayed by actor Jack Black in the film *The Big Year*. Greg was leading a trip for Wildside Nature Tours, an excellent tour company that travels to some truly amazing places. He gave a great interview and was supportive of allowing time for his clients to interview with me also.

Greg wasn't the only Big Year birder in Florida at the time. There is a lot of birding history in the area, and many dedicated birders call Florida home, including Sandy Komito (the roofing contractor, played by Owen Wilson in the film *The Big Year*).

Everglades National Park protects 1.5 million acres of sawgrass marsh, mangrove swamps, and pine forests spread across the southwestern tip of Florida. This landscape is unique —found nowhere else in the world. Here, meandering pine forests are interrupted by rivers of grass, which flow across the flat landscape. Alligators skulk in the swamps, masquerading as floating logs, while dozens of manatees laze in crystal-clear rivers fed by warm springs. Somewhere in the palmettos, lurking just out of sight was a bobcat, and its larger cousin, the Florida panther. This land is still truly wild.

The Snail Kite's curved bill is specially adapted to feed on freshwater apple snails

I hiked around in some of the surviving hardwood hammocks—native dense tropical forests with dense canopies that shade the tangled undergrowth beneath. These hammocks form small islands of native habitat across southern Florida, and I figured that any rare birds from the Bahamas would show up in this habitat. Using data from eBird, I targeted specific locations where rarities had shown up in the past, such as Key-West Quail Dove and La Sagra's Flycatcher.

These particular hammocks were mixtures of tropical and temperate tree species—live oaks, red maples, mahogany, and gumbo limbo. I recognized the red peeling bark, making them appear to be sunburned—which has helped earn them the name "tourist tree" in the tropics.

I joined up with local birding guru Larry Manfredi, following some advice I was given from another birder earlier in the year. Larry's backyard was landscaped for birds, and he kept his feeders full, attracting a variety of species to his yard including the Shiny Cowbird. This glossy black bird is native to South America but has steadily made its way north since the 1900s, and has expanded its range into southern Florida. Larry has graciously invited many birders to his feeders to see this bird, and while we waited he provided a fascinating interview for The Birding Project.

We sat and talked in lawn chairs in his backyard, watching his feeders as we discussed birds, his story, and Florida birding. We watched a group of Bronzed Cowbirds on his backyard feeder, while a group of Brown-headed Cowbirds poked around in his lawn. Before long, a male Shiny Cowbird landed on the feeder, giving us the "Cowbird Trifecta"! This small area is the only place in North America I could see all three of these species together at the same time.

After a quick lunch at a local place down the street from Larry's house, we drove around and targeted a few more birds that were new for me for the year. It was fun to have company, after birding the past few days on my own.

Nearly 100,000 years ago, the shallow sea that covered modern-day Florida began to recede as a huge glacial ice sheet formed over much of Canada and the northern United States. This transition caused sea levels to drop, exposing the Bering Sea land bridge, which opened the access for many species of mammals, birds, and humans to cross to this continent. In Florida, this same event revealed the Keys, a coral island chain stretching from just below Miami southward nearly to Cuba.

Highway 1 stretches from Miami down to Key West. The spectacular drive took about three and a half hours, but it would have taken longer if I had a fishing rod with me.

I stopped at Long Key State Park, where I saw the Zenaida Dove in February. I remembered seeing a large amount of trash washed up along the beaches, but given the singular focus of my visit, I was unable to do anything about it. Now I had time to combine a beach cleanup with some birding. The park employees at the office gladly gave me some trash bags to fill as I wandered around.

I started my trash sweep along the beach near the campground, where a Black-faced Grassquit had been sighted regularly for the previous two weeks. There hadn't been many recent reports, and I wondered if most birders had seen it, and nobody had kept looking for the bird as of late. I remained diligent as I picked up trash in the area. I did catch a glimpse of a small dark bird in a bush that I left unidentified—it sure looked like a grassquit.

My trash bag filled quickly with a variety of discarded items made mostly of plastic. Straws, silverware, a yellow shovel and broken bucket. Bottles and cans were abundant, along with styrofoam cups. Several water shoes, a flip-flop, and an assortment of other pieces of garbage made the bag heavy. I wondered if all of this trash came from cruise ships, or maybe it was carried by currents from resort beaches in the Bahamas. I was disheartened to spot a plastic Gatorade bottle floating in the distance through my binoculars. No matter how much I cleaned up, there was always more trash.

Hours later, I'd done all I could with the time I had. As I walked back to the parking lot, I rounded a corner along the sandy Golden Orb trail. A bird darted out underfoot—nearly causing me to trip as I danced awkwardly to avoid stepping on it. The bird flushed in front of me and landed nearby, giving me a better look—it was the Zenaida Dove! I breathed a sigh of relief and tried not to think about what would have happened if I had stepped on this rare bird.

I returned to the main office to ask about where the nearest dumpsters were. The grateful park employees took my bags from me and compensated my effort with multiple vouchers waiving the admission fees to any Florida State Park. I thanked them, grateful to spend more time birding this spot. I knew that as migration picked up, these would come in handy.

A legendary painter and ornithologist, John James Audubon visited the Dry Tortugas 184 years ago in early April. He spent nearly a week drawing the Sooty Terns, Brown Booby, and Brown Noddy, which nested on the islands in unfathomable numbers. On Bird Key, Audubon painted Sooty Terns and wrote about encountering Cuban egg collectors who gathered tern eggs by the boatload to sell at markets in Havana. In years since the bird colonies have declined, undoubtedly the result of indiscriminate egg collecting, and the total loss of Bird Key which was swallowed by the sea following a hurricane.

Over the years many birders have made the crossing by

boat or plane from Key West to the Dry Tortugas, to see a handful of birds found nowhere else in the ABA area. My plan was to drive to Key West and spend the night and take a ferry out to the Dry Tortugas the following morning. Spending the night in Key West on a budget was going to be a challenge. I'd been cautioned by Florida birders before traveling to Key West that finding a place to sleep in my car was going to be difficult. The word on the street said camping (or sleeping in a vehicle) was illegal outside of designated campgrounds. There were established campgrounds throughout the keys, but nothing on Key West. Hotels were over a hundred dollars a night, and there was no Walmart after leaving Miami. People even said that they'd heard of people being fined and jailed for sleeping in their car on Key West. "No Overnight Parking" signs were plentiful, and so it took a little creativity to find somewhere to sleep where I wouldn't be bothered.

Throughout the night, I parked and moved my car several times in order to remain as low-profile as I could. At about midnight, I noticed a vacant space in a parking lot full of cars, so I pulled in the same direction as the rest of the cars, crawled into the back, and fell asleep.

The first thing I noticed when I woke up the following morning at 4 a.m. was the police car parked nearby with its headlights on. I could see the glow on the officer's face from his computer. My heart started pounding, wondering if he was searching my license plate, or waiting for me to pull out of the lot so he could pull me over. Instead of getting out of the car and going through my normal pack-up routine, I decided to wait and make a clean getaway without drawing attention to myself. When it looked like he was on the phone, I started up my car with my headlights off, slowly rolled backward, and left the lot through the side entrance. I glanced nervously in the rear-view mirror for flashing lights to come on, but they never did. I made my escape! I breathed a huge sigh of relief.

I arrived at the ferry terminal long before it opened, and made sure I was first in line at 6:30 a.m. to ask about cancellations. The boat ticket wasn't cheap—$180 round-trip for the day. I knew that occasionally a last-minute space opens up to camp at the primitive campsites on Garden Key. If this could save me from making another trip later in the year, it was worth it.

To my surprise, someone had canceled the day before and I was able to fill their spot—what luck! After figuring out payment and permitting, I had less than 30 minutes before the boat departed to run back to my car and grab my gear. In preparation for this scenario, I'd packed a bag the day before, making sure I had my mask and snorkel in addition to my spotting scope, tent, food, water, and some extra clothes.

As others were boarding, I stood at the counter, waiting for them to process the changes in my status from a "day visitor" to an "overnight camper". A fee was refunded after showing my Parks Pass. I also negotiated a student rate, showing them my emails confirming my current status at Webster University's graduate program. Every dollar I could save was important.

One of the perks of boarding after everyone else was being introduced to Captain Meg. Following a tip from a Florida birder, I asked her if she could stop by Hospital Key along the way so I could see the nesting colony of Masked Boobies at a close distance. She promised if we were on time—depending on the conditions—she would try.

As I boarded the *Yankee Freedom III* I realized this was going to be the first proper pelagic trip I'd done so far this year. Despite riding the ferry to Victoria on January 1st, as well as the shuttle boats to Little St. Simons Island, this high-speed catamaran would take us to the Dry Tortugas, some 70 miles offshore from Key West. The two-hour boat ride passed quickly as I scanned the seas in front of us for birds and tried my best to photograph them—a futile attempt despite the relatively calm sea conditions.

Following through on her promise, Captain Meg brought the boat as close as ethically possible to the sand bar without disturbing the nesting Masked Boobies. I was on the bow of the boat and had explained to everyone around me as we approached Hospital Key why we were slowing down and what we would see. This was the only place in the ABA Area where this species breeds—and this species was both a year bird and a life bird for me. When Captain Meg came on the loudspeaker and told everyone why we had stopped, she added that I was doing a Big Year, and this bird put me one species closer to my goal. I was greeted with congratulatory pats on the back from many on board. Birds really do bring people together.

I was still overcoming my excitement from seeing the boobies up close when I realized the fort was in view. Rising out of the aqua-blue water was a dark long wall of Fort Jefferson, appearing like a Lego structure jutting upwards from the flat horizon. As the catamaran got closer, I began to notice individual birds flying to and from the bushy sandpit that extended from the largest island—Garden Key.

After we disembarked, I found the campground and dumped my bag in the sand under a canopy of sparse trees which offered some protection in the event it would rain or be windy at night. I figured I better set up my tent, to stake my claim and keep my campsite from becoming a picnic area for some day visitors looking for a shady spot. I carefully hid my camera lens under my sleeping bag and brushed the area around my tent smooth with a stick, so that if anyone disturbed my things I could see their tracks. (I wasn't sure it would work, but I thought it was a clever idea.)

Despite knowing that I had three days to spend here, I was eager to begin birding and see if I could find some new birds. The feeling returned—the scavenger-hunt-like adventure of knowing I had all day to find new birds. I ran around the inside of the fort, just to check everything out before I began the seawatch to try to spot the prized bird of the Tortugas: the Black Noddy.

Fort Jefferson was constructed in 1846 and served as a military post for the Union, and later served as a prison, housing about 2,000 people at one point. Some of the historical plaques stated that in July 1865, Dr. Samuel Mudd, along with three others, was imprisoned in the fort for aiding John Wilkes Booth by setting his broken leg and giving him a place to stay for the night following the successful assassination of President Abraham Lincoln.

Mudd was convicted to a lifetime sentence imprisoned within the fort's walls, from which he tried to escape unsuccessfully. In 1867 Mudd was personally pardoned by President Andrew Johnson and released from the fort after displaying his leadership during an epidemic of yellow fever on the island.

The inside of the hexagonal fort was largely open, with scattered groves of buttonwood trees and hedges of some sort of shrubberies. It was in these trees that most of the migratory birds sought refuge, gleaning insects from the leaves and branches, desperate for any energy they could gain. A small man-made bubbler attracts many migrants, who stop to drink and seek food before continuing on the long migration across the Gulf. Sadly, I found many deceased birds around the grounds, ranging from cuckoos to a solitary sandpiper. The perils of migration began to dawn on me as I saw firsthand the carnage of exhausted birds that couldn't finish the journey.

Farther into the fort was the large open field that was once the parade grounds. Now the only thing marching were Cattle

Egrets, who carefully stalked insects and lizards. I watched as several Cattle Egrets made their way over to the bubbler for a drink, and to hunt the warblers who were also in search of water. Although I didn't observe a successful capture, I was told later that this spot is one of the only documented areas where Cattle Egrets regularly prey on small birds.

Surrounded by translucent turquoise water, I spent that afternoon perched on the top of Fort Jefferson beneath a spiraling swarm of frigatebirds, scoping the coaling docks and beaches for any sign of the Black Noddy. This was the only location known in the ABA Area to see this species, which is smaller with a thinner bill than the more plentiful Brown Noddy. This species of tern is hard to find, hard to identify, and is not guaranteed to be seen every year. My persistence paid off. I found a bird that matched the description in my field guides, and digiscoped it and hoped it was my bird. The harsh light made viewing my photos difficult, but I had good looks and was fairly confident I had identified it correctly. The rest of the afternoon passed quickly walking around under the burning sun. I thought back several weeks to the cold mornings observing sage-grouse— this was definitely a nice change!

Overhead, Peregrine Falcons patrolled the skies, able to make a meal from any one of the birds below. Periodically a falcon flew over Bush Key, sending a tornado of terns into the sky. The hunting here was good, as evidenced by the piles of tern and noddy corpses stacked on alcoves among the fort's walls. I could tell spring migration was picking up, as fresh feathers from Yellow-billed Cuckoos rained down from the radio antennae, a favorite perch for the peregrines. Smaller falcons—the Merlin and an American Kestrel—patrolled the parade grounds inside the fort, snatching up a tired barn swallow or bunting that made the mistake of flying across the open parade grounds.

After eating two packets of dry instant oatmeal and a handful of fruit snacks for dinner, I settled down for the night, carefully wiping the sand off my feet before climbing inside my one-man tent. I wanted to try a night snorkel in the waters around the fort under the stars, but without a dive buddy, common sense got the best of me and I stayed out of the water after dark. I enjoyed the evenings laying under the stars, listening to the strumming of a ukulele floating from somewhere through the trees. If I listened closely, over the crashing waves I could hear the distant cacophony of the colony of terns across the harbor.

Camping on Garden Key truly allowed me to experience the islands in a more intimate way. The campground was tucked in amongst the dense vegetation a short walk from the public dock along the southern edge of Garden Key. Every morning I jumped in the clear water, warmed by tropical currents and yesterday's sun. In the afternoon the island was mostly quiet after the boat had left, taking the day visitors back to Key West.

The days passed lazily, birding early in the morning while the island was quiet until the *Yankee Freedom* arrived and visitors flooded the island—crawling all over the fort and sprawling out on the beaches like seals basking in the midday sun. Inside the fort, some birds became harder to find. Having seen nearly all of my target birds, I realized nothing "new" would likely show up for the remainder of the day. I welcomed visiting birders and interviewed high school-age students from a local school. They had traveled out on a field trip with their teacher, and it was fun to help the students find life birds.

On the third day, I spent the morning chasing warblers around the trees on parade grounds. As soon as I thought I'd seen them all, I spent the remainder of the morning searching for a Black Noddy on the coaling docks. I realized how lucky I was on that first afternoon to spot one so quickly.

During the afternoon downtime, I grabbed my snorkel gear and walked along the narrow brick walkway that surrounded the fort. I had tossed my dive bag in my car's roof box months ago without thinking much about it, and after carrying a mask and snorkel around for a month, I was excited to use them! Standing on the brick wall of the fort's moat, staring down into the crystal clear water, schools of small baitfish swarmed beneath my feet, and farther out, an oblong silhouette was surely a barracuda lingering in the shallows.

I was a little nervous jumping into the water, not because of the barracuda, but because of a nine-foot American Crocodile that has lurked in these waters for the previous 13 years. Nicknamed "Cleatus," the lone crocodile had been seen earlier in the day under the bridge to the fort, which I had walked over minutes earlier to get to the best snorkeling. I was told that it was an anomaly to find a crocodile so far out at sea in the salt water. To this point, he hadn't caused much of a problem with visitors. I'd survived birding in alligator-infested swamps, so this really wasn't pushing my luck. I slipped into the water and began swimming along the outside wall of the fort's moat—keeping an eye out over my shoulder all the while.

Underwater, it was an entirely different world. Along the moat wall, a patchwork of small corals and sponges grew attached to the wall. Excited to be in the water, I began swimming quickly and realized I wasn't seeing more than a few schools of fish. When I slowed down, I began to see more. Colorful Christmas tree worms poked out from the coral heads, their frilled, round layers looking exactly like miniature Christmas trees. Hundreds of fish comprised of dozens of species darted in and out from cracks and caves in the rocks. An underwater cacophony of snaps and crackles reminded me the reef was very much alive and active.

Farther away from the wall I discovered some coral that had bleached, a sign of warming waters. As sea temperatures rise, the coral jettisons the algae living within its tissues, and turns ghostly white. Sadly, more and more reefs across the Caribbean are facing this problem. After floating around for a while, I could feel the back of my calves getting sunburned, and decided it was time to get out of the sun again.

As dusk fell, a pair of nighthawks winged northwards over the water while I was preparing dinner at my campsite. Straining my ears, I listened for their raspy calls, which sound like the word "beard" spoken at a whisper. I couldn't hear anything over the breeze and the motor of fishing boats nearby. *Maybe they're Antillean Nighthawks,* I thought to myself as I made a mental note to check the airport on Marathon Key on my drive back to Miami. I remember reading somewhere that no bird in the Dry Tortugas should be overlooked or written off. The potential for rarities here was high, with Cuba less than 50 miles to the south.

The following day before I left the island, I walked out towards Bush Key and set up my scope at the end of the roped-off walkway to study the terns from eye-level. Past the ropes, a mockingbird jumped out from a cluster of sea grapes and ran along the sand with its tail held high, like a drab brown road-runner. Immediately something about the bird seemed "off"— and I realized it was quite likely a rare Bahama Mockingbird. I would need a better look to be sure and add the bird to my list— but it never showed itself again.

I had fallen under the island's magical spell. Time melted away and was nearly lost until I realized with the boat's arrival that I was supposed to return to Key West. The morning passed quickly, and soon I was on the boat watching the fort get smaller and smaller until it was swallowed by the sea. An announcement was made over the boat's speakers about the large swells we would encounter on the crossing back to Key West, and instructions were given about what to do if passengers felt queasy.

Three days of sun and birding from dawn until dusk had tired me out, and I was ready to get back to my routine of driving. I wolfed down the last packet of my off-brand fruit snacks, stretched out under the boat seats, and fell asleep thinking about the birds I'd just seen—and dreaming about the birds I would see next. Little did I know that my wildest dreams couldn't predict what would happen in the next 48 hours.

After dumping my bags in the car, I set out to explore the streets of Key West. I had a half-day remaining of the garage parking I had paid for, which gave me some time to explore. I walked around downtown Key West, enjoying having cell service again. I caught up on emails and figured out my plan for where to go next. Spring migration was really picking up, and I wanted to be along the Texas Gulf Coast and spend more time birding around High Island.

I strolled past colorful cottages, including the home of author Ernest Hemingway. Gangs of Red Junglefowl picked at the edges of landscaping before disappearing into the thick brush of people's front yards. White-crowned Pigeons cooed from somewhere in the branches above. A Thick-billed Vireo had been reported in Miami, and I decided a try for that bird was worth a stop on my way to Texas, which would be my next destination. I'd fallen behind pace on my interviews while on the Tortugas, despite my efforts to talk with birders who came over on day trips each day. At least at a rare bird stakeout I would have some other birders to interview.

I frivolously tapped the Garmin GPS stuck to my windshield, searching "Miami" despite knowing there was only one way to get there: Highway 1. There are only a few events that get serious birders as excited as a rare bird. Chasing a rare bird can be an emotional roller coaster, accompanied by the constant dread that something bad might happen to it; after all, a lost, hungry bird could very well end up in the talons of a larger, hungrier bird. This was the fate of a rare Ross's Gull in January 2017. After straying from the Arctic to California's San Mateo area—delighting hundreds of birders, the wayward gull was unceremoniously plucked from the sky by a Peregrine Falcon.

Whether I saw the vireo or dipped (which is birder language for a "miss"), the presence of other birders was almost guaranteed. As I rolled up at the stakeout spot, I was right. Birders from all over Florida were walking the trails or standing around waiting for the Thick-billed Vireo to appear. I leisurely chatted with some birders, getting more interviews done for The Birding Project. We stood around for hours, long enough that I retrieved my hammock from the car and hung it up between two trees. The afternoon passed with flocks of migrant birds moving overhead. I interviewed more birders and caught up with Larry Manfredi, who had brought a friend to the stakeout. The most noteworthy event was a raccoon that walked between Larry and me while we ate lunch. Curious, the little bandit reached into my bag, feeling blindly for something—anything to eat. I scared him off.

"There's the bird!" someone excitedly said, in a low voice as to not scare the vireo away. Peering through the brush, I saw the plain wings, back, and tail of a small bird. It jumped higher in the tangle of vines. The head was still blocked, and I couldn't get a look at the face or bill. Moments later it dropped into the thick foliage and was gone. Everyone around me exchanged high-fives, congratulating one another on finally seeing the bird.

I stood quietly by myself. Despite getting my binoculars on the same bird they were seeing, I didn't see it well enough to count it. That's birding.

Minutes later, Larry Manfredi got a text about a curious-looking bird at Fort Zachary Taylor in Key West. Larry surmised that it *might* be a Cuban Vireo, an endemic bird that has never been recorded outside of Cuba in Florida before. The chase was on!

I drove shirtless on the drive to Key West, hanging one arm out the window in hopes of cooling off and building my tan. There wasn't much of a breeze, despite being right next to the ocean.

I considered the irony of this bird showing up the day after I had left. At least I was close enough to chase it—for Olaf and any other birders doing a Big Year, this surely would have meant spending money on a plane flight.

When I arrived at Fort Zachary Taylor, I used my voucher for free admission to get into the park. Once inside, it wasn't hard to find the growing mass of birders at the location the vireo had been seen.

With my binoculars in one hand and my shirt in the other, I walked briskly over to the group of birders, who were gathering around a dense thicket next to a wooden fence. Before I had the chance to put my shirt on, the bird flew out just feet away from us, responding immediately to the playback of a Cuban Vireo call. While using bird recordings to lure birds into sight certainly works, there is a concern with this practice during the breeding season, when birds expend extra energy to defend their territory. This wasn't breeding season and this wasn't a nesting bird, so everyone was surprised when the playback brought this secretive bird into view for everyone present!

Many people left after they had seen the bird well, and many new birders arrived. The gathering crowd grew larger, and the skulky bird went back to being invisible, occasionally calling from deep within the foliage out of sight. I tried to point out to new birders where the bird had been seen, and even found an opening where it was visible, assisting others in getting a look. After taking several sub-par photos of the bird, I walked down the line of birders and interviewed half a dozen people and heard their stories.

Despite not having a schedule, I felt like I was behind where I wanted to be. Texas was calling. The excitement of having seen some good birds and interviewing a lot of people propelled me onwards, and I drove from Key West to Mobile, Alabama, a nearly 14-hour trek that put me back into the heart of Walmart country. For several hours I slept in the superstore's parking lot just off the highway, before returning to I-10 and continuing on towards Texas.

Spending vacation on a boat isn't for everyone, yet cruise ship lines constantly sell the experience using catchy slogans. These lucrative sayings promise travelers an "Escape" or encourage one to "Let Your Dreams Set Sail." They're kind of cheesy, but true—to an extent.

When I visited the Princess Cruises' website in March, I was promise I would "Come Back New." I added a few words to their slogan to fit my goal: to come back with new birds. I hoped I had made the right choice!

I jokingly told people that taking a cruise was the single best decision I never made. In January, Andy insisted that if I were to do a Big Year, I *had* to be on this particular ship—it wasn't an option. I countered, telling him that if he figured out the dates and ports, then I would put it on my credit card. I knew he wanted to go, and having me as a companion made it the perfect reason to split costs and make a trip like this happen. At first I wasn't wild about the idea. According to my own calculations, I could reach my goal of seeing 700 species without going on any offshore pelagic trips—yet I was willing to keep an open mind.

10

COME BACK WITH NEW BIRDS

IN MARCH, Andy and I met in Fort Collins, Colorado to snow-shoe several miles in search of Boreal Owls near Cameron Pass. Despite perfect weather and a full moon, we heard nothing, and got really cold. Following this adventure, we warmed up at Krazy Karl's, a local pizza joint. While waiting for our food, Andy told me more about these "repositioning" cruises. The best ones left San Diego or Los Angeles in May and paralleled the Pacific Coast northwards, about 50 miles offshore. This was a perfect route to find seabirds, including jaegers, albatross, and petrels, which were normally hard to find close to shore. This cruise ship provided an extended time out at sea on a stable boat, for prolonged periods of time. Also, other birders would likely be on the boat as well. This method for seeing pelagic birds was growing in popularity, and Andy predicted it would continue to grow as more birders learned about it.

Months had passed, and the 4th of May had arrived. The day began above the city, in the mountains of California's Los Angeles National Forest. Andy had flown out to L.A. the day before and joined me on a day-long California birding blitz in my car. We'd camped out somewhere just off the road in the National Forest, and were up before the sun searching for a White-headed Woodpecker. I'd seen this species years ago in Washington, yet seeing it again I was surprised at how small it was. Scores of Mountain Quail darted across the road in front of the car, and a Hermit Warbler carefully picked his way along some overhanging branches. The year birds kept coming...

We birded all the way down from the mountains to the ocean, stopping in some sketchy-looking neighborhoods, where I had found a Spotted Dove in North Compton just a few days before. We found munias in someone's backyard, and then headed to the airport to pick up my dad, who had flown down from Seattle. He jumped at the opportunity to fly to L.A. and pick up my car, driving it back up the coast to Seattle to await my return. Gestures like this reminded me how lucky I was to have my family's support.

We headed to the docks, where our ship, the *Ruby Princess,* was waiting. This 951-foot long boat stood nearly 200 feet tall, and was the only clue we had driven to the right port. We pulled up to a large, mostly empty parking lot, which had me second-guess if it was the right place. It kind of felt like being dropped off at the airport, except the large plate-glass windows were missing. The cruise ship terminal was a long windowless building that had a low curb appeal on the outside, and felt like an airport on the inside.

After waiting in some lines to check in, then more lines to go through security, we boarded the ship. This was my first time stepping on a cruise ship, and it was like entering a new world. After walking across the drop-down bridges and through the square door, my identification card was scanned and the adventure began. Walking into the ship's piazza was like being transported into a European city. People were buzzing around everywhere, a hum of excitement vibrating through the pulsing crowds. Rows of shops lined the hallway, with large glass windows full of fancy jewelry and clothing. Screens flashed like fireworks, advertising sales and on-board promotions, and piano music floated out from somewhere deeper into the abyss of the ship. After wading through an army of wheelchairs outside the glass-walled elevators, we opted to find the stairs and climb nearly a dozen sets of stairs to our deck. Then, we had to decode the ship's map to find our cabin. In the following days I got lost more times than I care to admit.

Unsure what exactly to expect, I opened the door to our interior cabin. Inside were two twin beds, two nightstands each with a lamp, a single chair and built-in desk, a small bathroom, and a closet. To save money, Andy and I booked this double-occupancy room for a promotional price of $199 per person. The extremely minimalist design was all we needed. After living in about 17 cubic feet solo, our 162 square foot cabin was plenty of room to share! Wasting no time, we dropped bags, unpacked our binoculars, and headed down to the bow of the ship, where a growing group of birders was gathered.

Before our ship had even left the Port of San Pedro, a line of high-end spotting scopes lined the front of the ship. Birders stood busily chatting about different topics ranging from migration to pelagic trips. As the boat departed the harbor, ambitious birders scanned every buoy, rock jetty, and building top for birds. The list of birds began to grow. Our 4 p.m. departure time was not ideal, as I learned it would place us in productive offshore waters along the continental shelf during the night— but I was grateful to have the opportunity to bird until dark, which gave me some time before bed to explore the ship.

The long interior hallways of the *Ruby Princess* were palace-like, with rich dark wood paneling, mirror-lined hallways, and grand chandeliers hanging in open foyers. Red carpet paved the way to a ballroom or lounge more extravagant than the last. Looking at the schedule, each of the three days was packed with activities: magic shows, stand-up comedians, musicals, and movies. Like a floating luxury hotel, the ship had something for everyone: an art gallery, a sports court, a putt-putt golf course, and a variety of pools and hot tubs.

With Andy, birding was the number one priority and meals were typically an afterthought. Only after the sun went down did we make our way back to the room to drop off our optics before climbing the steps to dinner. After spending months subsisting on a food budget of mere dollars a day, having an all-you-can-eat buffet of food was otherworldly. A variety of dining choices were scattered across the ship—including reservations-only upscale formal dining rooms for passengers who spent way more money to be on the boat than me. Still, I was surprised by the endless options at sea.

Alongside the other birders, I dined at Horizon Court, an "anytime dining" experience that fit our birding needs nicely. After a morning seawatch from the bow, I could run upstairs and catch the tail end of breakfast before the cafeteria was switched over to lunch. Chefs tirelessly grilled, sautéed, marinated, tossed, cut, chopped, and prepared food in plain sight all day. The options at each meal seemed endless—it was almost possible to dream anything I wanted, and if I looked around long enough, I was likely to find it on the ship.

It was a shame to pass up lobster, king crab legs, fillets of salmon, and delicious cuts of beef, pork, and lamb. I subsisted on lots of fresh fruit, and small doses of a smorgasbord of whatever struck my fancy in the moment. I winced as I thought about what happened with all of the food waste.

It was truly a magical day—waking up in the mountains and going to sleep out on the ocean. It became the final day of the year I would see more than ten new year birds in a single day. I was poised to pass the 600 mark in the coming week —*and it was only the first week of May!*

The next morning Andy's alarm went off earlier than I had expected. As he turned the TV on to check our location and the weather, I realized it wasn't even going to be light out for the next hour. *Thanks, Andy.* Insistent we do a walk-around on the ship to look for birds, Andy was excited to start the first full day of this new birding experience. Afraid of missing out on discovering something cool, I joined him. We shook down every fake tree we could find, but found only one bird—a single Eurasian Collared Dove, perched on a railing at the back of the boat. *At least we found something,* I thought to myself, as we headed to the dining room to find breakfast, which I knew wasn't going anywhere.

Nearly 35 birders stood on watch along the bow of the ship, with a firing line of cameras and scopes set up that would make any optics aficionado jealous. This was much different than my last pelagic trip out of Westport, Washington. I can still remember feeling awful when the bouncing swells made me seasick. The poor decision of not eating breakfast and staying up late the night before caused me to pass out, and I fell and hit my head on the deck. I remember falling into a peaceful sleep, and not wanting to wake up when the other birders grew concerned. After I did wake up, and they told me what happened, I said it was no big deal and wanted to continue heading out to sea. The captain had different thoughts. Fearing I had a concussion, he returned to port and left me with instructions to go to a hospital and get checked out. Luckily, a birding friend from Missouri who also happened to be on the boat—kindly offered to stay with me. We ended up going birding.

One of the major benefits to birding from such a large boat was the stability. Plenty of birders brought scopes and tripods, which were set up along the bow. With so many sets of eyes, if a bird flew across in front of us, everyone would know about it. There was also little to no motion. For people who get seasick, being on a large boat is much better than being on a small boat. The ship moved, but with more of a gentle rocking motion that was easy to get used to. Many birders avoid pelagic trips on smaller boats due to the long time it takes to motor offshore to deeper water, often heading directly into the swells, guaranteeing a bumpy ride.

On the ship, the crowd of birders and tripods on the bow attracted the attention of many other passengers. Walkers and joggers asked what we were looking at, and many people thought we were whale watching. I let these curious people look through the new Maven scope, which was shipped to a friend's house in California—just in time for this trip.

The first albatross winged by shortly after 10:00 a.m., crossing the bow and drawing gasps and generating excited chatter among the birders. Despite being nearly a football field away, we watched the long glider-like wings of the Black-footed Albatross carry the giant bird over the tops of the water with ease. Sabine's Gulls followed in pairs or groups of four. It was refreshing to see this boldly-patterned gull over the open ocean —a much higher-quality habitat than the inland lakes and reservoirs where I'd observed this species in the past.

We encountered the striking Sabine's Gulls in California's offshore waters

I returned from lunch carrying two entire pizzas. It took a little convincing for the dining manager to let me singlehandedly abscond with that amount of food, but they did. Soon after I returned to the bow and passed the pizzas around to the line of birders, the birding picked up. Monotone voices suddenly jumped an octave, as the first *Pterodroma* petrel of the trip flew low across the bow—a Hawaiian Petrel! Usually found miles from shore in deep waters, the path of the repositioning cruise had carried us just far enough offshore in California waters to encounter this rare bird. The afternoon only got better, with another Hawaiian Petrel, over a dozen Cook's Petrels, and several Murphy's Petrels also making an appearance. Surprisingly, there wasn't a lot of wind, which petrels use in their dynamic soaring. This was exactly what we had been hoping for. Seeing this many birders so excited made the experience all the more worthwhile for me.

The next two days passed in a similar fashion to the first. We spent nearly all day watching the sea, hoping for another glimpse at the rare seabirds we had encountered the day before. Despite spotting several new species, the intensity of the day before couldn't be duplicated.

I kind of backed off the birding a bit, knowing that there weren't any other real special birds I could get before we arrived at our next stop: Victoria, British Columbia. I soaked in the hot tubs, watched movies by the pool, and ate all the food I could knowing I would soon return to life on the road.

When I went outside early the next morning, I noticed that land had appeared on both sides of the ship. We had entered the Strait of Juan de Fuca, a passage of water between Washington state on our right and Canada to the left. Despite having another day left on the cruise, I planned to bail in Victoria and take the ferry across the strait into Port Angeles. The extra day it took to sail to Vancouver and then return home could be eliminated, and I was quickly learning that on a Big Year every hour counts. A Yellow-billed Loon had been seen recently offshore from Port Angeles, and I figured the ferry ride over would give me the chance to try and spot it.

In Victoria, we had a few hours at port, and a group of us planned to get off the boat and go birding with Anne Nightingale, a lovely local whose knowledge of the area was willingly shared as she drove us to the Victoria International Airport, home of the infamous Eurasian Skylarks. Anne didn't disappoint, and several of us got our lifer skylarks, singing and performing their display flight.

While the other birders boarded the cruise ship, I walked down the street and jumped on the ferry headed for Port Angeles. Diligently scanning the entire passage across to Port Angeles, the Yellow-billed Loon was less than 1,000 yards from shore—side by side with a Common Loon. I couldn't have planned it better! My grandparents picked me up and drove me back home, where my car waited for me. What a trip!

About this time, I solidified plans to visit Attu. John Puschock from Zugunruhe Bird Tours was offering a once-in-a-lifetime opportunity to visit the farthest Aleutian island in Alaska, which was a legendary birding destination.

Attu was largely unknown to me until I read Mark Obmascik's book *The Big Year: A Tale of Man, Nature, and Fowl Obsession*. I had read about the "greatest day of the century" on Attu, where whipping westerly winds deposited hundreds of rare birds on the island. In 2010, 20th Century Fox made the book into a comedy film starring Owen Wilson, Jack Black, and Steve Martin. Despite being sprinkled with avian faux pas (it is a comedy, after all), this film portrays birding in a positive way. In the few short months I had been conducting interviews, several people confessed to picking up binoculars for the first time after seeing the film.

Going to Attu was expensive, and I couldn't afford it and knew it. I wasn't ready for the financial commitment the trip required, but knew if I let the cost deter me, then I'd always regret missing this opportunity on my Big Year. Where there's a will, there's a way, and I negotiated a payment plan to create a way. In the meantime, I listed my beloved Canon 500mm prime lens for sale, knowing that I could recoup the $5,000 I had invested in it, and put that money towards Attu.

At this point I learned there were other Big Year birders goin to Attu—other than Olaf. I was curious who they were, but couldn't think about the trip too much just yet. I had bigger fish to fry—interviewing birders at the Biggest Week in American Birding.

11

THE BIGGEST WEEK

As a species, humans seem to be attracted to natural phenomena. There's something hypnotically alluring about forces so large and powerful that the human observer can't help but feel small and insignificant.

Both earthly and celestial events—the tides, solar and lunar eclipses, the aurora borealis—transfix the human imagination and capture our curiosity. These large-scale events occur in cycles of repeating intervals—sometimes annually, monthly, or even daily. These cycles are deeply connected to the natural world in ways humans are only beginning to understand. The migration of birds is an annual phenomenon that has occurred so long it is practically as old as time.

Bird migration has been studied extensively, yet much still remains a mystery. That humans are in awe of migrating birds is no secret—and at locations across the globe, humans gather to behold this amazing spectacle.

Coastlines, mountain ranges, and rivers create natural corridors birds follow as they move *en masse*. These "flyways" funnel the current of passing birds into an invisible riverbed flowing across the landscape. California's Point Reyes National Seashore, the Bosque del Apache in New Mexico, Point Pelee in Canada, and the Delaware Bay are just a few of North America's major migration hotspots.

Before birds cross Lake Erie on their northward spring migration, they stop to rest and refuel along the lakeshore. With the right weather conditions, thousands of birds can accumulate, forming a feeding frenzy, resting and fattening up for their "hop" across the lake, which pales in comparison to crossing the Gulf of Mexico, which many of these birds did a mere week or two prior to showing up on Ohio's lakefront.

This region attracts birders from all over North America who come to Ohio to witness the spectacle that is spring migration. This influx of birders brings a huge economic boost to the surrounding communities, injecting almost $40 million into the local economy. The ten-day festival along Ohio's lakeshore hosted by the Black Swamp Bird Observatory is arguably *the* Biggest Week in American Birding.

Growing up, I heard from birders about The Biggest Week. I mistakenly let other people's opinions affect the way that I felt, swaying me away from attending the festival in Ohio. I was much less plugged into the birding community as a whole, and my opinions were influenced by just one or two people. They had said that most of the birds seen at Magee Marsh could be found in other less-crowded places.

In high school I can remember several migration days clearly—mornings spent in urban parks in downtown St. Louis, where trees seemed alive with birds. These parks acted as a "migrant trap"—offering tired northbound birds a protected place to rest and refuel in the middle of the concrete jungle. Mixed flocks comprised of a dozen species of warblers, tanagers, vireos, orioles, and flycatchers could be found on a good day—though now that is much harder to see.

In March, the Maven team asked me if I'd like to attend the Biggest Week festival, and offered to fly me to Ohio and cover my food and lodging while I was there. My answer was obvious, and I looked forward to visiting the famous Maumee Bay and Magee Marsh I'd heard about over and over again. Where the birds go, birders follow. Well on my way to my personal goal of seeing 700 species this year, I hoped this festival would be my biggest week of interviewing birders.

I stood along the famed Magee Marsh boardwalk, beneath the mostly bare branches overhead. It seemed to me that spring was lagging behind in Northwest Ohio. The empty forest canopy had just begun to erupt with hues of yellow-green, but the palette of the forest was still dominated by wintry gray and brown hues of skeleton-like oaks and hickories that still had yet to bloom. Fledgling Great Horned Owls were just beginning to exercise their freedom—awkwardly climbing branches and venturing farther from the safety of their nest. Soon, Red-tailed Hawks would take over and reclaim their nests. In the evenings, the intermittent *peent* of the American Woodcock confirmed that indeed spring had arrived, and the birds would be arriving soon.

As I walked through the parking lot past cars with license plates such as "WARBLR" and "PEREGRIN," I stopped to admire a large nest in an old tree, nearly 100 feet tall. A pair of Bald Eagles sat nearby, keeping a close watch on the scores of binoculars and long telephoto lenses trained on them from down below.

The next few days I spent wandering the Magee Marsh boardwalk, because that's where the majority of the birders were. In order to interview 365 people during the course of the year, I planned to get ahead of the pace of one per day, in order to overcome the upcoming shortage of birders I knew I would face in Alaska.

I spoke with event organizers, international birding guides, and kids who had skipped school to attend the festival. I talked to Amish birders dressed in wide-brimmed hats, punk rock birders covered in tattoos, World War II veterans, and young couples whose love stories centered around the birds. The diversity of the people along the boardwalk was astounding.

I continued to photograph hands holding binoculars. Some people carried high-end binoculars made in Germany, while others birded solely by ear without optics. At Magee Marsh the warblers were close enough to the boardwalk that no binoculars were necessary. One thing was certain, the birding community was vibrant, full of unique individuals, each enjoying birds differently together.

I surveyed the growing crowd in the parking lot. Having seen a good number of rare bird "stakeouts," I've learned to pay attention to the crowds, reading the people to determine if they are looking at anything interesting or not. This crowd was definitely focused on something, but on the ground rather than in a tree. Approaching closer, I noticed what they were watching: a small bird crouched motionless among the leaves. Less than 20 feet away was a female American Woodcock, a robin-sized bird that relies on its cryptically camouflaged feathers to avoid being spotted by predators. She selected a resting spot between two parking lots, among some short grasses in a patch of poison ivy.

Woodcocks have large eyes located high on the side of the head to help spot predators. The field of view from each eye overlaps, giving a near-panoramic view of its surroundings. I'd read that as this species has evolved to favor visual acuity, the ears have moved under—instead of behind—the eyes. This truly amazes me, as does their ability to probe for earthworms, using a bill tipped with loads of sensory receptors.

An American Woodcock rests in a parking lot near the Erie lakeshore

As I studied the woodcock's wavy plumage, 41 miles to the west a birder named Steve Jones had just photographed a shorebird with a long droopy bill, and red breast. The shorebird associated with some Dunlin, but something wasn't quite right. When Steve posted his photos to local Ohio birding groups for help with the ID, it was like striking a match. The bird was a Curlew Sandpiper—an Old World shorebird normally found in Europe and Asia this time of year. Hundreds of birders abandoned their plans and fled to the flooded field northeast of a couple of farm roads.

As The Birding Project grew, so did the list of people I wanted to interview. I had a "target list" of other Big Year birders, authors, and people who had influenced me since I was a kid—birding rockstars. One of the names topping this list was familiar to anyone who has used a modern field guide, read about bird identification, or read his autobiographical Big Year book *Kingbird Highway*—Kenn Kaufman.

I hoped if I spent long enough in the field, I was bound to meet Kenn Kaufman. I couldn't wait to tell him about my adventures, and thank him for writing *Kingbird Highway*. I'm sure he gets that a lot, but I was convinced it wasn't every day someone came and told him that because of his book, they chose to live out of their car and do their own Big Year. I rehearsed this conversation in my head, debating if I should tell him I wasn't going to resort to eating cat food—my daily doses of instant noodles were already pretty bad as it was.

I still hadn't decided what I was going to say Kenn when I had the opportunity to meet him following a rousing talk given by Dr. J. Drew Lanham about land ethic and Aldo Leopold. After the talk, news broke on Twitter that a Curlew Sandpiper had showed up an hour away, followed by a Kirtland's Warbler had been found at Magee Marsh. Both birds were rare for Ohio, and would be fabulous additions to my year list.

Following Drew's talk, I finally had the opportunity to get Kenn by himself. This is one of his busiest weeks of the year, and I was honored for him to talk with me. To be honest, I was a little starstruck as I summarized the aim of my interviews for The Birding Project.

"You're doing a Big Year, right?" Kenn questioned. Wait— who was interviewing who here?

"Yes, but I'm trying to focus on the people too," I added, over-summarizing my stump speech on the *Engage* part of my Big Year.

"These are two *really* good birds for Ohio." He paused, letting his words sink in. I did care as much about the birds... In the moment I *really* wanted to interview him.

"I know." After a moment of consideration, I realized Kenn was right—and he and I both knew it. We agreed it would work better for both of us to reschedule our interview for The Birding Project. I thanked him for his encouragement and promised I would talk with him another time.

The parking lot at Magee Marsh was now nearly full, and finding a spot was difficult. The east end of the boardwalk was *swamped.* I wove my way through the crowd until I stood shoulder-to-shoulder with a man giving directions out loud about where exactly in the tree the Kirtland's Warbler was being seen. I smiled as I watched the half-ounce bird hop around, more interested in insects than the growing crowd of gawkers below.

It was nothing short of a miracle that this bird had flown from its wintering grounds in the Bahamas to here, en route to her breeding grounds on Michigan's Upper Peninsula where a very specific type of habitat remained. Grounded by weather, hunger, or perhaps a combination of both, this bird foraged in the most heavily birded stretch of habitat along the Erie lakeshore.

Now, I just needed someone to carpool with to the Curlew Sandpiper. Standing nearby were two Ohio birders, Dan and Jacob, talking about going to chase this rare bird. I chatted them up, explained I was doing a Big Year and asked if I could join. I'm not sure if there's a record for shortest time to see Curlew Sandpiper and Kirtland's Warbler back-to-back, but if there is, we probably held it.

A long day of birding had nearly drawn to an end, as I sat with new and old friends at dinner, recounting the exciting events from the day. I had seen two very good birds for Ohio. Seeing a Kirtland's Warbler here saved me the expense of driving to Michigan later to see them on their breeding grounds. What luck! I also had finally met Kenn Kaufman, who I'd wanted to meet ever since I read his book. Despite the conversation not going as I planned, I trusted it would unfold in the future.

Moments later, my phone lit up, as a text message arrived from John Puschock, owner of Zugunruhe Bird Tours and leader of the expedition to Attu. The message read *"Where are you?"*

When a Kirtland's Warbler shows up in Ohio, it causes quite the stir

12

NORTH BY NORTHWEST

A SINKING FEELING developed in my stomach as my euphoric birding high suddenly came crashing down. In a couple of days, I was scheduled to go to Attu with John and an intrepid group of birders that had assembled for this once-in-a-lifetime birding trip. John was asking about my whereabouts because everyone else was already either en route to Alaska or on the island of Adak, ready to go.

The boat had left Homer and was scheduled to arrive within the next two days. My stomach churned in knots as the reality set in: they were going to leave for Attu without me! Somehow the impossible had occurred. To maximize birding time on Attu, the trip had been moved up several days, and all the participants had been notified—except me.

I knew there was no possible way I could get to Adak in the next 24 hours. The mountain of rescheduling my three flights seemed insurmountable on its own, with last-minute change fees being more than I could handle financially.

Stepping away from dinner, I took a minute to myself to handle the fear that had overcome my thoughts. *You'll never make it in time. Think of the birds you could have seen. What an expensive mistake. This sucks.* I silenced these thoughts, focusing instead on all of the good I had experienced over the past few days. Sustained by people's passion for birds, and my own love for what I was doing, I recognized that nothing could interrupt that love from being expressed. Whether I was on the boat to Attu or not, I could still share my joy with others.

I calmed down, knowing that I was in my right place in this moment, and going forward into whatever the next adventure was—maybe Attu, maybe not. I closed my eyes and said a quick prayer.

I made no changes to the itinerary I had scheduled a month in advance. Over the next 24 hours, I flew to Seattle from Ohio, picked up my gear from home, ate a home-cooked meal, and drove to Seattle for a meeting I couldn't miss.

After my meeting ended I drove to the airport and made the red-eye flight to Anchorage. I woke up in Anchorage and boarded the morning flight to Adak. Each passing hour was calm but excruciating. I kept waiting for a text message from John saying "We're heading to Attu"—but it never came.

Some people believe everything is up to chance. Others believe in coincidences, while many believe in karma or even credit the working out of events as the plan of a greater power. In my life, I've had many experiences work out perfectly in a way I could never have planned or imagined—serving as a reminder of a greater force at work. You can call it what you want, but I acknowledge it as unfoldment. What happened next is a testament to that—the boat broke.

I never found out exactly what crippled the boat, but it involved the transmission. I don't recall. Whatever it was, this mechanical failure had stranded the boat in Sand Point Alaska, waiting for the replacement part to be flown in from Florida.

The rest of our birding group had spent enough time on

Adak and had already seen a plethora of good birds. Due to the delay, now they just wanted to get off Adak and be en route to Attu. I didn't blame them. The real question was, would I be able to get to Adak in the time it took to fly in the part and make the repair?

Light turbulence rattled the tray tables as our plane descended towards Adak. Last I'd heard, John and the group hadn't left yet, and I summoned hope that someone would be there to meet me at the airport. I felt nervous anticipation, as the newcomer in such an elite group of birders.

Neil Hayward, who held the current ABA record of 749 species, was co-leading the trip. I'd seen pictures of Neil online and in *Birding* magazine but had never met him in person. In Ohio I'd heard of an Australian character named John Weigel, who also was doing a Big Year. I didn't know much about John Weigel aside from what I'd picked up from the swirling rumors. I tend to ignore birding rumors anyway.

Another current Big Year birder, Laura Keene, was on the trip. She was from Ohio, and her reputation as a photographer preceded her—her Ohio friends made sure I knew she would be on the trip with me. Out of everyone going to Attu, she was the person I most anticipated meeting. I didn't know anything of the other participants but assumed them all to be birding veterans or hot-shot up-and-coming birders.

Pressing my forehead against the plastic window cover, I strained to see anything other than a wall of gray outside. Rain droplets streamed across the window, leaving jagged horizontal trails of water— quivering as they grew bigger until following the same horizontal tracks and disappearing from sight.

Without warning, we broke through the clouds and the jagged cliffs appeared below us. Like a scene from a postcard, the rocky coastline disappeared, replaced with fields of lush green grass, and then dark gray roads.

Just before we landed, I noticed a bright flash of white as a small group of waterfowl flushed from an airport pond, flying directly away. One particular duck really struck me as odd—it was nearly all-white with a distinct black-and-white pattern on its back. This bird and another of the same size broke off away from the smaller Green-winged Teal and I realized they were both Smew! I tried to should to alert the other birders on board, but my voice disappeared under the loud roar of the engines, which now spun in reverse as we touched down, and the pilot hit the brakes hard.

I was relieved to spot John Puschock waiting for me in the airport terminal building, which was more like a single large multi-purpose room. He wore an expression on his face that I could assume meant the boat continued to be delayed. I didn't know how he did his job, but he handled the circumstances well.

While John explained our current situation—confirming my suspicions, I eyed the airport taxidermy display of seabirds, their awkward stiff poses making them prime candidates for a blue ribbon in a "bad taxidermy" competition. Outside, we loaded my bags into a beat-up Ford Expedition that looked like it had seen better days. (It was one of the nicer vehicles on the island.) John Puschock told me about the birds the group had seen already in the last few days—birds that I still hadn't seen yet this year and still needed to reach my goal of 700 species. Each one to me was just as important as any rarity to help advance me towards this goal. The previous week before Ohio I had passed the 600 mark. The year was not even halfway over, yet I felt so close to my goal. I secretly hoped the boat would continue to be delayed long enough for me to see most of what had been seen already by the others in the group.

Our first stop was an empty house, with different rooms that projected mixed signals of habitability. The upstairs had some furniture, but the downstairs was mostly empty, with dust-covered piles of stacked furniture. Down the street and around the corner was another nearly identical house where the other group was staying. That house had curtains and internet.

Our group walked around the abandoned neighborhoods of Adak, which was once an active military base when tensions were higher with Russia. The wind had taken its toll on the island, tearing siding from abandoned homes and blowing out windows. The untrimmed lawns, cookie-cutter-like base housing, and random graffiti contributed to the eerie neighborhoods. Neil joked about Adak being the site of the zombie apocalypse. The surrounding neighborhoods fit that description well, almost like an abandoned movie set for Hollywood's next zombie film.

Common Ravens ride the winds together in Alaska's Aleutian Islands

The functioning but run-down truck bounced up the dirt road past the airport up the hill onto the higher part of the island. Our driver pulled over at the Adak National Forest, which could easily be circumnavigated by foot in under two minutes. Decades ago, serviceman planted this grove of conifers as a morale-boosting exercise. Now these are the tallest trees on the entire island, and the grove is considered one of the best "migrant traps" for vagrant birds.

We stopped at several different spots on the island, allowing me to see many of the birds the rest of the group had already found. This gave Laura the chance to work on taking more bird photos. She explained later that she was trying to document as many species as she could with photos, which was a great idea I hadn't really thought of. I wondered how many birds I'd photographed so far over the course of thee year. I could quickly count the birds I hadn't photographed on one hand.

The boat finally arrived as we were birding the island, and after birding all day, we returned to town for dinner and awaited our departure time. John received a call from Bill, the boat's captain, saying that the crew was ready and we should load up. It was 10 p.m. but still light out—enough to feel like it was dusk.

We returned to our rooms and did some last-minute packing, organizing, and consolidating—people who brought large suitcases were asked to leave their bags on Adak, and pack all the essentials in smaller, more storable bags. Room on the boat was limited, and unnecessary luggage and items were left behind.

I'd been on small fishing boats before, and large boats the size of ferries, but stepping on the *M/V Puk-uk* was a new experience for me—I'd never been on a boat this size before. The diesel motors grumbled angrily through heavy metal walls, giving the boat a rhythmic pulse—like a heartbeat. A nervous energy was palpable, as people tried to stay out of the way while loading up gear, but wanting to be helpful at the same time. We were tired from a long day of birding and waiting, which now had subsided as the departure was imminent. I looked across the wharf and saw a half-sunken boat, tipped on its side. The scene wasn't exactly heartening or reassuring before heading out onto the Bering Sea.

Captain Bill went through a detailed safety briefing, describing in detail what to do in the case of various emergencies. He pointed out the locations of fire extinguishers, the ship's emergency radio, and described the cold water immersion suits we would need to wear in the event the ship sank. I pondered this unlikely scenario as the bright suits were brought out and unrolled. It was mandatory each passenger put one on. I placed my feet in plastic bags first, which made slipping inside the puffy suit slightly easier. I stood up, steadied by the help of others, and posed for a picture. Everyone took turns putting on the survival suits, which was about as easy as wearing a marshmallow. We joked around to mask the unspoken fear of the unknown, hoping this would be the only time we'd ever have to wear an all-orange outfit.

Before long, the vacant neighborhoods of Adak disappeared over the watery horizon behind us. We steamed onwards into the thick mists of the Bering Sea under the fading midnight light. The *Puk-uk* muscled through the icy chop, climbing to the summit of the swells before sliding down the other side. Each wave broken by the bow echoed throughout the boat, adding a bass-drum-like percussion line to the engine's constant rumble.

Everyone took their own preventative measures to ward off seasickness, before disappearing into their respective staterooms for the night. Left to my own decisions, I headed to my bunk and curled up under the warm flannel duvet and drifted off into a peaceful rest.

The breaking waves on the boat's bow woke me from a deep sleep the next morning. I lost my balance as I dropped off the top bunk, forgetting that on a boat the ground wasn't always in the same place. Using both hands for balance, I carefully stood up and walked around the ship on my new sea legs.

The smell of bacon wafted from the galley, where our chef Nicole was busily cooking bacon and was taking egg orders as birders awoke and emerged from their cabins. I eagerly ate a big breakfast, which was surprisingly gourmet for being prepared on a boat. Some seasick birders didn't appear at all, and I didn't see them for several days.

*Northern Fulmars come in two distinct morphs, but
many individuals can be quite pale or very dark*

Whale! Off our starboard side, hundreds of yards away, I
spotted a dark shape breaking the surface of the water. Swarms
of birds added to the grandeur of the sight. At a distance, the
whale seemed to linger on the surface a little too long. Why
wasn't it diving? As we steamed closer and our views improved,
the leviathan morphed into a recently deceased floating island
of blubber.

Hundreds of Northern Fulmars were perched on and
around the carcass, and the cloud of birds evaporated as the
boat approached. It was a Sperm Whale—a large, blocky-
shaped beast drunkenly tipped on one side—a drifting free-for-
all for ravenous seabirds. Nearly everyone came out on deck
and took a few photos before the rancid smell forced us
onwards on our journey towards Attu. The *Puk-uk* resumed its
forward march towards the distant wall of fog.

The Aleutian Islands stretch over a thousand miles from South-western Alaska westward into Siberia, forming a barrier between the Bering Sea to the north and the Pacific Ocean to the south. Jagged island peaks rise from the sea, flanked by rugged coastlines topped with lush green grass. Rugged shore-lines comprised of dark volcanic rocks have eroded into coarse black sand, which lines the occasional beach.

Nearly 20,000 years ago the Bering Land Bridge connected the continents of North America and Asia. Researchers predict that this landscape looked similar to the shrubby tundra covering modern day Alaska.

The underwater topography of this region yields highly productive waters, the foundation for an amazingly rich and diverse food web. Many birds are found here, including gulls and kittiwakes, puffins, cormorants, auklets, and many species of waterfowl. For thousands of years, the rich natural resources here have sustained native people who lived closely with the sea along these rugged shorelines.

For the next two days, we steadily made our way westward, past volcanic islands bearing names like Gareloi, Kiska, and Semisopochnoi. The steady pace of 6.2 knots wasn't going to win any accolades, but the slow pace was partially due to the stabilizers, which helped minimize the rocking of the boat. The Bering Sea remained even-tempered throughout our voyage, though it did summon several surprises.

Monotonous hours passed under constant steel gray skies, which appeared the same from dawn to dusk. As a respite from birding, I read different books from the ship's bookshelf in the galley. There were many different Alaska natural history titles, but also some historical books detailing the wartime history of the Aleutian Islands. I spent hours with the history books, learning all I could about the mysterious island that lay in front of us through the fog.

Closer to Tokyo than Anchorage, the island of Attu is located between the United States and Japan. During World War II both countries knew that control of the airfield was a strategic advantage that might win the war for either side. World War II abruptly ended over a thousand years of native habitation on Attu. Native Aleuts and Unangan people were rounded up by Japanese soldiers and sent to Hokkaido to live in prison camps for the duration of the war. Only 24 of the 43 captive natives survived and were resettled on the nearby island of Atka following the war.

On June 7, 1942, the Japanese forces invaded Attu in a surprise attack, capturing prisoners of war and occupying the island for almost a year. The following May, extensive air attacks cleared the way for 11,000 American troops to land on Attu. The 19 days that followed were some of the bloodiest of the Pacific Campaign, with nearly 2,400 Japanese killed and 549 American soldiers losing their lives.

A bloody battle ensued as ill-prepared American troops landed on these beaches and fought their way up into the mountains, suppressing the Japanese invaders. The entire battle lasted 13 days, ending in a banzai charge when Japanese soldiers stormed U.S. buildings clutching grenades, choosing to die honorably by their own hand rather than accept defeat.

Most afternoons the boat's wheelhouse was the center of activity, where birders gathered to visit and scan for new birds. The first day alone, we spotted hundreds of Laysan Albatross, sometimes 100 in a single hour! This species can be seen off the coast of California, Oregon, and Washington in much smaller numbers, along with dozens of Black-footed Albatross.

The real highlight was when we encountered a juvenile Short-tailed Albatross, and we enjoyed watching all three species almost simultaneously. This was the largest bird on the North Pacific with a wingspan over seven feet. This regal seabird nests in volcanic Japanese islands, and has already flirted with extinction. Fewer than 6,000 individuals remain, which surprisingly, is a 79% increase over the last 76 years.

As we made our way west, the large incoming swells rendered the boat's electronic stabilization fins nearly useless. Although I never got sick, I could only stay inside for so long before needing to get some fresh air. The back of the boat was sheltered from the wind, and small gangs of gulls followed the boat like stray cats, waiting for Nicole to empty the kitchen compost bucket of food scraps into the ocean.

I spent hours on end standing on the stern, keeping watch for unusual birds and taking pictures of birds in flight. Without warning, from out of nowhere a rogue wave knocked the boat dangerously sideways. Instinctively, my grasp on the boat's rail tightened and I held my breath as a wall of water grew closer as the boat tipped towards the waves. It would have been too easy to fall overboard without anyone knowing. From that moment on, I looped my belt through the handrail as an extra measure of safety.

The omnipresent beating of the boat's engine continued for several days. I fell asleep and awoke 10 hours later in the morning—unaware time had passed as the monotonous drone continued. The only indication I had slept a full night was the grumbling of my stomach, hungry for a delicious breakfast.

On the third day, I awoke before sunrise, long before any other birders were up. Sleepily, I dropped down from my top bunk, careful not to step on the snoring man below. As I crossed the galley, the boat gently tilted to one side, and I had to grab a pole for support, but doing so felt much more intuitive than it did a few mornings before. Confidently, I climbed the stairs into the wheelhouse, where the first mate was on watch, keeping us on course toward Attu. We talked quietly as Attu grew closer on the ship's navigational displays. With no headwinds, we were making great time. A steady speed of 8.1 knots put us two hours ahead of schedule. I think everyone was happy knowing that soon we would be on land—not just any land, but Attu.

13

BIRDING ATTU

IN MY MIND'S EYE, Attu would emerge from the mist, much like an opening scene of a Hollywood movie, complete with the cinematic crescendo of woodwind and string instruments. In reality, Attu rose from the sea long before we reached its shores, on an unusually clear and sunny day. Low-hanging clouds hugged the highest peaks, still draped in snow. It was beautiful. Days of waiting, long flights full of uncertainty, pages of reading, and years of anticipation finally came to a head, and I was overcome with emotion and excitement. We had made it!

We dropped anchor in Casco Bay, a short boat ride from a protected sandy beach ideal for landing our skiff, a rigid inflatable boat stored on the bow of the *Puk-uk*. The next hours ticked by slowly as preparations were made for landing. Personal gear was readied, and the skiff inflated and carefully lowered into the water by a hydraulic crane. It wasn't cold outside, but common sense dictated that I be prepared for any conditions. After all, nobody can predict a freak blizzard.

Nearly a dozen adults paced around the deck of the *Puk-uk* like kids on Christmas morning, impatiently waiting to open their presents. In this case, our presents were wrapped in feathers and delivered by west winds—hidden amongst the island's beaches, lakes, and marshes.

For a brief moment, I was the only person standing on the island of Attu. The others took more care in disembarking the inflatable boat in between waves. My rain pants were wet from jumping out prematurely and sloshing onto the shores through the waves. It wasn't hard to picture the young soldiers landing on a beach just like this, also for the first time—unsure what lay hidden behind the snow-covered peaks.

I was lucky; my fear wasn't getting shot at. The thought of beautiful weather and no wind terrified me. We needed west winds and big storms to blow from Asia in order to see Asian birds on Attu. That's what this island is known for: bad weather.

The bright sun glinted off Attu's snow-covered peaks. I immediately regretted leaving my sunglasses on board the boat. Most of the higher parts of the island were still covered with fields of snow, and a cornucopia of different tundra plants and green vegetation poked out of the melting snow at elevations closer to the water.

The robin's-egg-blue sky boldly defied my vision of Attu. In my mind's eye, somber skies and winged winds blew the wet salty air off the ocean and through the tightly gritted teeth of every jacket zipper. The steady rain, accompanied by blowing winds and bone-chilling numbness I expected to feel was conspicuously absent, replaced instead by puffy cloud banks obscuring wide views of an azure sky. With less than a dozen clear days a year on Attu, we had won the weather lottery, yet this news wasn't good for the Big Year birders on board. Fair weather meant fewer rare birds. The birding forecast improved later in the week, with predicted southwest winds that promised a good storm. I couldn't wait.

While the skiff headed back to bring the remaining birders to shore, I meandered inland away from the beach, through the knee-high tufts of soggy grass still thawing from the damp snowdrifts that covered the higher slopes and valleys. Wavy strings of Cackling Geese flew overhead, noisily protesting our arrival on their beach.

I flipped over a twisted piece of metal, expecting a Brambling to flush out from underneath the discarded aluminum section—perhaps an airplane wing? I pictured rare birds hidden under whatever cover they could find—but learned that wasn't how it worked. In the following days, we would walk shoulder to shoulder, in a long flushing line across the marshy habitat, flushing birds from the grass, beaches, or marshes around the accessible areas on one small corner of Attu. Perhaps 95% of the island would remain unvisited by birders.

Before long the second group of birders had arrived. They repeated the same preparatory dance we had done earlier: jackets were zipped, telescopic tripod legs extended, and hoods cinched down to keep the wind at bay. Finally, we were ready to bird Attu.

Our footsteps squished, sinking into the soggy grasses as we began birding. We poked around the outside of the Lower Base building, a concrete exoskeleton that housed birding groups since the early 1970s. For over 30 years, Larry Balch's company Attour, Inc. made it possible for over a thousand birders to experience Attu. It was their systematic approach to birding accessible parts of the island that turned up many first North American records, such as the Great Spotted Woodpecker and Pin-tailed Snipe.

Behind the bunker-like concrete walls of the old dormitories were scattered metal remains that proved that indeed, people had once lived in this now uninhabitable concrete cave. Mineral-rich stalactites dripped from the ceiling, deposits from decades of damp water and decay. The room still held a pile of old chairs, a sofa that had seen better days, and the rusty skeletons of old furniture.

I stepped into the room through a gaping hole in the wall, where weather and time had long since broken the large glass window. An owl pellet sat on the windowsill. I smiled, enjoying the mental image of a Snowy Owl sitting in this empty window, seeking shelter from the angry Aleutian winds that were likely responsible for much of the damage in front of me. Perhaps the owl perched there after consuming a large rat, whose bones protruded from the gray pellet of fur that lay scattered nearby.

As I walked down the eerie hallway, I passed different bunk rooms. Inside these rooms were names scrawled on the walls or backs of the thin plywood doors. I walked into the "Rat Hole," which was the name given to this particular room. Reading the scrawl on the walls was like seeing a yearbook signed by birders spanning decades of birding tours on Attu. Many names were unfamiliar, some I'd heard before, and a couple of names were birding legends.

1984 PHOEBE SNETSINGER – 689 ABA Phoebe was diagnosed with cancer shortly before her 50th birthday. Fearlessly, she spent the next 18 years traveling the world in search of birds, recording an astounding 8,393 species. This feat earned her a record as the first person to see this many of the world's ~10,000 species and chronicled her dangerous journey in her book *Birding on Borrowed Time*.

Several names appeared many times, year after year, with totals rising with each new mark scrawled on the wall. I recognized many of the names from books, movies, and birding lore. Even inside the building, the Aleutian weather had taken its toll—peeled paint and faded ink attempted to erase their birding feats, but the reputation of these birders survives amidst birding lore—these are legends.

SANDY KOMITO – 780 ABA Sandy was no stranger to Big Year birding. In 1987 Sandy recorded 721 species, and his record stood for 10 years, until 1998—when over 12 birders made a run at his record—including himself. That same year, Greg Miller, a newly divorced computer programmer made an attempt at the record while keeping a full-time job. Al Levantin, a successful CEO on the brink of retirement also took a serious approach at Komito's record that same year, and the results were book-worthy.

BENTON BASHAM— 774 ABA "Ben" Basham was one of the founding members of the ABA (American Birding Association) and was the first to break 700 species in a Big Year. I'd heard his name before in Texas, yet never met him.

I photographed some of these walls for a blog post, knowing that in a few years the names and numbers would be erased by wind and weather. I was unaware that in a week, my own name and number would be added to these storied walls, along with the names of those in our group. At the time, I didn't know that birding history was taking place—I was living it.

That afternoon, we hiked 10 miles, mostly around Casco Cove. After being confined to a boat for several days, it felt good to stretch my legs. I could tell others felt the same. The wind had picked up a little bit, making finding birds difficult.

It was easy to spot the many Aleutian Cackling Geese. I inadvertently flushed an eider off her nest. Noticing an awful smell afterward, I inspected the nest more closely to find that the female had defecated on her eggs—perhaps a mechanism to reduce predation? I also thought maybe it would help her in returning to find her well-camouflaged nest if she were disturbed at night.

We ate our packed lunches along the rocky beach of Massacre Bay. I sat on a twisted piece of metal that was part of an airplane wing. Several sections of landing gear were strewn about in the tide line, along with miscellaneous items: truck tires, a metal lunch tray, rope, and ocean debris that recent storms had washed ashore. The sandwich I had made earlier that morning was squished from sitting in my backpack, but it sure beat eating ramen noodles on the back bumper of my car.

The handheld radio crackled once with news of two possible Brambling. This species of finch from Asia would be the first rarity we would chase. I was closest to the report and spent the next two hours pacing arduously back and forth through the area the birds had disappeared into. I walked over many wartime ruins—bunkers buried in the ground, hidden passageways, trenches, and remains of structures from World War II that made traversing the terrain here deceptive and dangerous. Several times I fell into a pit, long since covered by grasses and vegetation, concealing it better than the troops hoped for the day it was dug. Before long, John P. had relocated the male and female Brambling on the beach, picking insects from the wrack line of kelp and debris washed up on shore. I had good looks of both birds in my binoculars.

After a long day, we returned to the same beach where we had landed, to be shuttled back to the boat for the night. Lounge chairs were set up on the deck, a reward for the miles walked over difficult terrain, and cold beers were ready to be enjoyed. I opted for my new favorite beverage—a Hansen's juice drink. Guava was my favorite flavor, and I'd drink one in the morning and try to scavenge any that remained in the fridge in the afternoons. For dinner, Nicole whipped up a veggie lasagna with salad and cookies. A good meal certainly took the edge off the day's grueling pace—a luxury even the participants in the early days of Attour would envy.

That evening, Neil showed me how to use the Adobe Lightroom program. I'd been so busy this year I hadn't really edited any photos and wasn't too familiar with this new photo suite that had changed and updated since I had used an earlier version years ago. Led by Neil, we collectively went over the bird checklist for the day. I was grateful nobody was shouting out the name of some rare bird I missed—I knew it wouldn't last for long.

After completing our checklists (and me verifying I had "my" numbers right in eBird), people talked, the wine came out —and I went to bed. It was a long day. I was grateful I had made it to Attu.

Emperor Goose found along Attu's Gilbert Ridge

The next morning was spent getting all of the bikes ready, for our first *Tour de Attu*. Bike wheels, seats, and frames emerged from the boat's storage, filling the deck until piece by piece we had a fleet of bicycles. After transferring all of the bikes to the lower base building, John P. and Neil patiently went over each one making sure it was ready to ride—inflating tires, adjusting the seats, and checking the brakes. I didn't mind helping out, hoping to make things go faster so we could begin birding. Despite our delayed start, the birding picked up as soon as we got underway. That afternoon the group enjoyed seeing a pair of Rustic Buntings. I got great looks at the female, and was excited to see this life bird!

I was grateful to have a bike—we were able to cover a lot more ground, and I loved gliding swiftly across the old runway, riding down the middle as if I owned it. The thick carpet of moss made it difficult to pedal on the tarmac, and at times, was quite slippery when wet. It had been years since some members of the group had ridden a bike, while others had trained leading up to the trip to be physically prepared.

I was glad I was doing this while I was still young, with full balance, high stamina, and mental toughness that I had been hardening for months. I'd lived out of my car, hiked hundreds of miles to find birds, and now on Attu, my excitement and energy level was through the roof. I could barely contain myself.

I rode along the runway beneath loose streams of Cackling Geese cruising overhead—they were prolific. This wasn't always the case, however. In the 1800's Russian fur traders introduced foxes to the Aleutian Islands, in hopes of returning and harvesting fox pelts for market. Goose eggs and flightless goslings provided easy food for the foxes, which thrived on many of the uninhabited islands. Russian trappers returned to these islands and harvested the foxes, which had increased tenfold having subsisted on nesting birds. In half a century, foxes had eliminated a species that had evolved among these islands since the last Ice Age. It appeared the fate of the Aleutian Cackling Goose had been sealed.

In a fortuitous turn of events, the Alaskan conservation pioneer Bob "Sea Otter" Jones discovered a lost colony of Aleutian Cackling Geese on Buldir Island in the 1960s. In

1967, the Aleutian Cackling Goose became one of the first species listed on the newly minted Endangered Species list.

Bob Jones spent over a decade removing foxes to help restore geese on the Aleutian islands. He captured goslings to be bred and reintroduced on fox-free islands, and trained biologists to do the field work necessary to ensure the survival of these birds.

Over the next 30 years, Aleutian Cackling Geese were reintroduced to fox-free islands countless times until a wild population took hold, and goose numbers began increasing exponentially. Despite his hard work and dedication to these efforts, Bob Jones passed away before he could see the goose removed from the Endangered Species list in 2001. His legacy lives on in the dozens of clutches of eggs I carefully walked around, careful to not step on the eggs that would soon hatch into goslings.

To me, Attu was a proving ground, not to others, but to myself. I was going to try and spot birds, see them well enough to commit the field marks to memory, then identify them. I thought this was how good birders did it. I watched how Neil Hayward birded. A flash of feathers would come out from the grass, and immediately he was on it—with his camera. After getting a "doc shot" documenting the bird well enough to identify it, he raised his binoculars and studied the bird. Having a picture after a brief encounter with an Asian stray was much more valuable than trying to recall field marks.

I learned this lesson the hard way. After my bike got a flat tire, as I returned to swap out my bike I flushed a small brown bird, larger than a Pacific Wren but not as big as a Song Sparrow. I noticed the long legs and a white patch under the throat. That's all I got. My heart pounded as I radioed the others, who were ahead of me. Should I call them back? It flew up the river and vanished around the bend. I spent 10–15 minutes looking for it, but couldn't find it again. That night I was quizzed heavily on the small bird, which was a perfect match for a Siberian Rubythroat. This was birding on Attu

For the remainder of the afternoon, the group mostly stuck together, exploring the main places that we could bike to: Navy Town, the runway ponds, the revetments (large piles of dirt covered in vegetation, providing cover for wandering birds) and around the Peaceful River. The group enjoyed great looks at several Wood Sandpipers, an Old World species that caused some excitement early in the day when encountered, but by late afternoon, we'd seen over 20 of them, and many in our group had lost interest. I carefully studied this bird, as it was a magical feeling to know that I was close enough to Asia that I was in their breeding range. I also studied it carefully, memorizing the field marks so I could tell it apart from the similar but rarer Green Sandpiper.

Partway through the afternoon, someone radioed saying they had a tattler on the Peaceful River. I arrived as fast as I could, knowing that a Gray-tailed Tattler was a possibility here. I'd seen one before in the Pribilofs and was trying to remember the field marks to differentiate the two similar shorebirds as I set up my scope and found the bird.

Identifying the bird was like a puzzle: did the barring on the flanks extend far enough to be a Wandering? I laughed at the talk of nasal grooves (a narrow depression on the beak) when more experienced birders arrived. It was safe to call this a Wandering Tattler. This species is aptly named, since after breeding in Alaska and the Pacific Northwest, they wander during migration across the Pacific Ocean, easily turning up in Hawaii as in Mexico or Central America.

After going over the day's checklist, the group, led by John P's wisecracks, peer-pressured Neil into reading from his not-yet-released Big Year book *Lost Among the Birds*, which he'd brought along on this trip. Neil gave in and started reading at the beginning. I knew I was witnessing a moment of Big Year history—Neil recounting his impromptu record-setting 2013 Big Year adventures while John Weigel, Laura Keene, and I listened eagerly. The atmosphere was light, and it was fun to see everyone relax and unwind after a day of birding—I liked this group.

The following day passed much like the days prior. After landing on the island and prepping our bikes, we rode as far as the roads would carry us, along thin trails barely navigable by bike. We left the bikes and walked to Henderson Marsh. After birding the marsh, we set off for the long bike ride back. I decided to carry my bike and hike over the hill (others called it a small mountain) in a more direct line back to the runway. I didn't have a death wish, but after birding all day with the same group of people, I needed some time to myself. So much of my Big Year thus far involved other people, that it was kept in check by the time I was able to spend alone with my thoughts. It wasn't easy, but the longer I practiced listening to the internal voice within, the more comfortable I felt—and my unfounded fears I had been subjecting myself to were suddenly lifted.

The steep grassy hillside seemed impossible to scale carrying my spotting scope and mountain bike on my back, yet using my hands for balance I struggled until I reached the top. I was out of breath and grinning ear to ear. I'd challenged myself and succeeded—pushing my body and mind. I set the bike down in the grass, taking a picture of it to remind myself to push hard every day. Only after that did I take in the panoramic view. I was surrounded by mountains on one side, and an expanse of ocean on the other. *This must have been a key vantage point during the war, too,* I thought. No matter how many beautiful birds, mountain views, or waterfalls I looked at,

I never could shake the feeling that I was standing on a battle-ground. The more I thought about it, the closer tears came to my eyes. Thousands of people died here. Not just a relative *here,* but likely right under the grass on which I was standing. To make that realization more real, coffin-sized trenches filled with water were scattered about the top of the hillside around where I stood. Perfect rectangles, filled with dirty water, six feet long and three feet wide, they opened up to the sky, sunken into the ground. Maybe they were trenches or the tops of tunnels connecting an underground bunker system. I don't know. Perhaps they were graves, now sunken in the ground after years of snow and rain had softened the dirt and dissolved the bones, resting beneath the weight of a watery grave. I tried not to think about it as I carefully walked between them, with more respect for the scattered craters. I snaked my way down the hillside and across a scattered field of metal debris. It took conscious effort to step in places that were safe while keeping a vigilant watch for flashes of movement ahead. Anything could show up on Attu.

My legs grew heavier with each passing mile. My clothes hung heavy with sweat on my lean frame. Time passed regard-less of how tired I felt, and I returned towards Casco Bay in the most direct route possible. I descended out of the mountains carefully. I had to strategically select my route, avoiding river crossings, lakes, and swamps possibly too deep to safely wade through, while traveling in a more or less direct route, conserving energy.

I stood on the edge of a vast snowfield that spanned across two hillsides. Under my feet, I could hear the rushing of a stream. Each day, summer marched closer and more snow began to melt. The trickles were now streams, and I was certain a river of snowmelt existed under my feet, literally suspended by frozen water crystals. They were melting fast.

Ahead of me was an expansive snowfield to cross, which formed a snow bridge across the ravine below. I didn't know how deep this chasm was, but I was certain that if I fell through, I would be injured from the fall, and be out of radio contact. Crossing would only take a minute at most. Despite inspecting the terrain through my binoculars, I still had a bad feeling in my stomach.

Listening to this internal voice, I decided to radio back to the boat and ask for someone to watch me cross. That way, in the event I fell through the snow, someone would have eyes on me and a rescue (or recovery) party could be assembled immediately. John P. watched me cross safely over the weakening snowfield—and despite my concerns—I made it safely.

In the distance, a female Snowy Owl kept watch over our group from a telephone pole, snoozing lazily with her eyes mostly shut. Some people in our group approached the bird much closer than I would have felt comfortable doing myself. The owl sat stoically on the pole, shifting her gaze slightly to give the birders a cold unblinking stare.

The ethics of viewing owls seem to be an age-old topic of contention. Some birders and photographers ethically view these species from a respectful distance, giving the bird its space. Others use live mice to lure the birds in close for photos. I've noticed that if the owl opens its eyes, adjusts its perch, or flushes—the observer is usually too close.

On Attu, the Snowy Owls were remarkably tame. It was clear that we were the visitors on their island, and probably some of the only humans this owl would see the entire year. They went about their business with little care of where we walked, unless we inadvertently ventured too close to their nest.

*Female Snowy Owls are more heavily-marked than their
male counterparts*

The five days on Attu passed executing the same routine: exploring and searching for birds. Together, our group covered all of the accessible areas, on foot, by bike, in groups, and spread out. We had found some exciting birds, rare anywhere but Attu. Brambling, Rustic Buntings, and Wood Sandpipers were daily birds, and by the end of the fifth day, we'd shout "Rustic Bunting, flying left" and many would not even raise their binoculars. What we really needed was a big weather system to blow in from the west.

In a dramatic twist of events, a strong storm materialized, but from the wrong direction. We had been praying for west winds, but instead, the mounting storm was coming from the southeast. The *Puk-uk* was anchored in Casco Cove, which offered protection from every direction *except* the southeast. Strong winds were predicted for the duration of our trip, providing a grim forecast and possibly ending our birding trip early.

I was unclear if we were leaving Attu early to head back to Adak, or seeking the closest shelter in Ameria Bay—located about 30 miles to the southeast on the north side of Agattu, Attu's sister island.

As the sun sank towards the horizon, wrapped in a blanket of thick clouds, the wind began to pick up—foreshadowing the incoming weather system. I retired to my bunk before the final decision was made. Before I drifted off, I heard the boat's engine grumble to life followed by the sound of the anchor being pulled. I fell asleep before the *Puk-uk* left Casco Bay.

14

WEATHERED OUT

THE NEXT MORNING, the boat was strangely quiet. We were at anchor—but where? Heading to the bridge, I learned we were on the north side of Agattu. Everyone else had been awake for a while, and the remains of breakfast were still set out in the galley.

Outside, a steady shower of light rain was falling. We watched the Hollywood film *The Big Year* on board. I'd seen this movie dozens of times, but I had never seen the film sitting next to my compadre John Weigel. On my other side was Neil Hayward, the current Big Year record-holder whose record John was intent on breaking.

This was Neil's second time watching the film, which he said he enjoyed it much more this time around. When the Attu scene ended, I think we all were a little sour that our trip hadn't experienced a legendary fallout of rare birds from Asia, but it had been pretty incredible.

Peering out the galley window, I scanned the shore of Agattu. I desperately wanted to get off the boat and lobbied all morning for others to summon the energy to get out and bird with me in the rain. Finally, John P. agreed, and we launched the skiff. The adventurous souls landed on a steep gravel beach, and ventured inland a hundred feet when we realized we stood on a midden—an ancient garbage dump from the native inhabitants. Piles of marine mammal bones, scattered shells, and modern-day buoys and fishing nets mixed with trash bearing Japanese characters. We explored the beach a little, flushing the expected birds including Pacific Wren and Song Sparrow, and several Wood Sandpipers. This place was just as magical as Attu, perhaps even more mysterious.

After the storm passed, we hoped to have time to return to Attu for one final day of birding. The birding gods must have been smiling, since that night Captain Bill sailed back to Attu for two more days of post-storm birding. The weather on Attu remained dismal—which is exactly what we were hoping for.

Soon after sunrise, we landed on Attu with high expectations. We weren't disappointed. Not long after we flushed an Eyebrowed Thrush from some willows—a great bird for Attu. A second sighting later was likely a second individual. A snipe flushed, but only a few birders got good enough looks to deduce an ID: Solitary Snipe. I wished I had gotten on the bird sooner.

I was lured by the possibility of discovery, pushing my limits and moving faster on my own than I would at the group's pace. Historic birding accounts from Attu had mentioned White-tailed Eagles could be found nesting on the interior of the island, although this journey was much too far with the limited time we had. Instead, I focused on a more attainable goal: an endemic subspecies of Rock Ptarmigan (*Lagopus mutus evermann*i) This subspecies was quite dark overall, and its range was virtually restricted to Attu and Agattu. Perhaps 1,000 birds remain on Attu—I just wanted to see one.

Evermann's Rock Ptarmigan (left) is significantly darker than other subspecies found across Alaska

To get to the higher mountains, I hiked along the Peaceful River, flushing Common Snipe and Wood Sandpipers from the flooded valley. Rusted metal Marston Mats sunk into the spongy tundra, with wildflowers and tussocks of plants growing out from the holes. These perforated steel sheets were used as temporary runways during the war, and served as a reminder that humans had already touched this wild landscape.

The climb up the mountain took all the energy I could muster. I climbed into the clouds and followed the ridgeline even higher into the sky. Cackling Geese flew past below me, but I couldn't see them due to the fog. Suddenly, the ground in front of me moved, and I realized I had found the ptarmigan— quite by accident! Along the descent, I passed a Snowy Owl who kept watch over the valley below. Hiking back to meet the rest of the group, I found another male Brambling. The storm had delivered!

Our final day, tired hopes were as high as they could get. The trip had been exhausting for most, and knowing that we still had several days on the boat to get back to Adak was discouraging for some. I was ready to find some birds. The passing storm improved my morale, and I summoned hope that the winds had grounded some rare birds on Attu. John was optimistic as well.

Our plan was to be dropped off at the base of Gilbert Ridge and hike out along the ridge and end at Alexai Point. The skiff would pick us up and shuttle birders back to the boat. Shortly after stepping on Attu's shore for the final time, we began finding rare birds immediately.

As we hiked along the rocky beach, two tattlers were spotted among the rocks—giving great side-by-side comparisons of one Wandering and one Gray-tailed Tattler. While moving among the rocks to photograph the tattler pair, someone spotted a Common Sandpiper—a first for our trip. As we continued our hike, and a flock of seven Brambling flew overhead along the beach, equaling the total number of Rustic Buntings we had tallied so far.

We flushed waterfowl from the ponds on Alexai Point: Tufted Ducks, Eurasian Widgeons, and the Eurasian subspecies of Green-winged Teal. We also found shorebirds, including another Long-toed Stint. After finding a White Wagtail on the beach, a group of shorebirds flew in from over the ocean, wheeled around, and dropped down into the black rocks below. I looked at my photos I snapped of the birds and noticed one had a slightly upcurved bill. I recognized it immediately, as Neil made the call over the radio—Terek Sandpiper!

The Terek Sandpiper was by far the most exciting bird of the day, and a bird Sandy Komito had missed in his many trips to Attu. I marveled as this unique bird fed on the rocks in the light rain alongside two Gray-tailed Tattlers, who largely ignored our presence. I wondered what else might be out there, that the storm would blow in.

We continued walking around Alexai Point, when I spotted a Common Sandpiper foraging along the high tide line along the beach. A beautiful Black-headed Gull circled over the bay as we were being picked up and transferred back to the boat. It was a fantastic day to end our trip to Attu.

The return trip to Adak passed quickly. Everyone was exhausted from the trip, and nobody was looking forward to riding the swells for hours on end. The only motivation to continue birding was the chance to see the rare Mottled Petrel, or perhaps another Short-tailed Albatross.

I tried for hours each day to photograph the Fork-tailed Storm Petrels zig-zagging by the boat. Suddenly, a larger seabird flew over, gliding on long wings. *That's different-* I thought, and reflexively took several photos of our only Mottled Petrel of the trip. Sheepishly, I showed the photos to the others, none of which had seen the bird from inside.

The trip concluded after sailing through Little Tanaga Pass, where thousands of Whiskered Auklets swirled over the turbulent water. I mentally added this to my growing list of incredible experiences.

Whiskered Auklets were numerous in Little Tanaga Strait

15

JOURNEY TO HOG ISLAND

THE MELODIC SONG of a male Bobolink trickled down from somewhere above the small patch of Illinois prairie. Shoulder-high clumps of bluestem towered above a plethora of plants—milkweed and prairie drop seed, and scattered shocks of blooming flowers. Butterflies were abundant, and the grasses were alive with the subtle symphony of of insect noise.

This patch of restored prairie—located in the Chicago suburbs—was mostly hidden from from the road by a wall of oaks and hickory. Beyond the forests were subdivisions, schools, and business parks—full of people who passed by this ecological time capsule on their way to work—never knowing it was there.

Numerous hours had gone into restoring this piece of property—returning it to a healthy balance of native plants which would have been found here before farmers plowed under nearly 22 million acres—over half of "the Prairie State". Today, less than one-hundredth of one percent of the tallgrass prairie remains in Illinois—broken into small pieces like the one where I stood.

A male Bobolink sings from a perch

Justin was the perfect person to be teaching me about prairie restoration. He wore an earth-toned t-shirt with a Henslow's Sparrow on it—an open display of his love for prairie birds and conservation. His enthusiasm and knowledge on the subject knowledge was astounding.

Together, we walked across the prairie in carefree fashion, stopping here and there to tell me about different parts of this native prairie. We examined a penstemon with oblong white tubular flowers, and admired blue dragonflies that zipped over the grasses. Curled up in the grasses was a reddish-brown fawn, perfectly camouflaged by rows of white spots.

After a tour of the property, Justin put me to work. We were within an ideal planting window for seeding the prairie, and Justin had brought several different containers and bags of seeds to plant during our time together. This was a great opportunity to fulfill the *Preserve* mission of my EPIC Big Year—the work I was doing was surely preserving bird habitat along an important migratory route.

The seeds had been collected and dried, and were now ready to be sown. I was surprised how small they were—like barely-visible black beads. It took a tiny pinch with my fingertips to grab the right amount to scatter in the proper areas. I was grateful Justin was able to recommend where and how to plant the different types of seeds.

The sun was quickly approaching its zenith, and the morning prairie cooled by the dew was quickly becoming hot and humid. With our work complete, I thanked Justin for the opportunity to participate in helping conserve this amazing piece of habitat.

In the years since, I have looked forward to hearing the familiar jumbled notes of this dapper bird every spring. It takes me back to the small patch of restored prairie—knowing that beneath a carpet of grasses that I helped plant is a nest full of young Bobolinks waiting to be fed.

I met Eva at The Biggest Week festival in May, at the booth for Hog Island Audubon Camp. The puffin photos on display initially caught my eye, but it was Eva's description of the island that piqued my interest.

Her eyes sparkled as she described the rich birding history of Hog Island and the top-tier bird programs the National Audubon Society offered there. I could tell simply from her enthusiasm that this was an incredible place.

Nostalgia washed over me as Eva described the beauty of the Maine coast during the summertime, instantly transporting me back to my childhood days spent exploring tidal pools, swimming in the sea, and listening to the lonely call of the loon.

Born in Maine, I knew firsthand exactly what Eva was describing. I had already planned to visit Maine later in the summer, and when she invited me to Hog Island for a few days, I was honored to accept the invitation. If I said "yes" to all of the generous invitations I'd received from birders throughout the year, my experience would have been quite different—but saying "no" allowed me the freedom to chase birds at will and not overstay my welcome in any one spot.

For some, the journey to Hog Island begins at the Portland Jetport, but my journey began a bit farther: the Pacific Ocean. In a week, I drove my Subaru from Seattle to Maine through severe thunderstorms on the northern Plains, then to Minnesota's famous Sax-Zim bog, and onwards to Maine. Of course, I made many birding stops in a wide variety of habitats, and added a handful of new birds to my year list. I also stopped in Ithaca, to interview the eBird team and John Fitzpatrick for The Birding Project.

At the boat dock in Bremen, a friendly volunteer directed me to park my car in a grassy lot on a hill above the Maine coastline. I'd arrived early, in order to give myself enough time to unpack my car and take with me only the essentials—leaving everything else nicely repacked in my car for when I returned. To get to the island, a boat shuttles guests from a dock across the channel—only a five-minute boat ride. I boarded the *SNOWGOOSE III*—a handsome black and white lobster boat tied to the dock. After shaking hands with the captain, and an affirmative nod from the mate, the engines churned to life and we were off.

Before settlers colonized the Maine coast, Hog Island was a seasonal home to the native Abenaki people, who visited the island's rocky coastline in search of clams. European immigrants who arrived later released livestock on the island for grazing, which is how Hog Island was named.

Hog Island was founded by the Todd family in the early 1900s on the basis of bird protection and conservation. With impressive foresight, the family purchased the island in hopes of saving it from the same deforestation that was happening on many nearby islands to create pastures for livestock. The Todd Wildlife Sanctuary served as the home base for an educational camp run by the Audubon society.

Over the years, Hog Island has developed many amazing programs for youth, families, and adults. Now, Hog Island serves as a full-time laboratory for the National Audubon Society, with its beginnings serving as the basis for a national environmental education movement. Their live-feed Osprey Cam has captivated the attention of birders around the world.

The first bird life instructor at the camp was Roger Tory Peterson, who went on to publish the first modern field guide and changed American ornithology. Alan Cruikshank was a pioneer in bird photography and another leading force in the early days of bird camps. Following in his footsteps, author and artist Kenn Kaufman has also left a legacy at Hog Island. The list continues, with influential conservationists, authors, and bird researchers all having a shared legacy of educating and teaching others about birds on Hog Island.

Stepping off the boat, I walked into a palpable culture of teaching and learning. The island was peaceful yet bubbling with activity. Purple Finches sang their cheerful song from trees surrounding the well-kept gardens, which were in full bloom. Camp was already in session; the flock of teens were out on a field trip exploring somewhere, and the adults were engaged in different activities around the island.

As my luggage was unloaded and taken to my room, I walked

around eager to see what everyone was doing. A group of adults were huddled in a circle around a picnic table. As I peeked over the shoulders of surrounding onlookers, I noticed one woman in the middle was delicately holding a female Ruby-throated Hummingbird that had just been captured and banded. She gently spread the bird's wing and described what 'wing chord' meant—the measurement from the wrist (bend in the wing) to the tip of the longest primary flight feather. She continued to carefully narrate each step she took while noting the appropriate measurements and data before releasing the bird.

The process of bird banding consists of attaching a light-weight aluminum band to a bird's leg. Each band bears a unique numerical sequence, in hopes of the same individual being re-sighted and reported. This helps researchers learn more about migration, lifespan, and survival rate of a bird population.

The afternoon passed quickly and the adults attended various workshops in small groups. Some of these groups learned how to track birds with radio telemetry, while others recorded bird sounds or carefully prepared scientific study skins. Overseeing each group was experts in each of these areas, working one on one and providing quality instruction to participants.

As I wandered around soaking it all in, I had the chance to speak with a variety of guests as well as Hog Island staff and visiting instructors. Each interview helped me understand a different aspect of what was so special and unique about this place, and what kept people coming back.

Meals were served in The Bridge, a large two-story white building that stood out, visible from the mainland. I quickly learned this was the main hub of activity on Hog Island. We were summoned to dinner by the ringing of a bell— surely the same bell that notified Roger Tory Peterson that dinner was ready all those years ago. In the dining hall, a large flat-screen television displayed a live feed of the nesting Ospreys, whose nest sat on a man-made platform outside, a mere 50 feet away. Inside, framed black and white bird photos hung on the walls. Upon closer examination, I discovered these images were captured by Alan Cruickshank, a pioneer ornithologist and bird photographer.

Dinner began with the sharing of an inspirational quote from renowned naturalist Rachel Carson, who was friends with the Todd family and supported Hog Island.

"The winds, the sea, and the moving tides are what they are. If there is wonder and beauty and majesty in them, science will discover these qualities... If there is poetry in my book about the sea, it is not because I deliberately put it there, but because no one could write truthfully about the sea and leave out the poetry." -Rachel Carson

This quote provided some delightful discussion at the beginning of the meal. When the food was served, to my surprise, it was some of the best "camp" food I had ever eaten. Flaky rolls, a fresh healthy salad, and a vegetarian option that was tempting even to me to try! I left it for the real vegetarians to enjoy... Dessert was delectable, and for the first time in weeks, after I had finished eating, I was full.

Following dinner, everyone assembled for the evening program in the Fish House, a long dark-shingled building whose exterior was covered in lobster buoys. This fishing stage could have come straight from coastal Newfoundland. That night, Dr. Stephen Kress gave a lecture detailing his work on Project Puffin. As he spoke, I took notes about the compelling story of his efforts with Audubon.

Dr. Kress shared with an eager audience about his work on

Maine's Eastern Egg Rock, which was the birthplace of Project Puffin. During the Project's inception in 1973, Dr. Kress carried a suitcase full of puffin chicks from Newfoundland and reintroduced them to this historical colony. Hungry farmers and egg collectors had decimated seabird populations along Maine's coast in the early 1800's, and fueled by fashion, the feather trade was the nail in the coffin for many seabird species across Maine. Dr. Kress used Eastern Egg Rock to single-handedly transplant puffin chicks, and through trial and error, discovered a string of solutions to the many problems that arose. As a result of his efforts, mistakes, and humility, puffins and terns were successfully reintroduced to Eastern Egg Rock and beyond.

The methods developed by Dr. Kress and his team have since been used all over the world—Project Puffin has expanded and helped restore seabird populations across the globe. This entire journey was fascinating and inspiring to me. I couldn't wait to interview him for The Birding Project the following day.

The next morning the SNOWGOOSE III sat at the dock, ready for the day's adventure: a boat trip to Eastern Egg Rock. Dr. Kress' presentation the night before was the perfect primer to introduce the teens to the amount of work that had taken place that allowed them to soon see Atlantic Puffins close-up.

I could tell by the nervous energy that this was the highlight of their session on Hog Island. For many, this would be their first time seeing puffins in the wild. The adult group would also get the chance the following day to visit Eastern Egg Rock, but landing on the island in a rowboat and meeting the biologists was a special privilege only for the teens.

As we left the bay all eyes became glued on the horizon, and binoculars that were slung over shoulders moments ago were now close at hand.

"Puffin!" Someone shouted as we neared the rocky isle, topped with scrubby vegetation, rising out of the Atlantic Ocean. The excitement level on the boat jumped quickly to a ten as cameras began clicking, and all binoculars were trained on a pair of puffins bathing in the water ahead of us.

As we approached the rock, long lenses were exchanged for iPhones, and the birds stayed put long enough for at least a couple "Puffin selfies" to be taken. Overhead, terns returned from the ocean carrying fish for their youngsters, nestled somewhere safely on the rock above the high tide line. We motored around the island, keeping a respectful distance from the birds and enjoying the amazing spectacle before us.

Before long, everyone on the boat had great views of puffins, which were flying by the boat carrying food, swimming in the water, and perching on prominent boulders on the island. We could see the Project Puffin researchers who lived on the island full-time. Hordes of terns—Common, Arctic, and several Roseate, also nested on the island.

Atlantic Puffins on Eastern Egg Rock

The afternoon slipped away like the receding tide, and before we knew it we had to head back. The return boat ride was full of excited "Did you see that's" and scrolling through back-of-camera photos of puffins in flight. The boat briefly stopped to admire seals hauled out on some small rocks and gawk at the lines of gulls loafing on what surely were soon-to-be nests. Back in Muscongus Bay, we pulled in a couple of lobster traps, passing around the defensive decapod whose chillipeds were disabled temporarily by rubber bands. For some teens, this was their first time seeing a live lobster up close.

Here at the southern edge of the puffins' range, these charismatic seabirds are susceptible to the increasing effects of a changing climate. Warmer currents of water in the Gulf of Maine have favored fish like butterfish and moonfish, which come from warmer southern Atlantic waters. Some puffins have caught these fish instead of redfish or haddock and brought these back to feed young chicks. For a puffling, these fish are too wide to be swallowed and the chicks slowly starve.

Everything in nature is connected. I saw this more than ever as the day had been a day of connection for me. In my interviews with others for The Birding Project, I heard personal stories explaining bird tattoos and listened to the accounts of how everyone had come to be on Hog Island together, at that moment in time. I realized that never again, in the history of the universe, would that same group be all on the same island together. That made a pretty unique moment in my eyes, and I was pleased to be a part of it.

Back on terra firma, we wandered through a maze of spruce trunks, which blanketed the interior of the island. Ferns, with curly stems and prehistoric-looking fronds reached skyward, embracing the sunbeams that filtered down through the thick canopy. Everyone followed the same trail in single-file silence, with Scott Weidensaul leading the charge. There was nothing distinctive about the spot in the woods where we stopped, but Scott knew we had crossed an invisible line into the territory of a breeding Swainson's Thrush.

I could hear the male singing in the distance as Scott opened up a yellow tackle box, carefully unpacking the contents onto his jacket spread out on the ground. This trick of the trade ensures that any small components dropped by accident can be easily found and recovered on the jacket, instead of disappearing into the moss-covered forest floor. Out of the tackle box came ziploc bags of light-level geolocators attached to pre-sized bird harnesses. Small yet expensive, these coin-sized instruments contain a small battery, sensor, clock, and a computer that records how much light the sensor is exposed to. Using this data, researchers can predict where the bird was using known sunrise and sunset times.

Several teens helped set up a finely woven black nylon net that is nearly invisible to the naked human eye, and imperceptible to a flying bird until it is too late. At a distance, all I could see were the aluminum poles, like twin silver saplings sprouting from the forest floor, with the invisible mist net stretching between them.

Scott placed the portable Bluetooth speaker close to the net near the ground, and with care not to snag a zipper on the nets, returned to the group. Tapping his phone screen, the speaker came to life—belting out the rising, flute-like song of the Swainson's Thrush, which echoed through the forest. Within moments, the territorial male flew in like a small brown missile, eager to investigate and drive out the intruding bird from his territory. The mist net did its job, trapping the thrush just above the ground, suspending it in the air for mere moments, until Scott nimbly arrived and untangled it.

Scott talked with the patience and detail of a master teacher, carefully explaining each step as he weighed and banded the bird. I watched the faces of the teens huddled around him, eyes wide with fascination as they absorbed every procedural detail he narrated.

The bird was fitted with two colored leg bands, a yellow over red on the left leg, and a silver aluminum numbered band attached to the right leg. These bands helped scientists identify the bird by sight, or if recaptured, the specific number on the aluminum band would be logged with the Bird Banding Laboratory, tracing this bird back to Hog Island.

Scott, with great care and the steady hand of a teen camper helping him, fitted the geolocator to the bird, ensuring the harness fit snugly but not tight enough to impede the bird, which would put on an extra layer of fat in the coming months, before migrating to Central America for the winter. The procedure was complete, and Scott objectively selected one of the many hands raised to release the bird. With care, the thrush was set on a flat palm, and in an instant had winged his way back to the safety of the spruce trees out of sight.

On Hog Island, material things like car keys and wallets become meaningless, and sensory experiences take over. The sights, smells, and sounds of the island define the memorable moments. Without the distraction of noise—cell phones or traffic or airports, the peace present all around me was more noticeable. As I sat in the sun, I noticed butterflies and insects on the flowers. It was nice to stop moving, and just be still.

My remaining days on Hog Island passed in joyful ignorance of time. For a moment I forgot all about lists and what bird came next and remained fully present with the people who surrounded me. Little did I know that the friendships on Hog Island would last over the course of the year—and beyond. Leaving Hog Island was just as bittersweet as departing Little St. Simons in February, but I felt strongly that I would be back.

16

RETURN TO ALASKA

DURING THE GOLD rush of 1900, Wyatt Earp left Arizona and traveled to Utah, Idaho, Colorado, Texas, and California, before making his way north to Alaska. Along with thousands of other hopeful prospectors, Wyatt landed in Nome. In this burgeoning town, he opened a saloon and mined the miners—selling supplies to the prospectors for two years before heading back to the Southwest with a load of cash. Today, Nome is still a frontier town—ruled by a lust for gold.

The village of Nome lies on the southern coast of Alaska's Seward Peninsula, just below the Arctic Circle. Sleep is optional under a summer sun that never sets. After midnight, kids still play in the streets and fishermen stand around in the rivers, hoping to hook "the big one."

This frontier town is now a gateway for birdwatchers, who use Nome as a jumping-off point for birding tours along the Seward Peninsula. This corner of western Alaska is home to a diverse assortment of high-latitude species such as the Bluethroat, Arctic Warbler, and Northern Wheatear. Nome's three main road systems lead deep into a variety of normally hard-to-access habitats—allowing birders to spot uncommon nesting birds like the Bristle-thighed Curlew.

Nome is also the only airport with flights to the village of Gambell on St. Lawrence Island, which is well-known among serious listers as being one of the best single locations to find rare birds—many never seen in North America before. The cliche saying from *Wizard of Oz* is grossly overused—yet rings true for birders: there really is no place like Nome.

I looked out the window as we made our first descent into the village of Kotzebue. The landscape below was brushed with tones of gray—the bleak sky was reflected in hundreds of tiny tundra ponds which glittered as they reflected the cloudy sky above.

This marked the first time this year above the Arctic Circle. I'd visited Nome several years ago on a summer birding trip, after I'd heard about how unique it was as a birding destination. Following a quick stop in Kotzebue, we took to the sky and headed towards Nome.

The less-than-half-full Alaska Airlines jet descended out of the leaden sky onto the concrete tarmac so smoothly that nobody knew we landed until we were already on the ground. It felt good to be back in a town that I already knew my way around.

I walked down the main street, where a tall wooden arch carved from large tree trunks stood by the side of the road, marking the end of the Iditarod sled dog race, which had concluded just months earlier. I have a friend from Colorado who has run the Iditarod multiple times, and from the stories I've heard, it's a true test of endurance—kind of like a Big Year...

Jordan arrived at the airport later in the afternoon. He'd flown in from Seattle, and it was nice to see a familiar face. We'd met earlier in the year on the Attu trip, and it's safe to say that traveling by boat to Attu with someone bonds you for life. Our taxi ride from the airport was in a mini-van packed full with passengers, so I rode in the trunk on top of everyone's bags, without a seatbelt—typical of an Alaskan frontier town.

Subway offered a fast and cheap dinner option and was the town's only chain restaurant. We enjoyed our pre-birding meal next to the large glass windows overlooking the sea, which only months before was covered with ice. Also the town's only movie theater, one counter made sandwiches and the other served popcorn and candy bars.

After dinner, our rental car—a white Ford Explorer, waited for us outside the Aurora Hotel. We drove around birding just outside of the city until after 10 p.m. Despite the sun still shining low in the sky, we went to bed. The next day would be full of new birds.

Following a hot breakfast we set out on the Kougarok Road, a well-maintained dirt road that stretches nearly 86 miles from Nome into the frontier. Our goal was to spot the Bristle-thighed Curlew, a shorebird that breeds inland on the Seward Peninsula in Alaska. In a miraculous journey, it flies a nearly 2,000 mile roundtrip flight from the South Pacific to the rolling expanses of tundra to nest and continue the survival of the species. This task is growing more difficult as the global population declines—fewer than 7,000 individuals remain.

We continued along the gravel road heading inland, where each turn revealed sweeping views of glacially carved valleys. Near the Nome River bridge, we spotted multiple Arctic Warblers— a life bird for Jordan. The road passed through shrubby willows and wet lowland ponds as we headed inland towards the slopes of the higher hills and tundra meadows.

A Long-tailed Jaeger wings over the Arctic tundra

The soggy tundra was recently liberated from winter's cold blanket of snow by the warm sun and the lengthening summer days. The landscape around me exhaled an oxygen-infused sigh of relief from a long winter. This landscape was alive and buzzing with activity. Mosquitoes swarmed in hazy clouds, Musk Oxen waded in clear salmon-filled streams, and moose calves ambled awkwardly among the thick willows.

The next breath, an inhale—was coming. The pressure was palpable, as the wildlife we encountered were purposefully driven to reproduce and feed before the days begin to shorten. Soon, the tundra will hold its breath for yet another long winter ahead.

After driving nearly 72 miles, we pulled off the road, opposite a large dark hill named Coffee Dome. The hike through the unstable tundra tussocks wasn't as bad as what I've read in blog posts and magazine articles. Perhaps my young legs and experience hiking on remote Alaskan isles had conditioned me to the terrain.

From the road, the smooth arch of the hilltop appears lush and green, but every other step invites a twisted ankle, for the ground randomly disappears under the vegetation in a mosaic of potholes, puddles, and burrows.

The bright blue sky also contrasted many written accounts of Nome. It was an unusually clear day. Long, drawn-out rows of clouds sat over the distant mountains, existing only so I couldn't say "there's not a cloud in the sky." After being fooled by a Whimbrel, we eventually located the Bristle-thighed Curlew among the open meadows. The birds nearly disappeared when perched on the ground, obscured by wildflowers and clumps of cotton grass.

Along the Seward Peninsula in Nome, rare birds were never far from my brain. Siberia wasn't too far away, and this peninsula was always a good spot to be on the lookout for "overshoots"—birds that migrate farther than their intended destinations.

Semipalmated Plovers were common here, yet I had convinced myself I may have found a rarer Common Ringed Plover along the distance shoreline. A short burst of photos allowed me to send images of the potential rarity to John Puschock via Facebook when we returned to the hotel that night.

After reviewing my photos, John responded by telling me there wasn't anything that suggested it wasn't a Semipalmated Plover. Bummer. I spent time that evening going over photos and online field guides to be sure I knew what to look for if I ever did come across a Common Ringed Plover.

The next day we drove the second road from Nome, which crossed a variety of habitats en route to the village of Council. On the cliffs above the road, a female Rough-legged Hawk fed several downy chicks.

The road to Teller drops down a mountain where there's often Musk Oxen browsing on the tundra vegetation, and winds down to parallel some lagoons on one side and an open bay on the other. I noticed a plover on the gravel beach running parallel to the road. We stopped and I got bins on the bird, which I immediately knew was a Common Ringed Plover. I studied the bird and all the field marks were there. I took photos and Jordan and I both got some killer views of the bird before an ATV driving along the beach flushed it, and the bird disappeared out over the water.

Teller is a must-visit spot for anyone visiting Nome. Many villagers here still rely on sustenance harvest of salmon, and during our visit, we saw crimson strips of salmon hanging out to dry on wooden racks. I've seen Red-throated Pipits here in the past, and there's a pair of White Wagtails using a birdhouse in someone's backyard.

The Red Knot is a champion migratory shorebird. Three subspecies occur in North America, all threatened by over-fishing and climate change. I'd first learned about this imperiled shorebird when I read *Moonbird* by Phillip House. Phillip's book documents the journey of "B95"—a banded Red Knot named for the vast distance he migrated within his lifetime—to the moon and halfway back. I'd seen Red Knots on Little St. Simons Island, as well as in San Diego earlier in the year. However, the five birds I saw in San Diego likely continued their journey north and nested somewhere across the subarctic, perhaps near Nome!

As if by chance, while returning along the Nome-Teller highway, I spotted a guy dressed in "field clothes" kneeling by a stream washing dishes. I introduced myself to this stranger, who said his name was Luke. Along with a crew of biologists, Luke was studying Red Knots, and after visiting with him for a bit, Jordan and I were invited with them into the field.

Before long, we found ourselves hiking up in the hills, honing in on a nesting Red Knot following the beeps of radio telemetry equipment as they grew louder, until we stopped. Even with the bird being pointed out to me, I still couldn't see it with my naked eye.

The male Red Knot showed amazing camouflage. This plumage was far different than the bright red plumage I expected to see. Males share incubating duties with the female, who departs the breeding ground first, leaving the parenting duties to the male.

The remainder of the time we spent driving the roads, searching intently for all the wonderful birds that make Nome an amazing birding destination. We had excellent looks at Northern Wheatears hopping among the scattered boulders of a glacial moraine. We spotted an Arctic Loon and Arctic Warblers. High on the cliffs sat a Gyrfalcon scanning the valley below for prey.

Jordan saw multiple life birds, and I added 12 birds to my year list. It was an amazing trip—summer in Nome just can't be beaten.

The Bristle-thighed Curlew can be found near Nome

After leaving Nome, I flew directly to Illinois from Alaska, to pick up my car from a friend's house in Chicago. I prepared for the long drive ahead of me to Albuquerque, where I would attend the wedding of one of my best friends from high school. This cross-country road trip would help ease me back into the routine of living in my car.

Following my stay in Nome, I actually began to adjust to sleeping in a bed. Following the wedding, my plan was to head back into the dry heat of summer, into North America's furnace: Arizona.

17

HEAT AND ADVERSITY

BIRDING in Arizona in July during the peak of the summer heat was not part of the plan. However, I'd learned much earlier in the year that plans often have a way of becoming obsolete, and melting away into the hot summer heat. The birds were in Arizona, so I would be too.

Following the driving directions from Southeast Arizona to Lake Havasu, my iPhone took me through Quartzsite, Arizona, a small town just off the interstate. I'd heard of this town—the "rock capital of the world" in my college geology class. Though hundreds of RVs gather there in the winter, apparently nobody wanted to be there in the hot July heat.

Along the highway were signs for a bookstore called Reader's Oasis. My dad has always collected rare books, and I thought the store would be worth checking out. There were no other cars in the parking lot, so I figured it would be a good spot to stretch my legs and see if there were any interesting bird books. I stepped out into the triple-digit heat. A cat blocked the front door, spread full-Superman across the doormat in the shade.

Walking inside, I needed a minute for my eyes to adjust to the shadowy interior. Tables of books, shelves of books, glass cases with books, everywhere I looked there were books. I paused at the front counter, hoping someone could point me toward the natural history section, but not a soul was in sight.

From deep inside the bookstore, some old jazz tunes played. I began wandering around. There was a lot to see, and I carefully scanned rows of books near and far as I took in my surroundings while slowly walking the different aisles. As I rounded the corner I wasn't prepared for what I saw next.

In the corner of the store, facing away from me was a body. Dark, leathery skin hung loosely draped over the thin naked frame. Dark crispy skin hugged each rib, the pelvis, and shoulders, clearly sun-baked for years on end. A long gray ponytail protruded from under the wide brim of a cowboy hat, covering a bony spine.

I'd been to curiosity shops and museums and seen human remains, preserved by peat bogs or ice. Maybe the bookstore had a mummy on display? The body slowly began to move, as if the wind had blown and it was about to tip over.

"Can I help you?" My heart skipped a beat and I let out a gasp as I realized this was a living, breathing human! Relieved I hadn't just walked into a crime scene, I struggled for words as they body turned around to face me head-on.

I blankly stared at his face, averting my eyes from the lower half of his body, which in my peripheral vision I could tell wasn't covered with anything other than what appeared to be a crocheted sock. My brain raced to find the words to expedite my departure, as I couldn't just turn around and walk out the door.

"Do you have any bird books?" I asked. He thought for a minute, perhaps trying to remember where the bird books were, or where he'd last seen his clothes.

"Yep," he motioned to me with a slight nod, and then led me through the maze of stacked books into another room. As he walked he began to ramble, telling me about one thing or another. I think his name was Paul. He sure was a talkative fellow. He had no real bird books of note, and I didn't want to overstay my welcome. Yet, he knew he had a captive audience, and continued to talk at me.

I spotted a cooler of water, and hastily grabbed a paper cup and filled it to keep busy as he continued to ramble on from across the rows of books. I strolled around, noticing some newspaper articles describing the curious place I found myself in—a bookstore owned by a naked cowboy.

Approaching a row of books, I grabbed one from the shelf and feigned interest, in hopes he would wander off. The jazz music continued, overshadowed by the rhythmic hum of an oscillating fan inside a metal cage. The nude owner vanished back into the landscape of the bookstore, his back as worn and brown as many of the antique books on the shelves.

Sensing my escape, I crept cat-like towards the door, waiting until I had one foot out to shout "Thanks!"—and made a hasty exit into the bright light and suffocating heat. Realizing I was still holding my paper cup, I splashed the remaining water on my face to cool off, or perhaps wake myself from this odd experience that only a nudist birder could dream.

I'd always wanted to see the Nutting's Flycatcher. A drab, brown flycatcher from Mexico, this bird had been seen only a handful of times in the ABA area—drawing attention from birders nationwide every time it popped up on the Rare Bird Alert.

My plan for seeing one was to chase it when it was first reported, however, the reports didn't come to the surface in the way they usually do, especially with four people all doing a Big Year.

I'd read in the past about a pair of Nutting's Flycatchers that had been found in the Bill Williams National Wildlife Refuge, near the border of Arizona and California. Located below Lake Havasu, the Bill Williams River flows from Lake Havasu through a narrow, pathless canyon. I figured the birds just might breed there, and with a few emails, my suspicions were confirmed. I shared the details—hoping others would reciprocate if they found themselves in the same position.

To escape the 109 degree heat, I spent the afternoon on wifi at McDonald's waiting for Laura to arrive. She continued birding farther south, but was on her way to join up with me and try for the Nutting's Flycatcher together. We met at McDonald's before finding the hotel Laura had booked. This would become "home base" for organizing our gear and planning the attack.

Despite my plan to sleep in my car, Laura wouldn't let me. She returned from the hotel office with key cards for two separate rooms. She told me she wouldn't sleep well knowing I was outside in the heat in my car, and so she used her hotel points to book a room so I could sleep more comfortably. We had a big day ahead, and I was eternally grateful for this kindness.

After getting my things unloaded from the car and into the hotel room (mostly items I was concerned about melting) Laura and I headed out to eat, then drove up to Bill Williams to do a recon mission for the following morning. It was nearly 8 p.m. and still, the temperature soared over 100 degrees.

The road to Bill Williams had been washed out along various sections by recent heavy rains, making the road a crippling obstacle to any low-clearance vehicles. Fortunately, my Subaru had no trouble navigating the bumpy track. It definitely warranted one of the "roughest roads of the year" awards thus far.

The dirt road ended in a cul-de-sac, surrounded by thick

vegetation and a rocky hillside. A ROAD CLOSED sign warned people that this is where the road ended. I felt well-equipped to venture into the dry, hot wilderness, adequately supplied with water, a headlamp, and an adventurous spirit.

Our exploratory trip was a success—we found our way back to the car and came out alive. On the hike, we definitely got turned around but at least we managed not to get sunburned in the heat of the day. We both ended up bushwhacking a little bit, but it was nice to get a feel for the general area we would return to in the morning.

The next day we returned, intent on finding our target bird. Soon after sunrise, we faced many birds, including a confusing trio of flycatchers. It was difficult in the thick scrub to get good looks at this confusing group of birds that weren't very vocal at all.

Ultimately we were unsuccessful and called it a day when it got too hot at 9am. A Berylline Hummingbird had been re-sighted several hours away, and with that box still unchecked on her list, Laura jumped ship and chased it.

I returned to Bill Williams, intent on finding a Nutting's Flycatcher. My efforts were not in vain, as I found the bird having a territorial dispute with an Ash-throated Flycatcher and recorded the call, just to be sure. One thing's for sure—most Big Year birders don't know all the birds. I sure didn't, and reveled in all I was learning throughout the year.

It was awesome to have a birding community to rely on with help for these tricky birds. I emailed my recording of the probable Nutting's Flycatcher to a biologist who was more familiar with this species' vocalizations, and she promptly confirmed the ID for me, which renewed my self-confidence and made all of the effort worth it—despite the heat.

It was so hot I could barely think clearly. I took another long drink from my Nalgene. *Could heat affect my happiness?* I wondered introspectively. Of course not! While an outside thermometer could be affected by heat, my happiness could not. Yet how many external things do we let affect us each day? Happiness, I realized, was a choice, not the result of external factors.

Birding can teach grander lessons beyond bird identification and behavior. Like birding, in life, there will be adversity. It's inescapable. At times, adversity comes when we least expect it, often when we are at a point of being most comfortable. Other times it comes as the result of a choice we make, like going into Arizona in the summer, I knew it would be hot. And by hot, I mean dangerously hot. Hot enough to cook an egg on the sidewalk, or the road, or the black leather seats of your car. Adversity itself was definitely not a choice. How adversity is dealt with is a choice—one each of us has full control over in our daily lives.

The truth about adversity is that it is beatable. I learned along the way that by looking *past* the difficulty, there is good. It is just like cleaning the lens of a camera—this happened to me all the time during the year. When the crud—dirt, dust, pollen, and oil build up on the lens, the resulting photos include the crud. This distorts the image enough that it can change how we perceive the image, but never changes the scene being photographed.

This exact situation happened to me earlier in the year, when I photographed a drab-colored warbler. *Why does that bird have a spotted breast?* I wondered, reviewing my photos at the end of the day. In every photo I had taken of the bird, the same pattern of splotches appeared on the breast. I knew that bird didn't have a spotted breast, but according to my photos, it sure looked that way. *Maybe the bird was dirty.* I was convinced something was going on because that species just didn't have a spotted breast. *Perhaps I'm misidentifying it,* I thought, doubting my ability as a birder.

Then, it hit me. I checked my camera and sure enough, the lens was dirty, not the bird. What appeared to my eyes to be true simply wasn't. I had to think—to be smarter than my senses. This is how adversity works. It clouds our vision and obstructs our goals, but cannot influence the greater scene, because it is not part of it. To overcome adversity in your life, you must focus on the good present *past* the difficulty at hand. After realizing that, anything is possible.

Nutting's Flycatcher

18

CALIFORNIA

STANDING along the palm tree-lined streets of the Ventura coastline, I gazed out over the ocean. Just beyond the Pacific horizon lies an island archipelago spanning over 150 miles. The Channel Islands consist of eight islands, five of which are now protected as part of Channel Islands National Park, and are frequently visited by tourists who wish to kayak through sea caves, hike the scenic trails, and go scuba diving. For bird enthusiasts, the Channel Islands offer a unique opportunity: the chance to see a bird found nowhere else in the world.

The Island Scrub-Jay is found exclusively on Santa Cruz Island, which measures only 60,645 acres, giving the Island Scrub Jay the smallest range of any bird species in North America.

Every Big Year birder must visit the Channel Islands; it is part of the game. A taxonomic re-shuffling took place just over two decades ago, splitting North America's Scrub Jay into three species. Listers suddenly got a new bird to chase, and since then it has been part of the Big Year game.

There are fewer than 3,000 individuals of this species.

More or less, everyone visits Santa Cruz Island the same way: on the Island Packers boat tour. The boat trip to the island was like a mini-pelagic trip. Dolphins surfed in the bow's wake before diving and disappearing into the clear blue water. Before noon, the boat dropped anchor at Scorpion Ranch, on the northeast corner of Santa Cruz island.

In the late 19th century, Santa Cruz Island was home to more sheep than people. Early ranching families brought live-stock to the islands and produced wool and tallow for markets on the mainland.

Decades of overgrazing by sheep and feral pigs (introduced by the Spanish) caused ecological havoc. Eventually, most of the land was purchased from private landowners, and serious conservation efforts began, with hopes of restoring the island to its natural state.

As the Island Packers boat pulled into the bay, I jockeyed for position on one of the first boat shuttles to the island, to maximize my time on the island for the day. I've never been one to run past educational placards, but I only had so much time to find birds and didn't want to miss the special scrub-jay. I was aware there might be better spots on the island to find them, but I was capable of covering a lot of ground in a short time and figured that would be a good strategy.

Following the boat transfer, I hiked up the road past a campground, and into the hills. I spotted a brief flash of brilliant blue as an Island Scrub-Jay flew into a dense cluster of scrubby trees. This species was much bigger than I imagined. Several birds quietly sat low in the island oaks, their eyes hidden by a dark black mask. The small band of marauders lurked in the shadows of the scrub, waiting for people to arrive and unpack their lunches. I had no doubt I'd see the blue bandits better later on.

I hiked up a ravine and scrambled up a steep slope to the

top of a mountain. After surveying the island, I abandoned my hopes to run along the trails to a different part of the island, in search of scrub-jays in the pine habitat. I'd heard that the Island Scrub-Jay had locally adapted to different habitat types on the island. Some birds had larger bills to feed on pine cones, and smaller-billed birds fed on acorns from the oaks.

I found time to take a jog around, and tour some of the old buildings and see the visitor's center before returning to the campground. As I sat in the shade a small Island Fox fearlessly ambled up towards me, cocking his head in a similar fashion to a dog expecting a treat. I studied the fox, which nearly disappeared into extinction in the 1990s.

In Los Angeles, the manufacturing of a volatile insecticide, DDT, spilled 17,000 tons of the pesticide into the Pacific Ocean. The concentration of the chemical increased as it traveled up the food chain, first into fish then into Bald Eagles, nearly wiping out the Bald Eagles.

As Bald Eagles disappeared from these islands, Golden Eagles moved in from the mainland, taking their place. Abundant feral pigs supported the population of Golden Eagles, which soon learned the foxes were also easy prey. Before long, the fox population plummeted and Golden Eagle numbers soared.

The Nature Conservancy and National Park Service completely eliminated 5,000 pigs from the island, and Golden Eagles were trapped and relocated away from the island. Finally, Bald Eagles were reintroduced and began breeding after an absence of over 50 years. This conservation success story made Santa Cruz Island a model for island restoration.

I sat in the shade watching the fox trot around a campsite. Nearby, the harsh *shrek shrek shrek* call sounded from a thicket of oaks. Tired from the day's adventure, I kicked my feet up, planning my next move. *I think it's about time to get a proper look at a California Condor.* This sounded like a good plan. I knew I still wanted to see Himalayan Snowcock and figured if both attempts were successful, I could see my 700th bird in Nevada or Wyoming.

California's Highway 1 is well-known for the beautiful coastal scenery, but fewer people know it is one of the state's best places to find condors. There are many pull-outs along the oceanside north of Lucia before Big Sur, and many of these are great spots to scan the sea cliffs for roosting birds in the morning or catch a glimpse of a soaring condor in the afternoon breeze.

Condor 204, also known as "Amigo," was hatched at the San Diego Zoo in the spring of 1999. The following year, he was released into the wild and has been cruising the sea cliffs of Big Sur since, defending "his" stretch of beach along Highway 1 where I spotted him. Amigo has an interesting story. Following his release, he paired with a female, 222, and had a chick, condor 470. The original egg laid by the female 222 was not viable, and so biologists swapped out the egg with a fertile one from a captive condor breeding program. The egg hatched in the wild successfully, and the offspring 470 grew up in the wild and is still flying free today.

Weighing in at up to 26 pounds, with a wingspan of 9.5 feet, the California Condor is a giant bird! As one of the largest flying birds, it has commanded the attention of people for hundreds of years. Early Native Americans held the "Thunderbird" in high esteem and believed it brought thunder to the sky with its giant wingbeats. California Condors had been driven to extinction in the wild as a result of shooting, egg collecting, and lead poisoning.

The San Diego Zoo has worked in cooperation with the Peregrine Fund to breed the birds in captivity and release birds back into the wild. Today, there are over 270 California Condors flying free in North America.

I sat precariously on the metal guardrail at the edge of the road, staring down towards the water's edge, hundreds of feet below. Scanning the rocky beach, I could see dozens of California Sea Lions, covering the thin slice of beach like spring break sunbathers.

One sea lion at the edge of the group had a large bird perched on it... a California Condor! It was distant but clearly identifiable. I ran back to my car to retrieve my scope to get a better look. This was certainly a condor. My timing was perfect because right after I focused the scope the bird took a hop, skip, and a jump and was airborne. Even from the cliff-side view, I could tell it was a giant bird.

I watched the bird catch the stiff sea breeze and fly upwards, away from me. Suddenly, the bird made a wide, swinging turn, and flew back directly towards me. With my mouth agape, I stood speechless and the condor landed in front of me, on a bare rock. This was unbelievable.

I observed the condor rubbing his head against a rock, cleaning any remaining bits of Sea Lion off the bare skin of his head. They will rub their head on grass, branches, or rocks to clean themselves after a meal. They also enjoy frequent baths, and regularly preen their feathers to keep them clean.

One of the main threats to condors is lead poisoning, which occurs when condors ingest dead animal carcasses containing fragments of lead ammunition. In addition to lead poisoning, I learned that littering is also a very real threat to condors. Adult birds forage for bone fragments and calcium-rich shells to ingest for nutrition and bring these items back to the nest to feed a chick.

A California Condor perches on the cliffs near Big Sur

Along Highway 1, the condors have been observed picking up and ingesting bottle caps and pieces of plastic "micro-trash" that they mistake for these shells and pieces of bone. Biologists have put out broken seashells in areas frequented by condors in hopes that they ingest shell fragments instead of landing on the road to collect human trash instead. So far, this has been a successful strategy, combined with spraying condors with water when they approach the road too closely. While walking along the highway, I picked up several pieces of micro-trash to throw away in a garbage can, reducing the number of pieces available for a condor seeking additional nutrition for its offspring.

It seemed that no matter where I traveled or what bird I was searching for, human had impacted it in some way. As a species, we have destroyed habitat, exploited birds for their parts, and then attempted to fix it, putting the pieces back together. I pondered this endless cycle, wondering if I would ever see a bird in a landscape untouched by humans, just doing its thing. With climate change, even the most remote wild places have been affected. Would birds ever catch a break?

The Pacific Coast Highway hugged the shoreline northwards toward Carmel. The stunning ocean views I'd heard about were nowhere to be found—instead, this supposedly scenic stretch of highway was like driving straight into Hell.

Thick gray smoke blurred steep seaside cliffs which vanished into the haze. Helicopters chased distant flames across the hillsides, out of sight. Everything was cloaked in a grayish-orange smoke, and ash fell like snowflakes at the end of a storm. Wildlands fire trucks parked along the highway and the sky glowed orange. California was on fire.

19

ROCKY MOUNTAIN HIGH

IN THE EARLY 1960s, Nevada's Fish and Game Commission had a problem. They had a state rich in diverse habitats: rolling hills, steep canyons, and alpine meadows, yet these habitats lacked an adequate supply of game birds. To many bird enthusiasts, no problem exists with this scenario, but in the eyes of a sportsman, it looks different. The Commission, made up of biologists who were also hunters realized that without game, the hunters would find other places to hunt. As hunter numbers decline, the stream of revenue money dries up, and conservation withers away. Hunters have always been an asset to preserving habitat and conserving species.

To address this problem, biologists from the Fish and Game Commission began a task force to identify game bird species they could transplant to these "game deficient" areas of Nevada. Following the successful introduction of Chukar to the foothills, the search committee learned of the Himalayan Snowcock, a larger game bird native to the mountain ranges of Asia. To learn more, a biologist was sent to the Hunza region of Pakistan, which he recognized was very similar to the rocky alpine slopes of his home state. Immediately, efforts were made to transport the *ram-chuk* or "King of Chukar" to the tallest peaks in Nevada.

In September of 1964, 150 birds were captured from the mountain peaks and transported by burro nearly 70 miles to the capitol city Baltit, then moved by jeep an additional 64 miles to the village of Gilgit. Only 96 remained—most were in poor condition, suffering from a variety of avian diseases, broken bones, and exhaustion. For two days, the birds were medicated and fed and placed on quarantine. These birds were evaluated after three weeks, and the snowcocks that were deemed unrecoverable were culled.

The remaining 76 birds were shipped to Karachi, Pakistan, and then to New York City. Sadly, twenty more birds were lost in quarantine. Finally, nineteen of the originally imported birds were selected to be released—the remaining birds kept in the breeding program. For the release, the birds were carried by an Air Force helicopter on a high-altitude training flight 9,500 feet above sea level, before being released in the snow-covered slopes high in the Ruby Mountain range outside Elko.

Unfortunately, despite serious efforts being made, additional birds couldn't be acquired in Pakistan due to a border conflict. The captive birds in Nevada were entered into a breeding program, which ultimately failed.

Surprisingly, the released birds took hold. Decades later, a population persists, surviving cold winters, hunters, and Golden Eagles—one of the main predators of the Himalayan Snowcocks in both their native and introduced range.

The Himalayan Snowcock has a cult following in North America, receiving much more attention than in its native homeland. To any serious birder or connoisseur of upland game, the name immediately conjures breathless mountain vistas and steep mountain slopes, both extremely beautiful and physically exerting to reach.

To reach my goal of 700, I knew I had to see this bird. Some birders will rent a helicopter and fly into the Ruby Mountains, spotting the snowcock in flight as it moves from mountaintop to mountaintop. Although this was the preferred method in *The Big Year* movie, this was definitely not the way I wanted to see this bird. It isn't debatable whether a low-flying helicopter flushes these birds from narrow ridges, exposing them to predatory raptors and causing them to expend valuable energy. From my time working in the backcountry of Glacier National Park, I've learned that nothing can shatter the solitude and peace that wilderness provides like a helicopter flying overhead.

Growing up attending summer camp in the mountains of Colorado gave me plenty of opportunities to improve at hiking. By 2016, I had tallied nearly 15 summers living in Colorado's high country. One "rite of passage" that most mountaineering programs did was climb a 14,000-foot mountain, commonly referred to in Colorado as a "fourteener." This annual tradition had more than prepared my physical and mental fitness to a level necessary to make the trek.

I glanced down at my phone as I navigated towards Island Lake in Nevada's Ruby Mountains. I'd left California's Napa Valley earlier in the day, and stopped at the Jelly Belly factory —a childhood dream of mine. As I drove east, I realized that I would arrive after nightfall to Nevada's Lamoille Canyon; I needed to do some reconnaissance on my phone to figure out where the trailhead started and which direction Island Lake was from the trailhead. I was the only car on the empty two-lane highway, so I used the time and cell service to plan my attack.

After miles of winding forest service roads, the road dead-ended at a parking lot. Stepping out of the car into the chilly night air under the stars, my legs nearly gave out after spending so many hours bent in the driving position.

I estimated it would take me less than an hour to do the two-mile uphill hike, carrying some gear in my pack. The many switchbacks on the trail made the climb less rigorous, but the lake wasn't my end-game. No, I wanted to sleep on the rocky alpine slopes *above* the lake. Since it was dark, I didn't bother to check my phone to see what time I reached the lake. I began the vertical ascent by moonlight, until I ran out of hikable terrain. After some searching I found a horizontal place to sleep — a level spot next to a huge boulder. The vegetation wasn't too delicate and I was tired, so I set out my sleeping bag on the short vegetation, careful to crush as few wildflowers as possible, and went to bed.

Half the sky was still covered with stars as a ribbon of dawn stretched across the eastern horizon beyond the jagged mountaintops in the distance. I awoke to a low whistle—the sound of Himalayan Snowcocks. The birds were calling from one side of the glacial cirque, a ring-like wall of mountains around me. Not wanting to get up yet, I lay in the grasses, feeling the wind rush across the ground as the sun rose out of the distant molten orange clouds. The mountains woke up, with White-crowned Sparrows singing their cheerful song.

As I sat up, three snowcocks flew from the rocky ridgeline on the far side of the cirque towards where I lay, flapping and gliding on their short rounded wings before disappearing above me on the cliff face. Temporarily lost from view, I managed to sneak closer and re-find them as they moved uphill, feeding among the short plants and wildflowers.

I watched the snowcocks long enough until my mind got distracted by other things. Taking a break from looking through the spotting scope, I looked down at the lichen-covered rocks. I was fascinated by these ancient fungi, some of which grow only several millimeters per year.

Lichen is symbiotic, meaning it is not a single organism, rather a cooperative relationship between multiple organisms— fungi and cyanobacteria, the latter of which is photosynthetic and produces energy and nutrients for both organisms. (The fungus builds the body both organisms inhabit.)

Growing together allows both organisms to survive living in extreme environments, like the alpine tundra. As well as being a food source, lichen is used for nesting material. I've found lichen in nests of hummingbirds, gnatcatchers, and other birds that use it to help camouflage the nests.

Looking again through the scope, the snowcocks had vanished. Perhaps they had flown (or magically transformed into rocks), but likely they continued their upslope journey, disappearing into the mountain landscape they were born to rule, identical to the Hunza of Pakistan, but a world apart.

Himalayan Snowcock near Island Lake

From the moment I opened my eyes, I knew that it was going to be a good day. It sounds cliche—but it was true. The month of August was only five days away, and the Himalayan Snowcock the morning before had been my 699th species of the year. (Following later taxonomic updates, I would find out it was actually my 700th species) I planned on reaching my goal of 700 within the next few hours. First, I needed to find a Starbucks. I wasn't very motivated to fire up my camp stove and boil water for two packets of oatmeal, and surely there was a Starbucks just down the street in Jackson, Wyoming. With several blog posts needing my attention, I made my way inside carrying my laptop and my oatmeal.

Before my oatmeal had cooled to eating temperature, the notifications began popping up. Facebook, email, and texts from friends began arriving asking me, "*Did you see the news?*" and "*Is this your whale?*" These messages contained links to a couple of different articles spun from a *National Geographic* article published the day before. I hadn't seen the article yet, so I clicked the link. I saw some very familiar photos of *a* deceased whale (it wasn't "mine") I had spotted in Alaska nearly two years prior. Seeing the photos took me back to that exact moment in time.

The crashing waves pounded the black volcanic sand of Zapadni beach, one of St. George's only "true" beaches. The rest of the island was flanked by steep cliffs, reaching nearly 1,000 feet from the ocean. These cliffs provided nesting ledges for millions of seabirds, including murres, puffins, fulmars, and kittiwakes. Due to so many birds in the vicinity (particularly Red-legged Kittiwakes), someone was on hand during the summer months to help ensure the runway was bird-free before the planes would arrive. That someone was me. After the cargo flight had departed, I went down to the beach to see if the winds had blown in anything unusual during the day. The morning check was unsuccessful, but in the evening, I noticed a large white mound on the end of the beach, nearly among the rocks. It definitely wasn't there earlier in the day. After lifting my binoculars, upon closer inspection, it was clearly a dead whale—possibly a Beluga.

I walked along the beach, keeping an eye at the carcass at the end of the beach. It was definitely a whale, and the following morning I reported it to the tribal marine biologist on the island and notified my friend Karin. My photos were passed up an email chain, since several features of this whale were inconsistent with the presumed ID. Tight-lipped researchers emailed me in the following months, asking for my photos and videos, and then went silent. Little did I know, they were taking DNA samples and gathering measurements on similar whale skulls that had been found on other Alaskan beaches. I was pretty much kept out of the loop until the paper was published.

The *National Geographic* article confirmed that this whale was, in fact, a new species. This was the first I'd heard the official news, and once this appeared on social media, this story overshadowed what surely would have been a more noteworthy day—reaching my goal of 700 species.

A week earlier I had connected with the Teton Raptor Center, through a mutual Facebook friend. I admired their combined mission focusing on research, rehabilitation, and education. Their emphasis on bird conservation.

Fulfilling the *Connect* mission of The Birding Project, I wanted to learn more about how these biologists were using technology on their owl projects to record owls and document their movements. After sharing a little bit about myself, we dove into a discussion around the history and biology of the owls. I learned about some of the intimate movements and dispersal of the local owls, before going out with a biologist to use the technology in the field. I learned about different types of transmitters used in tracking bird movements. They were deploying homemade acoustic recorders that actively listen for owl calls. With the results, researchers can refine their techniques in surveying for owls.

In Wyoming, the Great Gray Owl is a state sensitive species. Many of the active Great Gray Owls nest on state-managed land, which is also used for forestry. As forest treatment, including burning and cutting, becomes more active, it is important to have an understanding of how this affects owls and other species of wildlife. At the southern extent of the boreal forest, any effects from climate change will also be studied/noticed.

"There're a lot of things that we can learn from birds," Arthur told me, as we got out of the car. It was nice to stretch my legs after driving all the way from Nevada to Wyoming. The warm rays from the early morning sunlight beamed across the valley, illuminating the tall craggy peak of Wyoming's Grand Teton. The iconic mountain range would be the backdrop for the next milestone of my Big Year, which I would share with this complete stranger I had met less than an hour ago.

Arthur was a biologist, although if he wasn't carrying binoculars, I couldn't tell from a quick glance at his appearance. His right arm was covered in tattoos, and I couldn't help but stare at the multiple piercings on his face. His flat-brimmed hat covered his ears, hiding yet another piercing. In the city, I wouldn't have given him a second glance, but standing out here in the woods, Arthur looked strangely out of place.

As we left the road and walked towards the forest, Arthur continued to share with me what he's learned from birds. A lump formed in my throat as I realized I'd been quick to judge him based on outward appearance alone. The only thing "out of place" was my quiet judgment, which I soon realized just how wrong I was!

Arthur and I quickly bonded talking about raptors and our deep respect for birds. His warm personality shined through as he described the moment he was hooked, during a lecture on songbirds given by a college professor at Humboldt State University in California.

We silently hiked up into the hills, through dense stands of Lodgepole pines, whose trunks and branches were garnished with what looked like hanging clumps of wolf lichen. If it was, in fact, wolf lichen, it had been used in Europe to poison foxes and wolves. My mind drifted the rest of the walk, as I thought about wolves and just how delicate predator populations really are. Arthur raised the receiver, an antenna composed of several long metal rods, and waved it slowly from left to right. The receiver's job was to detect a high-frequency radio signal, given off by a transmitter attached to a Great Gray owlet several months ago. I've used this type of telemetry equipment before to track down lost falcons, and was familiar with how it worked.

Originally I wasn't very excited about using telemetry to find and count a Great Gray Owl. Although the owl was free and unrestrained, in accordance with the ABA rules, it kind of felt like cheating. However, this was *my* list and *my* story; to me, there was more to this quest than just seeing the bird. I wanted to see technology applied in the field research, directly influencing conservation action. It was time to head out into the field.

As we traversed the hillside, stepping over downed logs and blooming wildflowers, the beeps from the receiver grew louder. I could tell the signal was scattered by the topography and thick trees, so I began looking for the bird, relying less on the sound coming from Arthur's telemetry. My diligence paid off—I spotted a fledgling Great Gray Owl perched high in a tree looking down at us. The jumbled signal from the radio-tagged bird was still a ways off, but we had stumbled onto one of her siblings by pure chance. I was transfixed. Arthur and I both sat down, leaning against separate trees, both watching the owl. It was clear he had a deep respect for all birds.

We both sat there as the minutes passed, mostly in silence. I thought about reaching my goal of seeing 700 species for the year. Though I sat in a forest, my mind traveled across the continent, back and forth, replaying all the birds that had come before this bird.

What was the significance of 700? I had reached my goal ahead of schedule. Was this truly the 700th bird, or was it the Himalayan Snowcock I'd seen two days before? Or the California Condor two days before that? I thought about the subjective nature of listing and keeping track of these things. What if I had counted the Thick-billed Vireo I'd seen in Florida, or the Pin-tailed Snipe or Siberian Rubythroat on Attu... These were all birds that I'd put binoculars on, but didn't see well enough to identify and feel comfortable counting on my own. *Did the number really matter?* I knew that in the future, with a single lump or a split, the number—and my 700th bird—would change. So why did it matter anyway? Truth be told, it didn't—at least to me anyway.

Like me, Arthur was also driven by a desire to share birds with others.

"If you can find that passion and enjoy the outdoors, then more power to you." he told me. What mattered most was enjoying each bird and the people and place that were all woven together in a complex tapestry of my experience. After our encounter, we left the owls alone with the forest, talking excitedly about the sighting all the way back to the car, where I thanked my new friend for taking the time to share this memorable sighting with me.

After thanking Arthur, I headed into Yellowstone National Park. I still had wolves on the brain and figured it would be a good time to make my dream happen of seeing wolves in the wild. Yellowstone's Lamar Valley was one of the best places to see wolves, and as I looked at a map, I noticed the Old Faithful geyser was on the way to Lamar Valley. I'd never seen it erupt and figured today was a day of many 'firsts'—what was one more?

I joined the sudden influx of people gathered along the semi-circular wooden boardwalk, which moments earlier hosted only a handful of people. In a matter of minutes, several mini-eruptions of steam and hot water gushed from the ground around the base of Old Faithful, the center of attention for the growing crowd of spectators.

The eruption lasted a matter of minutes, though it seemed to stretch on much longer. Shafts of sunlight slanted through the tower of hot water as it grew, then paused, then grew again, followed by another pause, before reaching its peak. The eruption concluded with applause, which rang from end to end of the curved boardwalk, crowded with people.

After watching the eruption, I retreated into an overstuffed leather armchair inside the Old Faithful Inn. The famous log-cabin style lodge was built in 1902. On their free wifi, an hour passed with little notice, and soon it was dark outside. I packed up and walked back to my car the long way, past Old Faithful one more time.

As if I had triggered an invisible land mine, the geyser started to erupt as I walked past. First, a loud gasp of air, sounding like a surfacing whale. Then, a loud belch followed, as a roar of hot air escaped from the chasm somewhere beyond the beam of my headlamp. Like clouds of diamond dust, water vapor swirled in front of my headlamp creating a sparkling wall of light in my headlamp. Distant squeals of delight were barely audible, as the crowds from earlier had dissipated, and now I stood elbow to elbow among a crowd of ghosts.

The silence magnified the voice of the geyser, which roared, splashing water on rocks somewhere in the darkness in front of me. I turned my headlamp off and sat down on a bench to take it all in. Small shimmers of starlight peeked through shifting gaps in the clouds in the night sky, as if stuck there after being blown out of the earth into the sky above. At that moment I felt a connection to the earth, an overwhelming sense of smallness among the natural world around me, and I reveled in it.

The feeling lingered as I snaked northwards along winding roads into the heart of the park and pulled over at the top of a pass to spend the cold night under the stars, a welcome respite from the routine of parking lots and bright overhead lights.

As the morning sun spilled over the hills into the Lamar Valley, I was already on the road, but soon got stuck in traffic. Only one other car was in sight, but between us were nearly 30 bison, content on making their way to greener pastures at their own bison-like pace. My Subaru was no match for a thousand-pound animal, and I was more than happy to wait my turn.

I pulled off the dirt road onto the shoulder, behind a truck that likely belonged to a wolf biologist. Further down the road, several spotting scopes were trained on the hillside across the valley, where a wolf den was located, hidden among the scrubby brush. Biologists and a small group of volunteers carefully monitored the wolf activity across the meadow, and they were eager to have me join them with my optics.

We watched several distant wolves lounging outside the den, and caught a glimpse of the pups at the den entrance. Nearby, a Northern Harrier cruised low over the brush, overtaking a wolf by surprise. The canid spun and jumped high into the air, attempting to thwart the bird's "attack" which we surmised, could have been play. It was an amazing encounter, reminding me that this year wasn't just about the birds.

My journey had been amazing so far. Now that I had reached my goal, I had to decide if this was my destination. Did I accomplish all I wanted to? My objective had been to see over 700 species of birds in the year—and I had done it. So now what?

I was happy about reaching my goal. I'd sacrificed a lot to make it happen. Financially, I'd practically bankrupted myself, after selling my camera gear and optics, I had dipped into my personal savings account. I had persevered through adversity, living on the road for months, subsisting on ramen noodles and cheap food. I had completed a semester of graduate school and was one step closer to meeting my goal of getting my master's degree.

The part of me that was hungry for more adventure popped my bubble of contentment with a sharp needle of desire. I wanted to see more birds. Could I afford to stay on the road and continue birding?

If anyone could understand the dilemma I was facing, it was Laura Keene. I called her up, and she asked me an important question:

"When's the next time that you'll be in this same spot?" I was home in Seattle, and knew she wasn't asking me to think about her question in a literal sense. I thought about what she said very carefully. I had seen over 700 species, and still had five months left in the year. A lot could happen in five months. I thought of a new goal: Neil Hayward's record of 749. Looking at the ABA checklist, I still had plenty of birds remaining. Some were easy to see, some weren't, and a handful of birds I could only dream would show up. That would put me close to the record. I didn't want the birding to end for me. I certainly wasn't ready to toss in the towel and get a full-time job. I knew if I stopped at 700, I would always look back and wonder what would have happened if I had kept going. It seemed less important to go for every bird I could, but pick and choose which birds I chased, and do so in a responsible way. I certainly couldn't afford to keep birding the way the others were, chasing individual birds on planes and staying in hotels. If I continued the car chases, and took strategically-planned flights, and stayed cheaply at those destinations, I may just be able to make it work financially.

Several people had suggested organizing a crowdfunding campaign—an idea which I'd been resisting. I didn't want to be a charity case or ask people to give me money just to go birding. However, I realized that I was able to do something many would never have the opportunity to do, and many people were following my adventures on social media, and living vicariously through me. These people wanted me to keep going and were willing to support my cause.

I spent weeks at home in Seattle, working on putting together a short fundraising video and launching a campaign on GoFundMe. I raised over half my goal, and the other half in offline contributions, and then some. Also, some people contributed their air miles, which made several more trips to Alaska possible free of cost to me.

Why slow down now? I asked myself. Pressing on the gas, I continued down the road.

*The Merlin, a tenacious little falcon, is found across
Montana's open habitats*

At this point in the year, hundreds of miles and hours pass by easily. With my mind on cruise control, the mile markers fly by and don't mean a thing. Like a bird heading north, I just traveled until I hit an obstacle or was too tired to continue. For me, the obstacle came first, blocking my way north—a giant set of peaks comprising Montana's Glacier National Park.

Deceptively named, McDonald Creek drains the melted snow from the surrounding peaks into Lake McDonald in northwest Montana's Glacier National Park. In May, melting snow trickles downhill from the high peaks, building up as it gets funneled through narrow chutes between steep rocky walls, cutting down to the valley's bedrock as a torrent of ice-cold water. In the summer, downed trees and debris piles are the only remnants of the creek's violent springtime mood swings. As the water approaches the lake, McDonald Creek settles down and calms to become a meandering wide channel of rippling water, draining into Lake McDonald.

—

This corner of Montana held many memories for me—some cherished and others not so pleasant. As I rode past McDonald Creek, I squirmed in my seat to keep my backside from falling asleep, then took a sip from my Nalgene bottle while blankly staring out the window, recalling working along this same stretch of river in 2008, when I was part of a team surveying for Harlequin Ducks. I allowed the unpleasant memory to wash over me like cold water slowly poured over my head.

I remember the day began pretty normally, with my field crew briefing the objectives for our survey. We were tasked with hiking upstream, along the banks of McDonald Creek and tallying the number and sex of any Harlequin Ducks we encountered. Simple, right? Being naturally curious, and loving the challenge of finding difficult things, I asked about the chances of finding a Harlequin Duck nest. "You have a better chance of getting eaten by a Grizzly," the crew leader replied, in his loose Midwestern drawl.

Less than an hour later, we flushed a female Harlequin from the steep banks above the creek, and I discovered her nest with eggs, hidden under the low-lying branches of a western hemlock. The rest of the day I kept looking over my shoulder, fully expecting to see a hungry-looking bear over my shoulder.

That afternoon progressed without any bear attacks, but was not incident-free. Further upstream along our survey route the bank disappeared, replaced with a long low-angle slab of rock. The spray from the water, combined with some algal growth had transformed the rock slab into a sedimentary slip and slide.

We crossed the wet rocks carefully, yet I wasn't careful enough. Standing up, both feet began to slide, as if I was being invisibly pushed towards the water. I may have yelled for help, but couldn't tell if anyone heard me, as I was quickly pulled underwater.

I was swept downstream quickly, as nature's powerful hydrological forces took over. I struggled against the current and was somehow able to find a crack in the rocky cliffs, and hoped I could hold on long enough to be rescued.

Am I going to die? I wondered as the icy current of McDonald Creek strained my tired fingers wedged in the thin hand-width crack I had found in the rock. I tried to kick against the current to resist the swift pull of the water, but my wet pants and hiking boots dragged me down. My backpack, filled with extra clothes and a warm layer in case I got wet, was now filling with water and dragging me down like a wet parachute. I gasped for air as I tried to keep my head above water.

Slow to respond, the rest of my crew ran downstream to catch up to me, staying clear of the boulders and angled slabs of slippery rock we had just crossed. With a broken tree branch, they fished me out of the icy water.

Tired and hypothermic, I struggled to navigate back to the car unassisted, hallucinating along the way. A series of bad decisions on the part of our crew leader led to this not being a great day, but I was lucky it didn't go worse.

The next day, we began our surveys along the icy stream. Weeks of surveys in the wrong habitat for Harlequin Ducks wore on me. Sobered by icy water and difficult off-trail terrain, birding all day wasn't fun anymore, and the pessimistic crew members made it all the less enjoyable.

In a desperate search for better people to hang out with in

my free time, I contacted Dan, who worked for Montana Audubon. After we spoke on the phone, he invited me to join him for a day of birding in the park with two teen birders. Josh and Andrew were both several years younger than me but extremely sharp in the field; these guys were so much fun to bird with that we connected afterward through Facebook and agreed to keep in touch.

Now, eight years later, Andrew, Josh, and I embarked on an intentional repeat tour of Glacier National Park. As we snaked our way up the Going to the Sun Road, hugging the curves literally carved out of the rock.

A Dusky Grouse perched along the rock wall guardrail, the other side dropping off hundreds of feet below. I'd seen them here before nearly in the exact same spot! Dusky Grouse are unique in that they eat trees, mostly needles of coniferous (cone-bearing) trees. This was a new bird for the year, and one I had been hoping to see with my buddies.

The treeless mountain slopes of Logan Pass are blanketed in the summertime by wildflowers, and white fleecy mountain goats graze lush meadows across the alpine tundra. White-tailed Ptarmigan, American Pipits, and Gray-crowned Rosy-Finches lured us into the heavy fog in search of more birds.

Almost eight years ago to the day, Josh, Andrew, and I had walked the same wooden boardwalk, searching for ptarmigan together for the first time. This is where we'd first met, and it meant a lot to return to this spot with them and have them be a part of my Big Year. I was well aware of Andrew's artistic talents, and it was on Logan Pass that morning I decided that I wanted him to illustrate my book I had been writing about my adventures.

We were unsuccessful in our search for ptarmigan at Logan Pass and dropped down to lower elevations on the east side of the Continental Divide. The afternoon flew by as we searched intently for woodpeckers among the charred skeletons of burned trees. A wildfire had swept through this part of the park last year, burning over 4,000 acres of forest and forced officials to close sections of the park.

Following a fire, the return of new growth and birds breathes new life into the landscape. Both Black-backed and American Three-toed Woodpeckers favor burned areas, as does the elusive Northern Hawk-Owl: my nemesis bird.

While being in Montana was a highlight by itself, spending time with old friends and reconnecting was one of the best parts of my year. I left Montana having added several new year birds, and solidifying some friendships that continue to bless me to this day.

A male Harlequin Duck stretches his wings along McDonald Creek in Montana's Glacier National Park

20

HEADING OFFSHORE

I KNEW I had some relatively easy code 1 and 2 birds left on the east coast, and so I planned to do a pelagic trip out of Hatteras, North Carolina. I could fly standby to North Carolina for $79, then rent a car from Priceline for $11 a day, and do two or three back-to-back pelagic trips with Brian Patteson. That's exactly what I did.

The summer humidity was expected, yet was stronger than I predicted when I deplaned in Raleigh. Second-guessing my choice to wear my fleece-lined jeans, I changed clothes in the bathroom near the gate, and then exited security.

While waiting for the shuttle, I went to get out my drivers license and realized I didn't have it. My mind raced as I mentally retraced my steps. *Maybe it was on the plane? In Seattle? Left in an obscure pocket in my bag?*

At the rental car facility, I unpacked both of my bags in the seating area. With the contents of my bag regurgitated onto the floor next to the water dispenser, I went through every pocket —nothing.

After re-packing my clothes and gear, I explained to the

employee what my situation was. He assured me that it was against their company policy (and most other rental companies also) to rent out a car without a hard-copy of the driver's license. My ship had been sunk.

Adversity presents itself in a variety of ways, often when it's least expected. This was just an opportunity to adapt, improvise, and overcome. I weighed my options. I called the airport in Seattle. They called the gate with the plane in Raleigh. I waited... and the reports came back negative. I submitted a lost property request. I texted home. I emailed the pelagic trip coordinator. I went back to the airport, to figure out how I could get to Hatteras. I called the Montana DMV, and asked about issuing an expedited replacement license, or emailing a digital copy in lieu of the real thing. I learned I could download my driving record, but they would only issue a replacement if requested by mail and then they'd mail it to my address in N.C. That wouldn't work...

At the information kiosk, I was given a list of valet shuttle services. I made some phone calls and learned it was $255 to take a one-way ride to Hatteras. That price was on-par with Uber, which also was an option I almost considered. I called an air charter service. He couldn't fly in and pick me up until the next morning, which wouldn't work since I'd miss the pelagic boat that left the next morning.

I filed a report with the airport police just in case someone turned it in there. While at the airport I went to see if I could go back through security and check the bathroom I changed in- just in case. They didn't let me through but did send an officer to the bathroom across from Five Guys to check for me- nothing. In desperation I sent out a Facebook post- maybe someone would know someone who could pick me up? I called Brian and left a message—perhaps someone else was flying into Raleigh who was also on the trip tomorrow?

Near my wit's end, I called my dad. Several minutes later, he texted a photo of my temporary Montana driver's license to me. It sure didn't replace the real thing—but was better than nothing.

Armed with the text message, I returned to the rental car counter. My final plan was to show the picture and my driving record. First, I looked again through all of my things—slowly, systematically. Nothing new turned up. My driver's license was somewhere, and it would show up with time. Something small like this couldn't stop me from doing this awesome boat trip in the morning. That was my right place and right activity.

I walked up to the rental car counter again and didn't recognize the guy at the counter. I guess there had been a shift change in the last 45 minutes. I explained my situation again, but the rule stuck—they couldn't release my rental car without a driver's license. This time, armed with a digital photo of my license, I presented new information. I suggested asking a manager, and he reluctantly told me he didn't think she'd go for it, but he would ask anyway. The new guy came back out, and said his manager told him they could rent me a car!

The look on his face mirrored my own surprise. I silently rejoiced and hoped the paperwork wouldn't take long enough for the manager to change her mind. I told him I didn't care what kind of car I got, I was just happy to have a vehicle. He tried to sell me extended coverage and insurance, which I almost bought out of gratitude for him, but realized that the price of this alone was going to be more than I paid for the whole rental from Priceline—so I kindly declined.

Out in the lot, I checked my car for damage, taking a short video clip of the exterior (a policy I always do in case it comes down to disputing a later charge) and I jumped in and was good to go. The only thing between me at Hattaras was the set of spike strips at the edge of the rental lot, and a guy who collects the paperwork. I stopped the car and put on my best blank expression.

"Drivers license please" he demanded.

"I showed it to them inside—is it necessary to get it out again?" I asked.

"We just need to be sure that you are who you say you are, and that you have the correct vehicle. My mind raced. This guy looked like he meant business. I feared that I failed to produce my license, he wouldn't let me take the car off the lot.

I didn't know what I was going to say, so I improvised; unzipping my laptop bag on the passenger seat to buy me time.

"Do I need to fill out one of those forms that show where the car is already damaged?" I had left the form blank, and taken a video instead, but figured this would buy me some time and maybe he'd just let me go.

I got out and did another inspection of the car, marking all the spots on the form that had scrapes or visible markings. I used that time to think about whether I'd tell him I didn't have a driver's license.

I got back in the car and grabbed my passport, opening it to my I.D. page and I flashed it when I handed my paperwork back. "Yep, I'm Christian—looks just like me, right? I quipped as his eyes lingered on my passport page. He thanked me and may have said something else, but I wasn't listening as I already had my blinker on and was crossing the spike strips, heading out of the lot towards Hatteras.

On the highway my heartbeat returned to normal, slowing down right along with the traffic. I had a 3 1/2 hour drive ahead of me, but I knew that if I didn't get pulled over, I'd be able to get to Hatteras about 11:30 pm and find a quiet spot to sleep in the back seat of my rather-small economy sized car.

I used the drive time to call my parents, update Facebook, and touch base with Brain about my current status. I thought

I'd make it now—just a couple hundred miles to go. I hadn't eaten since I boarded the plane nearly 7 hours earlier. I stopped at a Subway and got two footlong subs using a coupon. I'd eat one today and save the other for lunch tomorrow on the boat. The drive was going quickly until I got to the Outer Banks. I carefully watched my speed, passing several highway patrol cars, hidden in the bushes alongside the single-lane highway through the Alligator River, crossing swampy waterways and tangled forests.

For the first time in a while, I turned on the radio, and immediately recognized the James Taylor tune following a few sweetly-picked guitar riffs.

> Dark and silent, late last night,
> I think I might have heard the highway call
> And geese in flight and dogs that bite
> The signs that might be omens say
> I'm goin', I'm goin'
> I'm gone to Carolina in my mind

The song couldn't have been more perfect for my drive along the Outer Banks. I let the nostalgia wash over me, as I set the cruise control and rolled the windows down, letting the salty sea air fill the car.

With less than 30 miles to go, I looked down the road and saw flashing lights. It looked like maybe there was an accident. My heart sped up as I slowed down, and suddenly it occurred to me what lay ahead: a DUI checkpoint. I had nowhere to turn around.

The officer walked up to my car as I rolled the window down. "Good evening, Officer". This was the most sober-sounding greeting I could come up with. I offered a smile followed by a nervous pause, hoping he'd take one look at me and wave me through. I'd driven through Border Patrol checkpoints dozens of times across the southwest and my experience talking with them made me much more comfortable in this exchange.

"Can I see your driver's license please?" he questioned. I paused, and offered a weak smile as I chuckled and silently thought *I had a feeling you were going to ask me that.*

"I actually don't have one on me at the moment," I replied. Given how I felt, the words sounded bold they sounded coming from my lips. The matter of fact tone surprised me and the officer's mouth curled into a slight smile.

"I had it when I got on my plane in Seattle this morning, and when I landed in Raleigh tonight, I couldn't find it. It's been a crazy day."

"Please pull right over there for me—would you?" He pointed to a small space in front of a white truck with all four doors open that was being searched by several other officers, while the occupants stood outside in the lights with blank stares on their faces. They'd been busted. I moved out of the roadway and pulled in front of another patrol car, whose flashing lights lit up the inside of my car like a cops episode and waited with my hands on the steering wheel in plain sight.

The same officer came over to my car moments later and asked me something concerning the letters on my license plate. I told him I was unsure—it was a rental and I didn't know what was on the plates. I tried to get my shaking fingers to unlock my phone, so I could show him my virtual drivers license.

He looked at it and handed my phone back, asking me to read my license number, which he wrote down on a notepad. I read him the numbers, and he asked me to get out of the car and stand over against a post. I complied, and another officer came up with a police canine and walked around my car, the dog sniffing the tires. I was surprisingly calm. I knew I'd done nothing wrong and was kind of excited to see what was going to happen.

I figured I'd get a citation for driving without a drivers license, and wondered how much the fine would be, or if I'd spend the night in jail. I cringed at the thought and realized that was unlikely to happen.

The officer told me I could return to my car after the dog made his loop and jumped back in the police SUV. I waited for the first officer to return.

"I was able to look you up in the system, and saw your face matches the Montana license in the system—you're good to go."

I couldn't believe it.

"Have a good night Sir."

"You too, Officer." I turned around and slowly went through the checkpoint, passing people lined up facing the other direction who didn't look as fortunate as me. The dog had alerted to something in their vehicles, which was being searched. With the flashing lights in my rear view mirror, I headed south.

I arrived at the marina after midnight, checking a satellite image to be sure I was in the right meeting spot for the morning, before emptying the contents of my backpack onto the back seat. This trick leveled the deeply contoured seats to form an adequate sleeping surface. I put my computer bag with valuables in the trunk and spent the next hour and a half trying to get comfortable on the back seat.

Relaxing my mind from the day's excitement proved to be quite the challenge. I reviewed seabird ID, checked Facebook, and was surprised at the outpouring of support and well wishes for my safe travels to Hatteras. I sent a few messages thanking people and let them know I had made it.

I rolled the windows down, took off layers of clothing—

anything to get comfortable. I fell asleep after 2 am and woke up a few times to change position. I woke up 10 minutes before my first of 3 alarms set on my phone (there was no way I was going to sleep late) and drove to the far side of the parking lot, where Brian's website instructed us to park. I wasn't the first person to arrive; it was 5:30 and there were already other birders parked and getting ready.

We boarded the boat, stowing our gear inside and gathered on the bow to hear a short safety briefing from Brian, who told us if life jackets were necessary on this trip then we all would be in trouble. He explained the clock system used on a boat to identify where birds were spotted, and a little bit about seasickness. Without much ado, we were underway.

We motored out into the channel, with the sky just starting to lighten up at the edges. I watched real-time as stars disappeared and the sun rose on the eastern horizon through thin clouds over the sea. Everything about being out on the Atlantic was exciting—it smelled familiar, with the cool sea breeze starting to warm along with the color of the sky.

As we got further from shore we began to pass birds. The first dots to appear on the horizon were terns, flying high and dipping and dodging, and with the direct sunlight shining on them, it was hard to tell if they were Sooty or Bridled Terns.

When the next *tern sp.* flew overhead, I snapped a few shots and zoomed in to take a closer look at the pattern of the underparts, and looking at the photo I determined it was a Sooty Tern. Brian called some of the further terns Bridled, which would be a year bird for me; however, as I couldn't see the distinguishing field marks, I couldn't make a positive identification on my own. Maybe after more experience, I'll become as good as Brian, taking a speck on the horizon and accurately calling it a Cory's Shearwater.

The water turned from a grayish cast to a deep aquamarine

blue as we crossed into the Gulf Stream. The boat cruised easily across drifting lines of Sargasso weed, which shone bright green against the deep blue water.

Occasionally a flying fish would break the surface, propelled by its tail across the water. This created a beautiful repeating pattern of ripples on the surface before the fish went completely airborne—using the wide pectoral fins to glide over the glassy water. Some fish glided nearly a hundred yards before splashing back down into the water. Photographing these flying fish became a challenge I quickly accepted.

The birding began to pick up when we got into a flock of Cory's Shearwaters mixed with the smaller Audubon's Shearwater. Suddenly off the port side of the boat a large white bird materialized out of the sun.

Shouts of TROPICBIRD! were yelled across the boat. I took a quick look through my binoculars, before taking some shots with my camera. Later on, we added Great Shearwater, and several Black-capped Petrels to the growing list of birds I hoped to find.

The strong sunlight reflected off the water, and soon my fatigued eyes needed a rest. I stayed hydrated but before I knew it I was growing tired, and went inside and lay down to take a nap for a while.

I awoke to multiple shouts of TROPICBIRD, PORT SIDE and jumped up, ran outside, and took a few quick shots of a second White-tailed Tropicbird—a different individual then we had earlier in the day. This bird had a longer tail, and the previous bird was molting and its central tail feathers were much shorter. What a cool bird!

I returned to the dock tired and hungry. After thanking the crew, I walked down the street in search of a nice dinner and discovered the nearby seafood places weren't within my budget. I didn't really like seafood all that much, and the new life birds I'd seen deserved a celebration—but I didn't think splurging on dinner was the best way to spend my money.

I stopped at a gas station and bought snacks for the next morning— Pop Tarts, some chocolate frosted mini-donuts, and a Gatorade. Nearby, the Gingerbread House Bakery advertised pizza, which sounded like a fitting way to celebrate the seven new birds I'd seen.

Betting the beach was better than my car, I slept at a campsite near the ocean. I prayed for a breeze to keep away insects, but there wasn't much wind in the dunes, so OFF! covered every part that stuck out from the sleeping bag.

I fell asleep under the Milky Way, which looked brilliant in a sky free of the light pollution. The Milky Way was not visible from Walmart parking lots—that's for sure.

The *Stormy Petrel* returned to the Gulf Stream the following day, on slightly rougher waters. A steady breeze blew, yet carried few birds across our bow. There were more flying fish, which were very interesting to try to identify and challenging to photograph.

I worked on capturing the fish leaping from in front of the boat with my camera to distract myself from my empty hopes of seeing a Trindade Petrel or a White-faced Storm-Petrel. Despite many flying fish, I saw no new birds.

In fourth grade, my class was given a biographical research project. I had to research a famous person, then memorize and perform a historical dialogue about that person while in costume. At the time I was fascinated by flight, so my natural choice was aviation pioneer Orville Wright.

Kill Devil Hills and the Wright Brothers National Memorial was only a quick jaunt up the Outer Banks from Cape Hatteras, and after leaving Hatteras I spent the afternoon reliving my childhood acting career, and also learned some new historical tidbits about the Wright brothers.

Orville Wright wrote in 1941,

"Learning the secret of flight from a bird was a good deal like learning the secret of magic from a magician. After you know what to look for, you see things that you did not notice when you did not know exactly what to look for."

Many people look *at* a bird without knowing what to look for. In part, that's why they are so magical. Unlike a magic trick, however, when you do know what to look for—the magic only builds, for the seeking and finding is just as rewarding as just the finding.

Finding something you've looked for after a long time searching can often be more rewarding than just stumbling upon something one was not expecting. Both can be equally as rewarding when one is seeking birds.

At this point in the year, I knew exactly what to look for. The learning curve, which was steep at the beginning of the year, had started to flatten out—although it certainly hadn't leveled. I had spreadsheets of birds I hadn't seen yet, with data of where to find them. This, however, did not take the magic away, instead, it enhanced it. These surprise birds, out of range, late to migrate, or simply accidental- were just as fulfilling and magical to me as the common birds in each area I visited. I was having a blast and would continue. The birds didn't "run out" - as I checked them off. There were always more- both target birds as well as common birds that I could enjoy.

The destinations held magic too. Perhaps the most magical of them all was Alaska, and I was prepared to spend a month in Alaska in search of new birds. Time to fly.

21

A GAMBELL

FOR MANY, life in Alaska revolves around the weather. When the weather is really bad, planes don't fly. Grounded planes mean food, mail, and medications don't get delivered to people who need them. Residents in small villages around the state are dependent on bush planes, air taxis, and Alaska Airlines for delivery of these necessities. Anyone who has visited the Pribilof Islands knows how fickle the weather—and flights can be.

For birders, the onset of a storm bad weather accompanied by west winds, is welcomed by birders. Each new weather system has the potential to blow Old World migrants from their intended destination in Siberia onto the shores of St. Lawrence Island, where each spring and fall birders lie in wait.

Every September, several dozen birders visit the small village of Gambell, on the northwest peninsula of Alaska's St. Lawrence Island. Many birders go the traditional route of signing up for a birding tour hosted by Wilderness Birding Adventures, and others take the more difficult approach of visiting Gambell as "independents".

The latter approach takes on the complex puzzle of logistics: lodging, food, and transportation. On my budget, I opted for the latter. At home, I meticulously curated a month-long menu and then went shopping at Costco, buying over 50 pounds of food and carefully fitting it all in a footlocker which would be one of my two free checked bags on Alaska Airlines.

I had read about Gambell from other Big Year accounts, which painted the village as a dreary birding destination teetering on the edge of nowhere. I read that on a clear day you could look across the waters of the Bering Sea and make out the jagged peaks of Russia with the naked eye.

With Russia in sight, I imagined the birding must be *really* good. I had to go and see for myself what this legendary birding destination would be like. Hopefully, it would be one for the record books.

Following a brief layover in Nome, I walked out onto the tarmac, flanked by two older birders, both seasoned Gambell veterans. We loaded up into a small twin-engine prop plane. Despite saying 'Bering Air' it didn't feel much like a commercial flight; the pilot looked younger than me, and his uniform consisted of a pair of Carhartts and a blue flannel shirt.

I sat in the back and leaned up against boxes of cargo for the entire flight. After taking off, I inspected the cargo closer, and I realized I was leaning against a box full of eggs. A stack of pizzas from an Asian restaurant in Nome was strapped down further behind me, filling the plane with the aroma of lukewarm pie.

We flew low over the blue waters of the Bering Sea until a distant strip of land appeared on the right side of the aircraft. I quietly assumed it was St. Lawrence Island until the pilot pointed out that it was Russia. We banked left and made a long sweeping turn down through the scattered clouds, and landed on the northwest tip of St. Lawrence Island.

True to what I'd read, the plane's arrival was an event that drew people from the community together on the airport tarmac to see what the plane brought—almost like the arrival of Santa Claus. A group of people welcomed the plane, but were clearly more excited about the arrival of a flatscreen TV and boxes of energy drinks then the three birders that the flight also brought.

I carried my duffel bag on my back, strapped my backpack to my front, and dragged the heavy bin of food through the gravel. Stopping for directions, I found out where I needed to go. All of the houses seemed plain gray and weathered, and the only difference separating these identical structures were the broken down piles of junk sitting outside. Old snow machines and four wheelers sat among piles of parts littering the properties. Leaving a track in the gravel behind me, I made it to the lodge where I would live for the next three weeks, sharing a space with one of the best birders in North America.

Since January I've met hundreds of birders, some just embarking on their learning journey, and others who have been deepening their understanding of birds over decades. One name surfaced again and again throughout the year, and I realized I needed to seek this man out and learn something from him. His name was Paul Lehman.

I met Paul in a coffee shop in California earlier in the year to begin learning about Gambell. Paul has spent 7 weeks on Gambell every spring and fall for over 15 years, documenting the birds on Gambell, noting their arrival and departure dates more carefully than an accountant reviews their numbers.

Paul's obsession with bird abundance and distribution extended to every corner of North America. His understanding of weather as a driving factor to finding rarities was amazing. For Paul, a rare bird from North America is often more exciting than a vagrant from Asia. Often confused with other "Lehman" birders (Jay Lehman did a Big Year in 2013, spotting 733 species) Paul's only competition is with himself—yet he boasts many "first" North American records.

I shared a room with Paul in the Lodge, a leftover mobile construction trailer that had been the housing for construction workers who built the new school. Paul was an astute birder, carefully analyzing a sighting and studying the bird. He knew better than anyone else, what should show up when, and was remarkable in the field. I felt lucky for the opportunity to spend so much time with him.

A handsome male Lapland Longspur is ubiquitous across Alaska

In Gambell, there's trash, there's birds, and there's trash birds. After spending enough time around birders, you'll eventually hear someone use the phrase "trash bird". I believe that this phrase is slang for a bird that is overly abundant in a particular area or region, nearly to the point of becoming annoying to the observer who must search even harder for a subtle, less-common species.

I don't use this statement as a derogatory insult to the birds themselves—(abundant birds must be doing something right!) rather use it simply as a term for overabundance or ubiquitousness. This distinctly American phrase (I have yet to hear it used by international birders outside the U.S.) in the Lower 48 usually references overly-abundant invasive species, like the European Starling or House Sparrow, which are both introduced from Europe. The sheer abundance of these birds, coupled with their biological competitive edge of forcing other birds out of backyard bird feeders, often earns these birds a bad name. I'll admit, the phrase can be controversial, as many people love all birds, regardless of how ecologically disruptive a species can be.

Two abundant songbirds are quite abundant and fit the "trash bird" stereotype across much of Alaska. In any extended birding trip, one grows tired of both species out the sheer abundance. Ironically, the surrounding beaches of Alaska's many rural settlements are littered with trash, which one encounters nearly as regularly as they encounter these two birds. The Lapland Longspur and the Snow Bunting.

In order to find rarities in Alaska, one must first be intimately familiar with both of these ubiquitous species. An experienced birder must know every detail of these common birds, in order to better detect an anomaly. I learned this valuable lesson on Attu—that when a small bird flushed, it would most likely be a Lapland Longspur. I quickly memorized the field marks, flight style, call note, and pattern of these "Lappies"—so when the Brambling, a much rarer Asian finch flushed out of the grass—I knew it at once.

Seemingly bored with life on their island, the boys would wander around the outskirts of town with BB guns in hand, looking for birds. While Lapland Longspurs and Snow Buntings were most numerous, it caused the visiting birders much fear that these free-range kids would shoot something much rarer, leaving it for dead where it fell—swallowed up by the thick vegetation or scavenged by a greedy gull.

I watched several times as the boys hunted, casually strolling around until something moving crossed their path. Then they go into "sneak mode"—moving slowly, one behind the other as they sneak up to get within range- (often 10 feet or less) before steadying their sights and firing off a small projectile at the unsuspecting victim.

Occasionally luck was on the side of the kids and the bunting fell—to a rousing cheer of the hunters. More often the shot went amiss, much to the relief of the onlooking birders. Sometimes the birders would yell at them, reprimanding them for their lack of stewardship and care for a creature's life. I don't think these birders understand that it's not our place to chastise their activities and the local's choices of recreation.

This was their island and their culture. Hunting was woven into the fabric of their society for thousands of years. It's true—they weren't killing small birds for meat, but rather honing their skills and firearm safety, so someday they could accompany the older boys and men on hunting trips, where ducks, geese, and seabirds would be on the menu. As much as I didn't like to see birds shot (and nearly become an unintended victim of ricochet) I couldn't blame them.

It was not uncommon to find decapitated auklets while walking the gravelly area around the village. Sometimes the carcasses were from recently-fledged young, exhausted by their first flight from the distant cliffs to the ocean. The young birds crash-landed on the gravel flying as far as their still-developing wings could carry them—landing on roads, beaches, roofs, or wherever the wind blew them. Ill-equipped for survival on land, many of these small birds died.

Some birders showed great compassion for these little auklets and would pick up the survivors and stuff them into their pockets, or a windblown cardboard box, and flag down the nearest passing ATV for a quick ride to the beach, where the bird would be released into the glassy waves. I did this as often as I could, finding through trial and error a proper technique was needed to release auklets, especially on a windy day.

The technique was to hold the bird like a football, and then wait until no gulls are nearby, and throw the bird out over the ocean with the intent of scoring a 40-yard touchdown pass. Often the bird will stay folded up, opening its wings at the last second before splashing into the waves. If the bird is not thrown far enough, it will be pushed back onto the beach by the wave action, and become a meal for the ravenous Glaucous Gulls.

Tossing an auklet towards the sea with gulls around is like putting a piece of fresh meat in front of a carnivore—the gulls will quickly swoop down and pluck the smaller auklet from the water, dunking it five or six times before swallowing it whole. Believe me, I watched it happen more than once.

The boneyards were Gambell's haystack, and rare birds were the needle. Each boneyard was an ancient trash dump of the bones of marine mammals. Layer upon layer of walrus, whale, and seal bones mixed with gray gravel and pieces of trash, buried days—or decades earlier. Nutrients from decades of decay fed the thick carpet of wormwood, which grew in thick clumps in the boneyards. From a wayward bird's perspective, the dense vegetation of the boneyards was a source of food and protection from the wind. Birders knew that the greatest chance of finding a rarity was in the boneyards.

I had the opportunity to sit and talk with one of the village elders. He told me he was born in the 1930s in Gambell. He told me his tribe is of Russian origin, and he recounted the free flow of people across the Bering Strait. He told me stories of reindeer herds that crossed the ice when the sea ice of the Bering Strait froze solid in the winter. He shared hunting tales, and reminisced about times before the Soviet Iron Curtain blocked the free-flow of people and tradition between people here and nearby tribes in Russia.

Days passed, and September began to slip away. Each day on Gambell began the same way—hoping for a wind-blown bird from Siberia to be found. It wasn't. The next day didn't produce any rarities either. And the next. From all the stories I'd heard about Gambell, part of me was expecting a magical place where Stonechats and Willow Warblers flushed out of the grass in front of me, and where tired shorebirds dropped out of the sky onto the gravel-covered beaches. Although it had happened before, this certainly was not going to be that kind of fall. The wind blew from the north, and east—every direction except west—the direction we were hoping for.

The northeast winds had an effect on the birders too. The constant drizzle of the rain, sometimes blowing sideways, seemed to dampen the attitudes of many (but not all) of the long-staying birders on the island. Some birders wore their feelings on the outside, constantly voicing their discontent. Others remained stoic. Back in the lodge, the frustration was palpable, hanging over our heads like a thin layer of cigarette smoke under the lights inside a pool hall. As the ringleader, Paul didn't whine—he had been around long enough to know that some seasons weren't as good as the others.

I spoke with many of birders during the slow times, taking advantage of the knowledge and stories from these more experienced birders. I was surrounded by the top listers in the American Birding Association, who had been birding this continent for decades. One told me about their childhood memories of hearing the now-extinct Bachman's Warbler.

There was also a rare moment when Olaf, Laura, John Weigel and I were all in the same room. I think this is one of maybe two times this happened all year, the first being the Adak airport after our Attu trip. All I'll say is the tension was palpable.

I wondered why these people were away from their families, their jobs, the comfort of their own homes and the routine of their daily lives. For what? A new species on their life list? One night, through the wall I could hear one birder lamenting to his wife over the phone exactly how bad this season had been so far on Gambell. The sorrow in his voice was clear, and part of me felt sorry for him.

Several birders have been coming to Gambell for decades, with hopes of being present when a rare bird is found that has never been seen on this continent before. More of these "first" ABA records come from St. Lawrence Island than anywhere else on the continent. Several of these birders had spent decades amassing incredible life lists in North America. That didn't sound fun to me. Monte showed me the latest bird he'd photographed in the ABA. Ebbe described his daily ritual, going on a walk and searching for a Stonechat.

The day we heard the American Birding Association had put out a vote to include Hawai'i as part of the countable ABA area, it was like a bomb went off. This news sparked great debate among the veteran birders, whose ABA lists were over 800, some over 900 birds.

Pent-up feelings of frustration from weeks of poor winds and no new birds added fuel to the fire, and a heated discussion ensued. Everyone had an opinion. Many of the guys on Gambell had spent decades birding the traditional ABA area, and now this re-definition of what "counted" had been changed. This addition disrupted the equilibrium in many men's life birding achievements: their ABA lists. To be honest, I wasn't very interested in why they were upset, specifically. I listened from the other room, focused on writing, or swapping stories with Laura about our Big Years.

A Yellow-billed Loon flies past the seawatch in Gambell

As the weeks passed, the one consistency I could depend on was bad weather. Not the good kind of bad weather that steers vagrant birds across the Bering, but the bad kind of bad weather. North winds, thick fog, and a constant drizzle that brings chills through several layers of winter clothing- that kind of bad weather.

During this kind of weather, the majority of independent birders stayed inside most of the mornings, when doing a seawatch was futile or walking through the boneyards was a recipe for wet rain gear, boots, and socks that would stay damp for the rest of the day.

Everyone knew that despite the weather, Paul Lehman

would head out like clockwork, and do the same sweep of the territory he'd done for the last 15 years. If he found anything, it would be radioed out and others could follow.

Despite the weather, I went out regardless. I tried to hold on to the optimism, hoping that by covering different areas that I would somehow increase the odds of finding something spectacular- every birder's dream while in Gambell. This, however, was not the case, and I spent many hours and miles trudging across the gravel and slogging around the lake, spotting only Lapland Longspurs and Snow Buntings.

My birthday arrived and had passed without any ado. Unbeknownst to me, Laura had gone shopping earlier in the day and baked a chocolate cake covered in sprinkles for my birthday. It was delicious. Laura later confessed to me that she had to substitute some ingredients to make it work—but I didn't care. I bought a new box of Reese's puffs and a bag of Jelly Belly jellybeans to celebrate.

Later that evening, I was sitting in the lodge along with Laura and others when a group of Steller's Eiders were found feeding offshore on the point. I ran out to the point and enjoyed great looks at this sought-after sea duck. They weren't in breeding plumage, but swam right up close to shore in the surf, diving and feeding actively. The Steller's Eider was my birthday bird, and year bird number 726.

The following day signaled the start of the other Big Year birders departures onwards to other birds. Laura and John left to fly to the Pribilofs, where a Jack Snipe had been found days earlier on St. Paul Island. Olaf also left, but I didn't know where he was going until later, when someone told me he had the Jack Snipe too. For me, Gambell wasn't over until I said it was. I was biding my time, waiting for one bird to show up that would conclude my fall stay on the island.

The McKay's Bunting breeds on St. Matthew Island, and in the fall birds disperse and spend the winter on St. Lawrence Island and the mainland around Nome. Many Big Year birders return to Nome in the winter months to find McKay's Bunting feeding from backyard feeders. I knew I couldn't afford a return trip, so I decided to wait this bird out on Gambell.

Shortly after Laura and John had left, I knew it was time for a change. I grew tired of the dismal attitudes of some birders who sat inside all day waiting for the winds to change, their pessimism leaking into every seeming conversation and interaction. It made an environment I no longer wanted to be a part of.

I moved out of the lodge and arranged to stay with some of the local teachers from the school. This provided a much more social atmosphere. The teachers got together and played games, ordered pizza from Nome which was flown over on the plane, and overall were much more sociable. We laughed, quoted movies, and enjoyed our time together regardless of the weather outside.

I went to school with them during the day most days, unless I stayed home and worked on blog posts or went birding. One afternoon, an internet installation specialist knocked on my door. I answered, and introduced myself to him. Derrik is from Savoonga, and came into the house to hook up the internet. While waiting for something to load, he pulled up a GoPro video on his computer.

"Want to see a whale hunt?" he asked.

"Of course!" I answered enthusiastically. I realized what a privilege this was- probably as close as one could experience to the real thing while remaining on dry land.

The next 15 minutes of video held my attention and I watched in amazement, as Derrik's GoPro head cam was a front-row seat to a Minke whale hunt. He narrated it for me, describing the pursuit as 10 aluminum boats sped across the glassy Bering Sea, with two shooters positioned in the bow of each boat.

This particular hunt took place two years ago, in the fall and was Derrik's first voyage as a newly-minted boat captain. I watched as a young kid, maybe 16 years old took a shot as the whale surfaced in front of the boat about 20 meters away. The misty gray spout of air shot up through the water, followed by a quick crack and puff of water spray, the whale dove, leaving behind a crimson bubbling wake.

"That's a clean lung shot" Derrik said, with a hint of admiration in his voice.

The whale quickly was overtaken by the boats, and several skilled men threw long spears tipped with a sharp nail-like spike on the end, which were tied to ropes attached to bright orange fishing floats. Past generations used the skins of spotted seals filled with air and sewn shut, creating large 4-foot long fishing floats. Now, whalers use bright orange rubber boat floats which work just as well, if not better and are more resilient. The knowledge of how to construct sealskin floats "the old way" has nearly been lost.

I watched with a mixed sense of sadness for the animal but knew how valuable this food source was to this community. The footage ended abruptly, before the whale expired and was towed back to the beach, where the community gathered to celebrate the catch and help with processing the supply of food.

To be honest, the lack of new birds had helped shift my thought from birding being my primary focus to engaging with the local community. I spent fewer mornings walking the boneyards, and more time in the school (I did take a radio with me, just in case a really good bird was found). I networked persistently until someone introduced me to Drew, the high school science teacher. I offered to give a presentation about birds to his class, which he gladly accepted.

One student, in particular, seemed to enjoy my bird photos more than most. Usually, for most of the class, he sat quietly at one of the back tables, maybe falling asleep when I wasn't paying close attention. When I showed my bird photos he became the most lively student in the room. He perked up when I showed photos of ducks and geese in particular, and would confidently shout out the name for these birds in his native Y'Upik language.

It dawned on me that the birds he was excited about were all birds the villagers hunted for subsistence. Emperor, Cackling, and Snow Geese. Sensing he was a hunter, I asked him one day to tell me about his hunts. Like many native communities in rural Alaska, hunting is woven into the fabric of the Y'Upik culture in Gambell. Chris learned how to shoot a rifle when he was five years old. He practiced on small game and upgraded to a shotgun when he began targeting ducks and geese. The price of food is high, and villagers often scour the beaches as seasons change, gathering the bounty the sea offers.

Spending time at the school soon led to teaching several classes with Drew and working with students in the classroom. The more time I spent in the school, the more interested I was in learning about the history of Gambell. I checked out books from the library, including *The Kids from Nowhere,* a fascinating book about the history of the school on Gambell. The kids in the book were now grown up, and I sought out their relatives and listened to their stories.

Before long I felt much more a part of this unique community. After school, I helped the Home Ec teacher make fry bread before a community dinner, and stayed after school on Wednesday's for the traditional dancing. A line of folding metal chairs was set up in the middle of the gymnasium, and drummers of all ages sat and played while singing traditional songs. I even got up and danced.

Finally, on September 18th the first wintering McKay's Bunting showed up in Gambell. I didn't find them myself, but was grateful that somebody else did. I chased these birds successfully, spying the frosted white bird that had likely just flown in from St. Matthew Island, the primary breeding location of this species. This was likely the last new bird I would see in Gambell, so it was time for me to go. I briefly contemplated heading to the Pribilofs, but that came at a dual cost. The financial burden of this trip would put me deeper into debt, but I was more concerned with getting stranded on the island due to bad weather, potentially risking missing my next commitment—making it to Houston for my brother's wedding.

A Snow Bunting (left) and McKay's Bunting (right)

My return to the Ted Stevens International Airport in Anchorage was slightly more overwhelming than I had imagined. Accustomed to the quietness of life on St. Lawrence Island, the first thing I noticed after landing was the noise. Sirens blared, lights flashed, and the engines idled at a dull roar as we deplaned onto the tarmac from the back of the Boeing 737-400 Combi aircraft.

I stopped at the bottom of the stairs, dazed by the sudden sensory onslaught. Standing drenched in sound, like a cold shower startling me and jolting me back to reality. I wasn't in Gambell anymore.

The noise inside the airport was slightly less assaulting, but was visually overwhelming. Swarms of travelers as far as I could see easily outnumbered the entire population of Gambell.

After checking the monitors for departing Seattle flights, I realized a flight had just left, and there wouldn't be another one for a while. Although I had a ticket for the first leg of the flight, I was flying standby to Seattle, and had to wait for the next open flight. I found an empty row of seats across from a half-empty gate where people were lazily sitting around waiting for the aircraft to arrive. Each of my bags got its own chair, and I took the last seat, greedily filling an entire row of seats. Turning my phone off airplane mode, I checked the flight loads, which were oversold to Seattle for the rest of the day.

Nearly all of my air travel this year had been on on a standby basis, meaning that I paid a reduced fare for a standby ticket, and if there was space available on a flight, I got on. If the flight was full, I waited for the next flight. I'd had plenty of practice flying standby, and after adopting the "we'll get there when we get there" attitude, I got used to it. One thing was for sure, I wasn't getting on a flight to Seattle anytime soon.

I turned my phone off airplane mode, and my phone lit up

like a winning slot machine in Las Vegas. Flashing notifications flooded the entire screen. Ignoring them, I tapped Facebook—and the first item in my News Feed was a post from Neil Hayward on the ABA Rare Bird Alert page: ACCIPITER ON ADAK. I stared at the photo, taken by Frank and Barb Haas only hours earlier. There was no doubt in my mind that I was looking at a Eurasian Sparrowhawk, which was not even on the ABA checklist.

Scrolling through the comments discussing the ID, I wondered how long the bird would stay on Adak. My train of thought was interrupted as an announcement was made over the speaker: *"We apologize for the short delay, but we are currently waiting for our plane to arrive before we begin boarding for Adak..."*

I couldn't believe it. My stomach did a somersault. *Could I...* Wait for a second, this wasn't the plan. I needed to get home to Seattle, and then to Texas for a wedding, I *could not* miss.

If I could... What if... My thoughts were racing. I picked up the phone to make a few phone calls, and to check the weather on Adak for Sunday, which was the next returning flight to Anchorage. If I could switch my standby ticket I was using for my Seattle flight and go to Adak instead, I would surely be the only birder on the entire continent able to chase this bird unless it stuck around. A single flight to Adak from Anchorage leaves every three days, and I knew this was my shot.

I felt inspired, or maybe even called to go to Adak. Part of it was the possibility of re-finding this bird, and some of it was making a split-second decision I knew I would regret at the end of the year, if I played it safe. I knew that re-finding a migratory raptor would be hard, but my wanderlust burned within and I couldn't sit at the airport all day. I had to get to Adak. Phone calls complete, it cost me only thirty-eight cents to change my standby ticket. I put it on my credit card.

Alaska Airlines flies to Adak every three days. Frank and Barb (who had found the sparrowhawk yesterday) were on the flight back to Anchorage. I made sure to talk with them and get any last-minute info that might be helpful in my search. They described where exactly they had seen it, and emphasized that despite looking in the morning before their flight, it had not been refound. Given the number of Peregrines and Bald Eagles on the island, I would be hiding too...

The airplane was virtually empty. I was able to choose whatever seat I wanted, so I sat in the last row at the back of the plane. There, I had time to digest the consequences of the decision I had just made. My luggage from Nome had been checked through to Houston, and I would pick it up whenever I arrived. I had only the clothes I was wearing, my Xtratuf boots, and the raincoat I carried with me. My spotting scope and camera were safely packed in my carry-on bag, along with a toothbrush. *That's really all I need* I thought to myself.

As soon as we reached our cruising altitude and the seatbelt sign had been turned off, my stomach grumbled. In all of the Anchorage airport excitement, I had forgotten to eat. Rummaging through my carry-on bag, I managed to find several Clif bars. I opted to purchase a meal on board- and save the food I had brought with me for later. After I bought some food, I told the flight attendants I had made a snap decision to go to Adak, and was ill-prepared for the next few days. They gave me two of their large bottles of water from the cart, and an entire bag of 36 mini-bags of pretzels, and a bar of chocolate. I poured both of my cans of ginger ale into my Nalgene bottle to drink later.

Having only been to Adak once, I kind of knew the drill once we had landed. I remembered one place to stay, the Bluebird — which was also a home-run restaurant. The owner, a retired Navy pilot, flew the same aircraft my dad did when he was in the Navy. I hoped he would remember me. I bummed a ride from the airport and ended up getting a room upstairs at The Bluebird. It had two twin beds, a small TV and DVD player, and a small bathroom. This was much better than the first room I thought I'd be staying in months ago on Adak. I dropped my stuff, and then put on my rain gear and headed out towards the old high school.

I immediately found the exact branch pictured in the photograph, except it was missing one thing: the sparrowhawk. Walking among the pines, I remained on high alert, checking each grove of trees for any raptor-like bird. Up ahead on the road, several Lapland Longspurs foraged for seeds along the grassy shoulder. The dark blur appeared out of nowhere, flying low with rapid wing beats, hugging the road as it chased down the startled songbirds. I held my breath as I raised my binoculars to get an unobstructed view of the bird, now flying even further away. *Peregrine Falcon.* The juvenile falcon definitely got my hopes up.

Over the next two days, I walked around the island, checking every cluster of trees I could find. The following morning was dreary but had hopes of turning into a good day. It was raining, despite patches of blue sky over other parts of the island. My ears immediately tuned into the flock of Lapland longspurs, flying overhead I walked to Adak National Forest, checked the neighborhoods, and hitchhiked out to Clam Lagoon with some ordnance disposal guys. They'd served in Iraq, and tried their best to describe all of the birds they saw over there.

I sat on a grassy hillside on Adak, overlooking the old high school building. Nothing had changed from the last time I was here in May. Surveying the scene before me, it more closely resembled the aftermath of a midwestern tornado than an abandoned military base. Pieces of metal roofing hang off the building, swaying in the breeze sounding like a bear breaking into the trash cans. Across the runway, I could hear beeping from construction vehicles hard at work, despite it being a Saturday. The sooner the job is done the sooner they can leave. I'm leaving tomorrow whether or not I see the bird.

There is something special about Adak—maybe it's the constant sight of Bald Eagles flying around or the undulating hillsides of green grass that move wave-like in the wind. There's also magic here, a mysteriousness that keeps you on your toes, requiring diligence to check and double-check each and every bird—it could always be something rarer. Despite giving it my best effort, I could not relocate the Eurasian Sparrowhawk. I pushed myself physically, birding hard each day.

The inbound flight from Anchorage arrived right on time. I wondered if I had instead gone to St. Paul if I would have made it out and back to Anchorage this easily. The construction crews were on board with me, flying back to Anchorage. I didn't regret this trip at all. I took a chance, to chase a rare bird and missed. It wasn't really about the bird; I had already seen more birds surpassing my goal. It was about the adventure, the spontaneity, and the challenge to figure out the logistical puzzle of it all. I was winning because I wasn't losing. Fear couldn't handle me. Love always wins.

Over the year, I had heard many stories from birders of the 'bird that got away'. As people told me about their "nemesis" bird, I would smile and nod, knowing that each person has their own bird that they just can't seem to connect with. For me, the Northern Hawk Owl was this bird. How could I not adore a bird whose name combined 'hawk' and 'owl'? As a child obsessed with raptors, this was the best of both worlds. After moving to Montana, I claimed 'HAWKOWL' as my vanity license plate, secretly hoping it would help tip the scales in my favor for finding this elusive bird in the state. It didn't, despite many attempts made searching in Glacier National Park, this bird still had an empty box next to it on my life list.

While in Anchorage, I enlisted the help of Isaac, a Facebook friend who I'd never met before in real life. Isaac had lived on Adak for 6 years, and provided some valuable coaching and insight during my sparrowhawk chase. We made plans to go birding together when I returned to Anchorage before I had to fly to Houston.

Following a smooth airport pickup, we left Anchorage and cruised along the gradual incline of the winding Glenn Highway. Below the road, the Matanuska River carved out a winding course through pines, spruces, firs, and aspen in a valley that was formed by the slow receding of ice and snow. Ahead, an impenetrable wall of clouds sat draped over the Talkeetna mountains, the fresh snow spilling out onto the cold slopes below. The gray sun, obscured by snow-filled clouds, shone pale winter rays through holes in the clouds, which created a patchwork of light on the distant mountainsides. The vibrance of fall color animated the landscape, slowly relenting to the stillness of winter.

Along the drive, our conversation broke the minutes of mutually-agreed-upon silence. We both were present with the task at hand, and spotting owls were much more important than making small talk. Miles of silence passed until one of us would turn our head quickly. "Bird!" We slowed down and moved to the shoulder for a closer look. The repeat culprit of several of our "bird" sightings were Canada Jays, an inquisitive bird commonly seen around trailheads and campsites looking for free handouts from hikers. However, in this setting perched atop a Spruce tree with head tucked, a jay can resemble a

Northern Hawk Owl closely enough to fool even the most experienced birders.

My eyes grew tired of scanning the tops of trees speeding along at 50 miles per hour. Growing bored, I used my phone's stopwatch and calculator to determine I looked at 16,800 tree-tops in an hour. After several bouts of stop-and-go, we slowed down to make a mental note of a gravel side road to check on the way back. Before we returned to full speed, Isaac slowed down, his gaze fixated on a tree ahead. "Look, there's your bird!"

Sure enough, perched in a tree mere 30 feet away from the roadside. I raised my binoculars and took a quick look to confirm- it was surely a hawk owl! We high-fived quickly and shared smiles, before pulling off the road further. I fumbled for my camera in the back seat, and once we reached a halt I took another look through my binoculars.

The bird seemed to look right through the window at me. I rolled the window down, and the owl promptly flew off. It landed a good distance further away, carried by a flight of several strong flaps, and then a strong upward pitch to set it atop a different blob-shaped tree, set back further from the road and obscured by plenty of blobby spruces in between. I snapped a couple of pictures then watched it stare intently at the ground, transfixed by some unobservable motion below. It dropped down and flew commandingly to a new perch even further away.

As Isaac parked the car, we discussed our options. Many birders I know would have called it a solid sighting, worthy of adding it to their life list. The thought of bears, bull moose in rut, and other hazards of swampy boreal forest may have turned many birders away from leaving the road and plunging deep into the forest, but not us. We split up to cover more ground and ventured into the muskeg—Alaska's equivalent of a bog. Despite our best efforts to relocate the owl, neither one of us were successful. We did find bunches of ripe blueberries wrinkled from the recent frost, which made for the perfect snack on the hike back to the car.

Shortly into the several-hundred-mile drive back to Anchorage, a Northern Hawk Owl flew right in front of us across the road, gliding up to perch atop a roadside spruce. I savored every second of watching this bird, who was much more accommodating than the first owl. After several minutes it too disappeared into the forest, preoccupied with finding his next meal.

Half an hour later, we were treated to a third bird perched on a power line, hunting actively. I watched this bird for over half an hour, and it flew towards me, clearly not concerned with my presence but remaining vigilant in the hunt. I watched it drop down into the tangled vegetation and emerge with a tundra vole, which it grasped in one foot as it balanced precariously on the top of the tree with the other. It took two bites to devour the vole, and I photographed the entire sequence. I moved further away to get a different angle on the bird and looked away momentarily to set up my shot. When my eyes darted back to the tree-top perch, the bird was gone.

The Northern Hawk Owl was a nemesis no more. More importantly than checking this bird off my list was an opportunity to meet and bird with another Facebook friend in real life, building a connection with the birding community. Most importantly, I was ahead of schedule to depart Anchorage and fly to Houston for my brother's wedding.

Northern Hawk-Owl

Throughout the entire year, there was only one date I couldn't miss—a single day that had nothing to do with birds. Family has always come first for me. Surely there were birds I had missed this year because I prioritized family (Illinois' Black-tailed Gull comes to mind).

In January, when Kevin and his fiancé Paighton asked me to officiate their wedding in October, I happily said yes. Missing rare birds came as an afterthought—one knew thought I could deal with later.

Three flights and 4500 miles from Anchorage, I arrived in Houston without a single wrinkle in my travel plans. Surrounded by family, the atmosphere of boundless joy and love made helping with wedding preparations a breeze.

For the first time in over a year I got my hair cut. The stylist at the men's grooming salon commented on the "carefree" and "windblown" look, which I definitely had going. As flattering as that was, I knew a change of style was needed for this special occasion. It was certainly worth it when I saw how happy it made those around me—particularly the bride!

With the exchange of vows only 72 hours away, the inevitable happened—a rare Variegated Flycatcher was spotted on South Padre Island, less than half a day's drive from Houston. Earlier, I figured that I needed at least five "mystery" birds —coded birds that I couldn't forecast would show up, in order to reach my goal of 750 species. This would be one of those birds—I had to chase it.

I silently did the math. I could make it to South Padre in under six hours, (*five and a half if I drove fast...*) and if the bird stayed put, I could drive down, see the bird, and return to Houston before dinner time the next next.

Surely, if I waited, the bird might be gone. That's the risk of waiting too long to chase any rare bird. Looking at a satellite image of the location, I predicted the bird wouldn't stick around long.

I spent a few hours in a conflicted internal dialogue. *You might not see this bird ever again in Texas. Family first! It's just a bird. Do you really want to leave your family?*

Of course, I didn't want to leave my family just to see a bird. I'd seen hundreds and hundreds of birds already, and if it meant missing this one, I wasn't going to upset the people that meant the most to me. Only *after* the wedding, *if* the bird stuck around *then* I would chase it. I casually mentioned the rare bird offhand, so it would come as less of a surprise if the day after the wedding I chased it. I could wait.

The wedding day went perfectly. The moment Kevin and Paighton began their vows, a mockingbird broke into song from the foliage adorning the trellis above our heads. I smiled. I savored each moment of the reception and family time afterward, leading into the after party to hang out with their friends on a ranch outside the city. Standing around the blazing bonfire, surrounded by my brother and new sister-in-law and their friends, my mind drifted south to the Lower Rio Grande Valley. Staring into the fire, I hatched a plan.

Four hours later, I sleepily swiped my iPhone, silencing the 2:15 am alarm. After barely any sleep, I was wide awake, caffeinated by the excitement that chasing a rare bird brings. My dad graciously woke up and drove me to a sketchy Greyhound station in downtown Houston, where I boarded a bus bound for the southernmost city in Texas.

Sleep largely evaded me, during the multi-hour bus ride, prolonged by the four or five stops made along the way. I wasn't going to complain; the one-way ticket cost about $30 which at this point in the year, was a small price to pay for a new bird over 700. Out the window, the sun rose over the fields and oil refineries to the east.

Minutes after arriving in Brownsville, Hilary, a college tennis teammate and fellow Bio major—picked me up. She lived in Brownsville and was working on her master's degree, examining genetic variation haplotypes of sea turtles along the southern coast of Texas.

We stopped to pick up a few of her friends and the group of us headed to the Bird Center on South Padre Island. My stomach churned in nervous anticipation as we got closer.

Arriving at our destination, I spotted a group of birders standing together in the corner of the parking lot, with binoculars pointed the same direction. Relief washed over me, as I realized I would get the bird. Immediately my thought shifted to how I could make this most enjoyable for others, who may not want to photograph and watch this rare bird for the next hour.

The flycatcher sat on a bare limb, making several short flights out from his perch, grabbing an invisible insect in the air and returning to his perch. These short "sallies" are characteristic of flycatchers. I spoke with several other birders, doing a few interviews before joining my crew for a stroll through the boardwalks of the nature center.

We were surprised when we went to pay admission, to learn that another birder had paid all of our entrance fees- in an act of kindness that left me grateful and eager to pay it forward the next chance that came along.

The four of us walked along the boardwalk, spotting different species of wading birds that were on the provided scavenger hunt sheet. Despite having seen hundreds of birds prior to this one, something about that bird and this particular day was really special. All of the pieces came together, for a fun day birding with friends old and new. I took one last look at the flycatcher on our way out, thanking him for sticking around.

Later that day was the last sighting of the Variegated Flycatcher, who was absent from his perch the next morning. I had come at the perfect time, or maybe it had waited for me. It's funny how things work out sometimes.

My heart was full; family, friends, and good birds had lifted my spirits. Figuratively speaking—I was on top of the world. To actually reach the top of the world, I needed to fly to Barrow Alaska, which is exactly where I went next.

22

ON TOP OF THE WORLD

THERE IS A PLACE WHERE LAND, sea, and sky meet. This ephemeral place is framed by wide horizons showcasing expansive views of tundra and sky. Shifting light, melting fog, and a steady breeze blowing from the icy water combined into a cocktail of incredible beauty that could only be found in the Arctic. This place is called Utqiagvik. Formally called Barrow, residents of this village voted to rename Alaska's northernmost town in October 2016. Following a narrow vote, the city reclaimed the traditional name—Utqiagvik emphasizing the cultural identity of the people. I stood speechless, on the northwestern edge of the continent looking over the horizon. With a deep breath I filled my lungs with the brisk air, soaking in the polar views I've dreamed of seeing since I was a child. Standing on the land's edge and looking out at the horizon, I surveyed the Beaufort Sea from beneath an arch of bowhead whale jawbones on the outskirts of town. Open water stretched as far as I could see, and despite my watchful gaze, no white gulls flew by.

All around, I could see evidence of a changing world. The sea ice had not come, despite being well into the first week in October. The creatures that have evolved to thrive in this frozen world have appeared on time. Numerous polar bears lingered on the outskirts of town, having swum across the Beaufort Sea in search of food. Only days ago near where I stood, a single female walrus washed up on the beach, her ivory tusks chipped from hauling herself out of the ocean onto the ice over and over again. She was sick, weakened by causes unknown and perished before my arrival. This changing world shows no mercy to nature.

My journey here was less perilous, but remarkable in its own way. I'd made a nearly 4,000-mile odyssey from the southernmost city in the continental U.S. to the northernmost city in the U.S - in just four days. I made this trip with my friend Zoie, whose job as a flight attendant helped me get to Alaska free of charge. In exchange, I provided the logistical planning of our trip—figuring out where to stay, how to get around, and where we could go to see polar bears and perhaps the mysterious Ross's Gull.

I stepped into the one-room airport terminal, scanning the unfamiliar faces for a friend I only knew from Facebook photos. She met my gaze with sparkling eyes and a beautiful smile that flashed for a moment like the northern lights. This was my first time meeting Leanna in person, having connected through Facebook by a mutual friend. We talked while waiting for the bags to be brought over, and within minutes she felt like a friend. Leanna welcomed us to her village with open arms and excitedly led us outside with a quiet grace and poise of a dancer. Her graciousness, local knowledge, and enthusiasm made the trip a great success!

We headed out for an afternoon drive, to explore the coastline and see what we could find. Scanning the horizon I spotted what appeared to be a large white pile of snow, but it seemed out of place on the barren tundra. I raised my binoculars for a closer look and as I studied this shape it dawned on me that this was a polar bear! Unlike the few images of starving polar bears that circulated on social media, this bear was healthy. It casually lay on the frozen shoreline, sprawled out in a similar way to a dog on the front porch. I took many photos, not knowing this wouldn't be the only bear I would see on this trip.

Offshore, bowhead whales make their annual passage past these beaches, following their fall migration routes from the Beaufort Sea calving grounds to feeding grounds in the Chukchi and northern Bering Sea. Each year several whales are intercepted by Inupiat hunters, who for generations have relied on the whale for survival. These people rely on the whale to supply their nutritional needs over the long winter months when the sun sets for a continuous 65 days and temperatures plummet well below zero.

To the west, just outside of town, we stood atop a bluff overlooking the sea below. Looking down the coastline, it was clear that the rising sea levels have taken giant bites out of the shoreline, eroding away soil that was once permanently frozen. Fragmented pieces of tundra, complete with a thin layer of grasses and flowers on top, slumped and slid in pieces onto the beach below.

Change has been a constant in the Arctic. In 2016, for the first time ever, a cruise ship crossed the Northwest Passage following the same route as the ill-fated Franklin Expedition did 121 years prior. In an attempt to sail from Europe to Asia across the Arctic, the ships were trapped, frozen in sea ice. Indisputable research shows that Arctic temperatures are rising ten times faster than any other time in recorded history. This is undoubtedly accelerated by human activity.

Over the last 40 years, the Arctic has lost sea ice to equal the size of Mexico. As ice melts, exposing dark land surface, more sunlight is absorbed than reflected, causing the surface to warm twice as fast as the global average. As the ice melts, newly-exposed resources which before were inaccessible becomes available, forcing countries bordering the Arctic to decide whether to conserve or exploit these new resources. Now, one of Earth's most hostile ecosystems is one of the most vulnerable—and time will unfold the next chapter of this unpredictable story.

We stayed close to town because earlier in the day several boat crews radioed back to the village with good news: they had just captured a bowhead whale. The fall whaling season is short, regulated by the International Whaling Commission, and there are strict quotas for harvesting whales. This was an important cultural event I didn't want to miss- and was grateful Leanna was willing to share it with me.

From a distance, I could see the large dark outline of the whale—already hauled out of the water laying on the old runway. The animal's body looked awkwardly out of place- a form evolved to weightlessly fly through the water now appeared grossly misshapen by gravity. I imagined it died hours ago, out at sea, before being brought to shore.

In this village, traditional skin boats have been replaced by aluminum boats for the Fall whale hunt. A changing climate has shifted the patterns of the sea ice, which arrives later each fall. Without the ice to channel passing whales closer to shore, the hunters travel further offshore to find whales, often exceeding 50 miles.

The tradition of whaling has adapted to modern regula-tions, yet the spirit of the hunt and gratitude for a successful harvest is still pure and strong. Families cheered and sang as the captain's boat arrived at the old runway. The captain and his crew pulled up, their boat carried by a trailer, cheers applause rang out, not to celebrate the whale's death but the safe return of the boat crews. Much can go wrong out on the Beaufort Sea, and everyone returning safely made this a successful hunt.

At the carcass, men went to work with curved blubber hooks and knives fixed to long handles. The outer layers of blubber were stripped away, and the prime section was handed off to the striker, the man who dealt the fatal blow to the whale. Along with the captain, they received the choice pieces of meat. Everybody helped; I was no exception. I grabbed a rope and helped peel away heavy blocks of blubber, which steamed as they were stripped back, releasing heat energy that was captured by small plants, then passed up the aquatic food chain until they were eaten by the whale. The slumped shape on the runway was no longer a whale, it was food.

Silver-haired women grouped around metallic bowls, working quickly with curved blades to cut fillets of blubber into small strips, which were washed and then boiled. Young girls wearing whaling crew sweatshirts or cheerleading sweatshirts assisted the elders in preparing this batch of meat, which would be eaten within the hour as they worked on the rest of the whale. Everyone worked together with remarkable efficiency, side by side with family members and neighbors. Within the span of a couple of hours, the whale was gone.

Ziplok bags of whale meat now filled freezers across the city and was loaded on planes and spread across Alaska's North Slope, shared with family and friends in need. The inedible pieces that remained on the old runway— jaw bones, the spinal column, and skull were scooped up by a bucket loader and driven beyond the city limits to the point, where it was shared with the polar bears and gulls.

The next morning we took a drive out to the point, hoping the whale carcass had attracted some polar bears and gulls. In particular, I was hoping to spot both Ivory and Ross's Gull—two high-Arctic birds that specialize on feeding on polar bear kills and fish stirred up from wave action on the shore. We saw many polar bears, and thousands of gulls, most of which were Glaucous Gulls.

Within the hour, the sky turned gray and the winter weather arrived. Snow started to swirl down from the sky as if to encourage us to get going. I took one more opportunity to get out of the truck and scan over the ocean.

A distant white gull caught my attention. *Was that it?* I squinted harder through my binoculars as if that would make the mystery bird bigger. Through nearly a quarter mile of blowing snow, a pale long-winged gull flew stiffly into the wind, crossing the point far out over the Beaufort Sea. Ghost-like it melted into the icy fog from which it came, disappearing as quickly as it had materialized. I lowered my binoculars in amazement.

At a loss, I had to accept that I would never know what that bird was. That was ok. It's just part of the mystery and magic of Utqiagvik.

Not even an hour had passed since the sun had slipped behind the mountains, painting the sky a brilliant palette of warm hues over a sea of Saguaros. As I lay on my back on the ground, the cold soaked through my shirt from the foundation of an adobe brick house in the middle of the Sonoran desert.

The brick walls formed a false layer of protection around me—there were no windows or doors, and the night sky was the only roof over my head. Nighttime in the desert was a special time when many animals emerge to live their lives in quiet secrecy.

The soft humming of insects merged together to sound like a desert ocean, rising and falling in fluid waves of different buzzes, rattles, and clicks which all ebbed and flowed together as one noise. The full moon overhead cast a soft glow over the cacti, which appeared fuzzy in the moonlight. The branching arms reached towards the sky as if trying to hug the moon.

I laid there listening to the desert noise as time slowed down. My stomach began to make noise in protest of how little I'd eaten—mostly having snacked on granola bars and water. My upside-down binoculars held my head off the concrete, cradling it and providing a makeshift pillow for this bird-watcher.

Months earlier, Laura had heard Ferruginous Pygmy-Owl right near this spot, and surely if they were calling now I would have heard them too. As I lay on the concrete floor, I nearly fell asleep, enchanted by the song of the Sonoran desert.

Walking back to the parking lot, I heard a curious noise—the squeal or scream of an owl that sounded much larger than the one I was searching for. I made some recordings of the ghostly squeals, that returned to haunt me months later when I discovered the voice memo on my iPhone.

I contemplated sleeping in my car, but I knew that I wouldn't hear anything if I did, and it was too nice of a night to sleep under a roof. I ended up sleeping at a trailhead on the concrete pad behind the pit toilet—which was both very clean and did not smell—and more importantly, it was elevated off the sandy desert floor—which turned at night into a highway for spiders, scorpions, and other creatures.

I spent all of the following day looking for pygmy-owls. I drove, hiked, and listened everywhere. A willing park employee volunteered an exact location of a nest—privileged information that I knew he probably wasn't supposed to disclose. I followed his directions, finding an empty cavity in a cacti and a curious Gilded Flicker pecking at the entrance hole.

Walking back to my car down the sandy wash, I flushed a small owl, that in a flurry of stiff wingbeats, flew low into the desert scrub and disappeared. I saw neither the rufous tail or false eye spots on the head— either field mark I told myself would clinch the ID. It probably was a fledgling pygmy-owl, but I hadn't worked so hard to count probably's.

Part of the fun of birding National Parks was just exploring. In Organ Pipe, I saw a small green patch on the map- a freshwater spring in the middle of the desert. Named Quitobaquito, this oasis contained several types of organisms found nowhere else on earth.

As I walked down a dirt road towards the spring, I found a small turtle in the trail. A beautiful little guy, with yellow stripes and about the size of a walnut. and moved him for fear of him getting run over by border patrol ATVs. I later learned that this was one of about 150 Sonoyta mud turtles, an endangered species found here and in a Mexican sewage lagoon and a couple of other ponds. This truly may have been the rarest organism I saw throughout the entire year.

Leaving Organ Pipe heading north, I drove through the town of Why, Arizona which made me laugh. I asked myself *Why not?* And stopped and bought a cheap popsicle for a dollar —paid for with loose change I excavated from beneath the passenger seat.

I woke up early in the morning and looked for pygmy-owls one last time. No luck. Leaving behind the dry desert of Arizona, I headed back towards California. It was a long haul, but I needed to make it by this evening. After endless miles of driving through nothing, I reached Dateland, Arizona.

When I noticed neat rows of date palms in the desert, my first thought was it might attract migrating birds. I was right, but not as right as I wanted to be—despite a thorough search I couldn't find anything out of the ordinary. I sampled enough dates to be considered a meal and bought a date shake, which was a strong candidate for dessert.

That afternoon I spent some time searching around the town of Weldon for Ruddy Ground-Doves, and drove through Yuma at 6:10 pm, and was parked in Angeles National Forest by midnight. I'd hoped to get better looks at Mountain Quail the next day, and maybe some photos. I selected a parking place at a trailhead in Los Angeles National Forest, not thinking twice about the fact I was parked next to a large dumpster.

I woke up during the night to loud crashing sounds, and knew it could only be bears. They were right outside my car, and by the sounds of it—were having a territorial dispute. There were growls, grunts, and groans, followed by some huffing and snorts. After the scuffle, a big boar walked right past my car, close enough I could hear the labored breath as it panted heavily. I guessed this was the loser of the altercation because the other bear stuck his head out of the opening of the dumpster. I turned the headlights on to see the bear better, and he ducked back into the dumpster. Figuring the bears wouldn't bother me in my car with such an abundant food supply nearby, I curled up and went back to bed.

Bears had never really been a problem for me before. While working in Glacier National Park, I'd run into bears on my surveys—and backed off. I even had to chase a black bear out of my campsite while cooking breakfast. I'd run into bears a few times this year already, in Big Bend National Park, and Madera Canyon, where a double black bear encounter (both adults) had sped up my heart rate when I got between them along the Carrie Nation trail while searching for the Aztec Thrush. (That was the only night I slept on the roof of a rental car) I had seen many bears both close and from a distance, and never felt like there was a huge threat to my safety.

I stood in the pouring rain and tried to come up with a plan on the docks of the Monterey Bay harbor. In a very atypical fashion, Debi Shearwater's final pelagic trip failed to turn up any new year birds. I was happy the boat had at least left the harbor of Monterey Bay, despite the inclement weather. I tried to focus on the positives as I walked up the gangway to come up with a plan.

From the start of the trip, Debi had provided an accurate assessment- she voiced her hesitation that these conditions didn't favor good birding. Given her experience on the ocean, I was skeptical too. Despite her doubts, we got out past the harbor, and tolerated the blowing rain and wind for about 4 hours as we braved the conditions close to shore. Laura, John, and I were all together on the same boat, all hoping that we could add a new year bird to our lists: the Flesh-footed Shearwater. Several Leach's Storm-Petrels blew haphazardly past the boat, at one point nearly colliding with the vessel. One poor birder was so seasick that he lay motionless on the back deck for nearly the entire duration of the boat ride. Other than the storm-petrels, nothing notable was seen, but it was nice to be out on the water again.

Within an hour of docking, plans were covertly being made to head back out. John and Laura were talking with Debi about it, but given the weather and sea conditions, it didn't make sense to head out right away, so we gave Debi some time to figure out if she could get a boat and crew together for the following day. Laura and I spent the afternoon doing a sea watch from Point Pinos, hoping for a shearwater flyby, but the rain continued and we both called it a day earlier than either one of us would have liked.

That night, Olaf called me.

"Do you want to go with me on a boat somewhere?" I've learned that an invitation from Olaf is never straightforward. Earlier in the year he told me he might offer me a seat on a fall pelagic trip, and I'd forgotten about his offer until now. I'd already been invited by Laura and John to go with them the following day on a boat in search of Flesh-footed Shearwaters.

I had to make a decision: should I go with Laura and John on their private pelagic trip to look for Flesh-footed Shearwaters, or follow up on Olaf's cryptic invitation to go with him "on a boat somewhere"? I wasn't sure why this trip was shrouded in secrecy, and upon further questioning, Olaf wouldn't confirm or deny that a Blue-footed Booby was involved. This bird tipped the scales for me. Was it worth the risk? Absolutely.

The following morning the rain had let up and gray skies were replaced with blue. I arrived at the docks and found out that Olaf had chartered the *New Captain Pete* and we were bound for the Farallon Islands. I had just been out to these islands with Debi on a pelagic trip—and we'd missed the Blue-footed Booby—so I jumped at a second chance at this new bird. I figured I'd be just as likely to spot a Flesh-footed Shearwater on our trip as John and Laura were on theirs.

As we approached the Farallon Islands, the jagged rocks rose from the sea, like a row of shark's teeth. The boat made a straight course to Sugarloaf Island, where the Booby had been seen the day before by the team of biologists stationed on Southeast Farallon Island. Hundreds of birds covered the rocks, mostly Common Murres.

With some careful scanning I found the Blue-footed Booby, laying down on a shelf. The incoming swells made describing and getting the others on the bird difficult, as the boat moved every direction. To add to the confusion, a Brown Booby was perched nearby, but soon everyone saw the bright blue feet. We took some pictures, and continued on our way.

In the fall the Farallon Islands are home to several different groups of pinnipeds, including northern fur seals, elephant seals, and California sea lions, which attracts scores of great white sharks each fall. Through my binoculars, I could look up onto the island at the top and see a marine biologist keeping watch for white sharks from an observation tower. They kept an eye on us, and returned my wave from the boat.

We spotted a sea lion floating lifelessly in the water. For several minutes we waited, watching it intently. Our boat captain said that the sharks, after making a kill, will come back and eat it. This crime scene lacked a pool of blood and through my binoculars I couldn't see any bite marks, so we surmised this sea lion died from unknown causes. With a successful chase under our belts, we began the ride back across the channel.

The Blue-footed Booby is a visitor from the Galapagos

I kind of felt felt like a double-agent. No sooner had I stepped off the boat with Olaf and returned to my car, I was on the phone with Laura and John. They both had successfully found a Flesh-footed Shearwater, and were en route to San Diego to head offshore in search of the Least Storm-Petrel. As its name suggests, this bird is smaller than other storm-petrels, and often is harder to find among rafts of hundreds or thousands of slightly larger Black Storm-Petrels.

The following morning I was headed out to sea again with Laura and John, but this time on a much smaller boat, captained by Dave Povey. Today, the sea conditions were calm and Captain Dave leaned into the throttle as we picked up speed and headed out towards the flat horizon.

Looking towards the horizon, I spotted a large shape in the water. Through my binoculars I watched as the shape shifted, flashing silver like a wounded fish. As we approached I soon realized this was no fish, but a lifeless balloon floating on the water's surface—animated by the swell. Dave carefully maneuvered the boat alongside the mylar carcass, and grabbing a metal pole with a hook on the end, stabbed the balloon, bringing it into the boat in one smooth motion. I could tell this wasn't the first time he's done this.

For the duration of the day, we stopped for any trash we could spot. We took turns wielding the hook, rescuing countless marine organisms from an entanglement they never saw coming.

Throughout the morning, we spotted more birds and more balloons. I quickly learned how to handle the hooked pole, and before long I was the designated retriever of floating trash. We deviated from our course for each and every floating object we could find. Half a dozen balloons, several plastic bags, and a floating sheet of packing wrap later, we certainly were doing our part to leave the ocean better than we found it.

We lurched forward as Captain Dave nudged the boat from idle, spinning into a 180 degree turn and returning to our invisible course towards the flat horizon. I thought more about how ocean pollution is affecting birds.

Half a century ago, there was no plastic in the ocean. Today, hundreds of millions of tons are riding the ocean currents, breaking down and emitting chemicals that smell delicious to birds and other marine organisms.

Plastic might be one of the biggest threats to seabirds. Scientists are already finding plastic in the digestive systems of birds, and now there are even photos of Albatross regurgitating food for their young, with plastic mixed in. Plastic get into the ocean in many ways- discarded items, boats dumping trash, but mostly from windblown trash from landfills.

I wondered why seabirds ate plastic. They seemed too intelligent to inadvertently consume it while feeding. This question lingered in my mind, staying with me until later, when I looked up the answer. As plastics break down and becomes coated with algae, it gives off a chemical—*dimethyl sulfide* which scientists found is the same chemical emitted by phytoplankton as they are consumed by predators. Phytoplankton are the main prey of many seabirds—so in a way, plastic smells and tastes like food.

Many sea birds have an incredible sense of smell. Millions of years of evolution has finely-tuned the olfaction of these birds to detect food. This case of mistaken smell causes seabirds to seek out plastic instead. Can seabirds and other marine life adapt fast enough to survive in our changing world? Time will tell.

Dave's voice snapped me back to the present moment. We had crossed the Thirty-Mile Bank, which meant to now be on the lookout for storm-petrels. These birds preferred to be offshore, where the California Current carries copious amounts of plankton, a storm-petrel's favorite food. When they're not feeding, storm-petrels congregate in large "rafts" on the water. Several boats of birders had recently scoured this area, but the rafts of storm-petrels remained elusive. Small groups of two or three storm-petrels zipped across the water's surface far away, but these weren't what we were looking for.

Our target bird, the Least Storm-Petrel, is smallest of them all (hence the name) It is much less common than the larger Black Storm-Petrel, which are more numerous off the Southern California coastline this time of year.

Black and Least Storm-Petrels off the coast of California

John hollered as he spotted a smaller storm-petrel, winging its way swiftly away from us, low over the water. Dave adeptly turned the boat and we gave chase. The bird flew as if it were haphazardly dodging invisible boats on the open ocean. It was extremely difficult to keep binoculars on the bird, now flying parallel to our course, as we caught up to it. Laura and I both switched to our camera, firing off volleys of shots as John studied the bird through his binoculars. I tried to get good looks at it too—it did seem smaller than the other birds we had seen on the water minutes earlier. Flying alone, it was hard to get a good comparison, but we figured we had the bird.

After exchanging high-fives, we idled before turning back towards the San Diego bay. I looked at my photos, studying the pixelated image of the bird we all had just seen well. It was a Black Storm-Petrel—I had no doubt. How do I tell John and Laura that we got it wrong? Birding can be tough, and moments like this, in the heat of doing a Big Year, were much tougher.

I broke the news, pointing out the subtle things we missed moments earlier in the field. This would be a new bird for all of us, and so the extra scrutiny and post-examination of the photos was important. We all reviewed the photos and reluctantly agreed that it wasn't conclusively a Least. I felt better, yet deflated. We'd used a lot of fuel chasing distant storm-petrels, and it was nearing the time to turn around. We could spend a little longer out on the bank, and began heading south. While looking at the horizon, I noticed a dark slick across the water in the distance. Raising my binoculars, I realized that I had spotted a large raft- no, a giant raft of storm-petrels!

Our spirits rose as we neared the flotilla of birds on the water. A conglomerate of shapes morphed into individual birds as we closed in and turned the engine off, as not to disturb the roosting birds. I had vastly underestimated the size of the raft, and now that we were closer we realized that in amongst the Black Storm-Petrels were many Least Storm-Petrels! Their smaller size and thinner wings were obvious, and it was perfect to see them side-by-side with their larger relatives. Our hard work had paid off, and luck certainly was on our side. There were also several storm-petrels with white rumps, two of which we saw well and one that disappeared among the birds—left unidentified.

After high-fives were exchanged, Dave brought out some celebratory chocolate-chip cookies. I liked experiencing the different traditions people used to celebrate life birds. Satisfied after spending some time observing the rafts of birds, we slowly backed away and returned to the bay, stopping only for balloons and trash. After returning to the dock we thanked Dave and snapped a few photos together, and returned to the hotel.

Back at the hotel, I went to John's room to check in on him. He was sitting at the desk, with his laptop in front of him. The screen cast a bright white light on his face, reflecting in the glasses which he only wore when he meant business.I peeked over his shoulder. John was looking at eBird maps of eastern Canada.

"Mate, how do ya reckon I'll get Great Skua if the ferries are all shut down?" John asked. I could sense the desperation in his voice.

"We could always charter a boat out of Hatteras at the end of the year and go for it like Neil did", I replied. I didn't want to do what Neil did because it had already been done. I wanted to do something that hadn't been done. I paused and thought more carefully, and considered the options.

"We could always just take a cruise ship. I'll bet we could find a Great Skua on a boat to Newfoundland."

"A cruise ship?" John clearly wasn't on the same page as me with this idea. I explained to him that we could probably just ride a cruise ship from New York up to Canada—going through Great Skua waters nearly the whole way. I was eager to explore offshore on an East Coast cruise, and see what birds could be found. As far as I knew, this was uncharted territory for Big Year birders. We would be pioneers, and if we were successful, maybe other birders could do the same in the future. A quick Google search showed a outgoing cruise from New York City to Newfoundland. I knew that things were about to get real exciting.

A Yellow-nosed Albatross had recently been seen in Massachusetts waters, and I still needed Great Skua and Dovekie. With big risks come big rewards—and John didn't need more convincing. I was clearly hooked on the high of big year birding, caught up in the 'dream and do' mentality. I figured we could tag on the Yellow-legged Gull while we were at it, saving us both a trip to Newfoundland later. With a few clicks, I booked a multi-day cruise from New York City to St. John, Newfoundland. This was happening, whether we were ready or not.

<hr>

We were late. I'd taken the lead on travel arrangements, and pushed the logistics down to the wire. John and I had left San Diego, flown all night to New York City, were picked up by my friends and driven to the cruise ship terminal via downtown New York City.

It took me a few minutes after being dropped off at the cruise ship terminal to realize our boat wasn't there. Where was it? I checked and rechecked all the screens. No boat. How did I screw up? I checked the reservations on my phone battery, which was dangerously low. Date? Today. Time? The boat left within the hour. Port? New York City. I googled 'Cruise Ship Port' and realized there are multiple ports, Brooklyn, Red Hook, and Manhattan. Then it dawned on me: we were at the wrong one.

In a flurry of activity, we wove in and out of traffic at a pace only a New York taxi driver could pull off. In a matter of luck we made it to the correct terminal and got on the boat.

Riding outside on the bow, we passed the Statue of Liberty

as we left the harbor. Darkness fell, and we returned to our cabin. I realized that evening looking at the map, that St. John (our destination) and St. John's (the location with the Yellow-legged Gulls) were two different cities in two different provinces. (Nova Scotia vs. Newfoundland) I realized my mistake and sheepishly told John. I think he was too tired to care. I was humiliated, and humbled. I chalked it up as a good geography lesson, and a mistake I wouldn't make again. We still had a chance at seeing a skua. After a brief meal, we returned to our cramped quarters of our interior stateroom, eager to get a good night's rest.

I opened my eyes, confused about where I was. It took me a few moments to remember I was at sea on a cruise ship. Putting on my clothes, I bundled up and went outside for a lap around the decks, looking for birds that had collided with the ship (a trick I learned from Andy earlier in the year) Returning later with John and with my spotting scope to find some birds, I began scoping from the promenade deck on the starboard front side, looking into a beautiful sunrise on the horizon.

A brown blur caught my eye—a Swamp Sparrow—quickly flew past me and landed somewhere on the ship. In the next hour, I had tallied a handful of migrant birds which landed on the boat, including a Downy Woodpecker. Later in the morning I walked around the boat to see how many species I could find. I discovered a Ruby-crowned Kinglet trying to hide in a fake bush, a couple of juncos, a Chipping Sparrow, and a Merlin who rode the ship. Birding on a cruise ship was turning out to be more fun than I thought!

As we steamed further offshore, the wind picked up to 40 knots, and a nervous announcement came over the speaker, changing our schedule. Due to the high winds, we would go to Halifax first. The course was altered and the boat sped up. This was concerning because we didn't quite make it to the shelf edge, and our altered course avoided some of the main underwater topography I was hoping we would encounter. Oh well—it was outside my control. Birding in the morning was pretty slow, with Cory's and Great Shearwaters making up the majority of seabirds we were seeing.

Due to the ship's altered course, we never got over the anticipated deep water and submarine canyons which yielded the best birding. Still, we watched. The afternoon passed slowly with no birds, and in the final hours we began to see gannets, some gulls, and finally large numbers of shearwaters. Birds seemed to be everywhere, as we barreled through a food-filled nutrient-rich upwelling of cold water. *With this many birds feeding, a Skua certainly shouldn't be far...*

Soon, John spotted a bird he thought was a Great Skua, and took a few pictures to look at before excitedly attempting to describe the the "close" bird. I scrambled to find what he was seeing, assuming the bird in question was close, among the rafts of shearwaters on the water, and began looking for a larger dark bird among them. When John realized I wasn't looking out past the shearwaters, watching the closer of two birds flying, it was too late. Looking at his pictures, it was clear I missed not one, but two Great Skua. Later, seabird guru Brian Patterson confirmed that John's photos were indeed both Great Skuas.

Our miscommunication had cost me a bird, which felt pretty bad. What if this was the only skuas of the trip? I was worried. At least John saw it, as this bird was much more important to him than it was for me.

The missed skua lingered in my thoughts as we pulled into port in Halifax. Having seen his target, John decided to jump ship. He stayed busy coordinating flights and his next chase: a Yellow-legged Gull in Newfoundland. I didn't have the luxury (or the funds) to continue with him from the cruise ship. That left me stuck on a boat, Skua-less.

On the return voyage, I birded hard. This meant eating little, moving little, and standing dawn to dusk looking out over the water, scanning for birds, with few interruptions.

Above the watery horizon, I noticed three dots in sky, flying towards the boat. As they grew closer, I could tell by the bouncy flight that they were Purple finches. All three finches flew directly towards the side of the ship, and I thought maybe they were going to land on the boat. I watched all three birds swoop in towards the boat, then fly head-on into the plated glass on the deck above where I stood. Two birds bounced off, fluttering down out of sight. I grabbed my scope and ran upstairs, dismayed to find the still-warm body, belly up, on the deck. The others sat stunned under a lawn chair nearby. I was heartbroken.

I realized firsthand that a cruise ship has an ironic role in bird safety. On the open ocean, a cruise ship can be a place of refuge for an exhausted bird, providing a place to land and rest. Also lethal, a cruise ship is virtually a floating skyscraper. Filled with bright lights it is disorienting and attracts migrating birds and seabirds. Sucking them in, it is a death trap. From a distance, astroturf-covered decks look like green lawns, and potted plastic plants appear real.

Confused juncos hopped around on the pool deck, picking at pizza crust crumbs. A Golden-crowned Kinglet clung to the bulbs of a the outdoor movie screen. Warblers huddled in the plastic bushes around the hot tubs on the pool deck. The ship's Merlin spent hours sitting on a wire, keeping a careful eye out for birds approaching the ship. I watched it hunt all day, targeting multiple Blackpoll warblers with a 100% success rate.

I found dozens of dead birds on the boat. Exhausted from their journey over the sea, they used the last of their energy supply to reach the ship, then collapsed. Some birds flew into plate glass railings, plummeting to the sea below. Researchers are barely beginning to understand the numbers of birds that perish. It's extremely difficult to get an accurate count, because stunned birds bounce off the windows and fall into the sea and drown. Birds that land on the ship and survive the impact often recover and continue on their journey.

Many dead birds are discovered and thrown overboard by cleaning staff early in the morning before the passengers wake up. I interviewed some of these workers, who admitted to this, and confirmed picking up injured birds and keeping them in cardboard boxes indoors until they had recovered enough to be released.

Half way back to New York City, the horizon was completely devoid of any birds whatsoever. I wondered about the Purple Finches—what was their story?

I imagined that somewhere in Canada, a young girl pressed her forehead against the glass of her living room window, staring out into her backyard at the bird feeder. Perhaps twelve years old, she had just begun to take an interest in birds. Noticing some birds she'd never seen before, she called to her mom in the next room.

"Mommy, what are those? That one looks like it's been dipped in purple paint!"

"Those are Purple Finches" her mom pointed out. "A male and three juveniles. Do you see how streaky they are?" As if on cue the birds flushed from the feeder. Perhaps they caught a glimpse of a Cooper's Hawk. The male would stay around the yard, which provided a steady supply of black oil sunflower seeds. The juveniles however, continued their wanderings, in search of food. The trio of Purple Finches winged southwards, all fueled up before crossing the open water. This was a family group composed of juveniles, all from the same area in Canada's boreal forest, nearly 60 feet high on the limb of a spruce. When cone and birch seeds are in short supply, Purple Finches migrate in search of food. The three birds disappeared over the open ocean, leaving sight of land and driven by an instinct to fly south, inherently knowing where to go.

My wind-burned cheeks and cold hands were proof that standing outside in the wind for nearly 10 hours each day wasn't easy, but the migrant passerines and Atlantic seabirds made it enjoyable. Throughout each of the days, I had a normal diversity of seabirds stretched throughout the day: gulls, terns, some waterfowl, shearwaters, jaegers, and gannets. The following day was the same routine: Walk the decks, eat a little breakfast, and then from 8 am to sunset, stare at the ocean.

I watched a flock of shearwaters scatter in front of the boat, which seemed to split the giant group of birds into two. Among the shearwaters were several large dark skuas, which flew with a stiff wing beat and plowed through the shearwaters, scattering them. Two were dark, nearly black- South Polar Skuas for sure. The third bird was different, with pale golden mottling on the head and back. This was a Great Skua! My persistence had paid off.

On this trip, I pushed the physical limits of what I thought was possible. The discipline developed from months of sitting for endless hours in the sitting position, driving for up to fifteen hours a day had directly translated into birding alone on a cruise ship. I never was bored, left to confront my thoughts and observe the watery expanses passing me by for hours on end. The birding was about what I expected it to be like, but I wasn't prepared for the emotional impact of seeing the destructive nature of the cruise ship. The time alone with my thoughts had provided contemplation, and time to think and plan ahead of my next move.

I returned to New York City, and once I reached free wifi, booked and boarded a plane for Newfoundland to meet Laura. Since I was doing a Big Year, I realized that if I wanted to see this bird and maybe a Dovekie, this was my chance. I would have spent money returning to the East Coast later in the year to look for Dovekie regardless, so I figured if I was going to spend money I might as well go for two birds at once.

After a connecting flight in Montreal, I was on my way to Newfoundland. Although the plane ticket was expensive, I justified the ticket, thinking of all the money I'd saved flying standby in the previous months. *This was just what a normal plane ticket costs,* I told myself. I wondered how the other Big Year birders did this for just one bird.

Fortunately, Laura and I found the Yellow-legged Gull on our own, mixed in with hundreds of other gulls near Quidi Vidi lake, roosting on some baseball fields. There are multiple gull species with yellow legs, but only one Yellow-legged Gull, a species that breeds in southern Europe and the Azores and rarely strays to eastern North America. In recent years, there have been annual sightings of this species in Newfoundland. Although Laura had already seen Dovekie, we drove out to Cape Spear—the furthest East point in North America to search of the small seabird. Together, we realized that our journey this year had taken us to Attu (furthest west) Key West (furthest south) and Utquiagvik (furthest north in U.S.) As we scanned the choppy water for an early Dovekie, we reflected on the amazing places we had been this year, both together and separately. Spotting seabirds wasn't in the cards for that day, but it was clear that winter was coming.

Winter in Alaska is cold, dark, and snowy. The wind greeted

me as I stepped out into the cold early-morning darkness from the small airport terminal in Kotzebue, it was windy. I pulled the hood of my parka up over my face, the long guard hairs of the wolf fur ruff tickled my own hairy beard. I'd purchased the vintage parka on Craigslist the day before in Anchorage, in a hail-mary effort to have everything needed for this spontaneous Arctic adventure.

The plan had come together rather last-minute in typical big year fashion. In a heroic effort, John Weigel had set a plan in motion to charter a small plane from Kotzebue, in an attempt to relocate the two Gray-headed Chickadees reported in eBird nearly two weeks prior by a winter camper, at 'Salmon Carcass Lake'. A late-season salmon run had deposited spawned-out fish carcasses on the lakeshore right before a big freeze, and the chickadees had taken advantage of the protein and calorie-rich food source. This was a shot in the dark, as the report was sketchy at best—but the observer was confident in their ID. I was skeptical, but upon being asked to go, I realized the magnitude of this opportunity, and my skepticism took a back seat to excitement.

The Gray-headed Chickadee might be one of the rarest breeding birds in North America. Believed to have crossed the Bering Land bridge during the last ice age, this species persists along riparian boreal forests, virtually as remote as one can get. To my knowledge, in prior years only a single Big Year birder has seen this species during their Big Year.

The wind blew through downtown Kotzebue, finding holes and cracks in the metal buildings and signs, producing an eerie chorus of flute-like whistles and shrieks. From the airport, the short walk down the road felt much longer, but it was a relief to step inside the warm office of the air taxi service who would be carrying us into the vast wilderness. I waited there for everyone to arrive. Before long, Laura, John Weigel, and Jay Lehman had all arrived and we made the necessary preparations to embark on a day trip further into the Arctic. The excitement was palpable as we stood ready, waiting for the pilot to finish loading the plane with food and gear for the day.

As the single-engine Cessna roared to life, I looked behind me at John, Jay, and Laura in the back. I flashed a wide grin, and then turned forward again to look out the window for take-off. Instead of heading straight down the runway, we veered left and took off at a surprising angle. In the early morning light, I could see the small town of Kotzebue below, as the plane banked left in a sweeping climbing turn.

Flying at a steady clip of 116 knots barely 500 feet over the frozen tundra, the following hour passed in silence as each of us wandered lost in our own thoughts. Occasionally the pilot would point to something down below us- a red fox standing in the middle of a frozen lake, or a set of wolf tracks meandering over a hill. I gazed out the window, mesmerized by the terrain.

Meandering rivers sliced deep gashes across the tundra, arcing and curling snake-like back upon themselves, almost as if they had reversed direction and were flowing back uphill. I imagined the landscape below in the short Arctic summer, when the hundreds of ponds below would be home to nesting waterfowl and shorebirds.

The steady whine of the engine changed tones, and suddenly the plane made a sharp banking turn. The ground was much closer now, and I looked down out of my window and realized that we were doing a flyby of our landing strip, which wasn't a strip at all but a relatively flat-looking gravel bar in the middle of a wide river surrounded by stunted Spruce trees.

On the next pass, the pilot dropped the plane onto the gravel, knocking down short saplings and narrowly avoiding thicker patches of willows, keeping the prop and wings clear.

Once the engine shut off, the pilot explained we would shuttle to the lake one by one in a smaller plane, since the frozen lake wouldn't hold the weight of all of us loaded into the Cessna. We disembarked onto the gravel bar, unloading our gear onto the rounded, frozen stones covered in a thin layer of fresh frost.

The pilot fired up the engine and took off, leaving the four of us standing on a gravel bar in the middle of the Arctic on our own. Minutes later, we heard the higher-pitched whine of the Piper Cub's smaller engine.

This plane was our shuttle back and forth to the frozen lake. Equipped with inflatable wide rubber tires, this was a true bush plane. It had a maximum capacity of one pilot and one passenger, who sat directly behind the pilot, nearly straddling him.

We took turns shuttling from this gravel bar to the frozen lake which served as the base camp for Operation Chickadee. Each time the plane took off with another birder, there was one fewer left on the sprawling gravel bar. I wandered over to the edge of the river, looking and listening for birds, until the silence was broken and the plane returned.

Soon, it was my turn to climb into the cozy cockpit. Examining the thin walls and frame of the aircraft from the inside, I realized just how lightweight and small the plane really was. The pilot gave me the thumbs up after I had buckled up, and with a loud roar, the plane spun 180 degrees and we were rolling down the gravel bar.

I watched the spruce trees across the river grow bigger as the plane lifted off the old riverbed, and flew just above the treetops. Several minutes later the plane dropped onto the frozen lake, crabbing sideways and touching down, skipping like a flat rock across the water. The inflatable wheels didn't spin at first upon contact with the ice as the plane glided to a graceful stop.

Our pile of gear sat at the edge of the lake, and by the size of the pile one would guess we would be here for a week instead of a couple of hours. A heap of duffel bags and backpacks in addition to a stove box, extra food, warm layers, tents, and gun cases.

As we waited for the Piper Cub to shuttle all four birders to the frozen lake, we wandered around, staying close to the others. In the snow, fresh bear tracks meandered across the frozen lake, and none of us was eager to venture too far alone.

The piercing cold sucked the life from the camera batteries, rendering the devices nearly useless. Our batteries became the first casualties of the trip. My phone battery had dropped dangerously low just from the cold, and I turned my camera on to find that only a 25% charge remained from the full charge I gave it the night before. Thinking back to March, and photographing sage-grouse in the cold, I took both batteries and held them in my hands, inside of my gloves. I tucked my phone down inside my shirt, in between base layers to keep the battery safe from the cold.

I began looking around and taking in the wonderland we had been dropped into. Within 10 minutes of landing I started scanning the trees. Several White-winged Crossbills and some redpolls vocalized from deep into the forest. A fluttering in a tree at the edge of the lake caught my attention, and I struggled to lift my binoculars with a parka and gloves on. I found the small bird in my binoculars.

"Chickadee!" I shouted. It perched in front of a spruce trunk for a brief moment, before hopping up and working its way across some branches, dodging in and out of sight. Laura and our guide were at my side immediately, and Dave got on the bird as it flew.

"I think that's it" I said excitedly. I didn't want to jump the gun on the ID as most people do when seeing this bird for the first time, so I described the bird as best as I could in the moment. "It looks like a Black-capped... but not quite" were the next words out of my mouth, as I described the features of this bird. For certain, it was not a Boreal Chickadee.

The bird quickly moved from trunk to the dense branches, and dropped from the spruce into a willowy thicket out of view. I was excited. I thought this bird was a Gray-headed Chickadee. Others didn't really get a good look through binoculars like I did. I wanted to run after it and try to find it, but the plane just landed so we didn't go anywhere.

I had to try to restrain myself because I wasn't the guide and didn't want to overstep my bounds and go running into the forest chasing this bird before everyone got there. We were still waiting on John, who had just been shuttled to the lake from our first drop-off point. John got out of the plane, and I told him the news. The guide called us together, ending my chickadee chase.

We listened to a short safety briefing focused on the dangers of exposure/hypothermia, and the precautions of winter travel on ice and snowy bear trails. We all got cans of bear spray, and our guide carried a loaded shotgun. I was literally standing in the tracks of grizzlies in the snow as I strapped on the can of bear spray onto my packs waist belt, within easy reach.

We went off in the general direction the chickadee was last seen- they guide played a call but had no response. My general aversion to playback went unvoiced, as I wanted everyone else to see the same bird I had just seen.

My hope and optimism wasn't mirrored by the guide, who suggested we continue to follow the plan and hike to to the lake where the chickadees had been seen last week. Inside I was devastated. *Why weren't we staying and chasing this bird?* I had a chickadee right *HERE* and we were taking time walking almost a mile in a different direction where there *MIGHT* be chickadees? I didn't get it.

I trudged through the snow behind the others, keeping my feelings bottled up. *Would we see more later at the lake and have it for sure, making my sighting not matter?* I was about 90% sure of the ID at this point. Two seconds longer would have been enough time for me to think clearly as I looked at the bird. I should have taken a photo, but my batteries were still inside my gloves were on and the bird disappeared before I could raise my camera. *It all happened so fast...*

We hiked to the lake, nearly a mile along bear trails. I stepped in deep holes in the snow made by grizzly bears, likely digging up voles from their burrows. My size 12 boot tracks matched the length of many of the tracks, which were frozen in the snow as permanent reminders for me to watch my back as I brought up the end of the line of intrepid chickadeers.

We hiked over a mile and a half to the lake, following meandering bear trails through the thick brush. The true size of a sow grizzly became apparent the moment I stepped foot in her frozen tracks in the snow. Leading the way was our pilot, who carried a short-barreled shotgun for self-defense in case we surprised any lingering grizzlies. Wolf tracks also crossed the trail, disappearing into the wall of dense trees and underbrush. On the side of the trail, I found a caribou antler that had been shed the previous spring.

The remainder of the daylight hours were spent chasing chickadees around the lake. The report of the Gray-headed Chickadees had come from the tributary to this lake, and the pieces of salmon carcasses were scattered about.

This was where the chickadee report we were chasing originated from. It looked believable. The lakeshore was buzzing with White-winged Crossbills, and all chickadees I saw were distinctly Boreals. I didn't see all the birds the others saw, and the flocks seemed to stay just ahead of us. After a good look at the first Boreal Chickadee, I explained to the group how different it was from the bird I saw earlier. As we trudged through the thick spruces, over piles of bear feces and salmon heads with eyeballs picked clean.

I replayed my sighting over and over again in my head. I wondered to myself *Could it have been a Black-capped Chickadee?* It was possible, and I knew I'd have to contact some experts on range maps and chickadee distribution. Our guide told me that Black-capped Chickadees didn't occur this far north of Kotzebue, and so that only left one option... I wanted a second and third opinion to be sure. I wouldn't make a definitive sighting until I could rule-out the remote possibility it could have been a Black-capped.

The possibility of vagrancy couldn't be overlooked, however I knew if it was indeed a Black-capped I would have seen the entire head pattern clearly. I thought a black cap would be distinctive against the trunk of the tree, but I didn't see a clear black cap. I also didn't clearly see a gray cap—a field mark that for me, would clinch the ID.

The bird I had seen occupied my thoughts as we kept searching. The daylight waned quicker than we all wanted it to. For that reason I wasn't the only one who wished to be here in the Alaskan summer, partly because of the extreme cold and lack of birds we experienced.

However, I'll take quality over quantity, and I had a poor-quality sighting of a potential high-quality bird... I think the consolation prize for all of us was being here. We made a trip that no other birder had made in winter—crossing frozen waters and boreal forest. The light, the views, and the adventure all packed into one day made this journey epic— regardless of the outcome.

We finished our excursion in reverse order as we started—

shuttling one by one from the lake to the gravel bar, assembling and boarding the Cessna, and flying back to Kotzebue. On the flight back we hugged the tundra as our experienced bush pilot banked the plane giving us topside views of musk ox and caribou herds from under 100 feet. Chickadee or not, the trip was a success! We all had stayed warm, surviving a hostile environment with bears, ice, and the joyous silence of solitude.

During the minutes I stood on a small gravel bar, watching the bush plane fly away carrying the other birders to the next recon point, I felt like the only person in the world—a world where the laws of nature decided who lived and who didn't, the rules which seem so obsolete when you are sitting at home in front of the computer screen, with a roof over your head, heat pouring out of the air vents, and a fridge stocked full of food. I'd been in the wilderness before, but until this day, I had never been *here*. And *here* was where the Gray-headed Chickadee lived.

One of the best parts about all of the travel across Alaska was the high quality of service and rewards offered by Alaska Airlines. Over the course of the year, I had put nearly all of my expenses on my Alaska Airlines signature Visa card. I earned air miles for the gas and groceries I had been buying all year.

The flight from Kotzebue to Nome to Anchorage passed quickly, but not without incident. Just as soon as we took off from Anchorage my ears just would not pop. For the first time in a long time I felt absolutely miserable. It seemed like someone was inflating a balloon inside my head. The increasing pressure that was building up in my head grew to a throbbing so intense that I could hardly think. Searing pain shot to the corners of my eyes from deep inside my head, and no matter what I did to clear it, nothing worked. Every position I tried I could not get comfortable.

Laura was sitting a few rows ahead of me, and wished I was sitting near her, knowing that she would take care of me. I tried quieting my thought, staying focused on the good present in my experience, and shutting out the pain. It worked; I fell asleep somewhere over Canada and somehow managed to get enough sleep that I could drive the rental car when we got to Chicago.

After landing in Chicago Laura immediately rented a car, and we both headed North to Michigan's Upper Peninsula where a confiding Fork-tailed Flycatcher had been seen along the shore of Lake Michigan.

Following what we remembered from the directions posted in the Facebook group, we drove past the spot at first, because the "green barns" were actually storage sheds. No bird was seen on the first drive-by.

After turning around and finding the right spot, I began scanning the bushes along the lakeshore. South of where I was standing the bird was perched up just above the tangle of brush along the lakeshore. I called to Laura who hadn't finished getting her coat on, and waved at her to come over across the road. I've got it!

We admired the dark cap and long curved tail plumes, snapping shots until the bird left his colorful perch and flew low along the lakeshore out of sight going north. We shared congrats and talked about how cool the bird was. Typically this species is seen in Florida, and in most cases disappears after the initial day its found. A record in Michigan was amazing!

I spotted a car pulled over down the road—obviously a birder. We flagged him down and told him we had the bird. In disbelief, he rushed out of his car. He'd been looking for hours and hadn't seen it and was just about ready to leave for the day and go back home.

More birders arrived and quickly the word spread that the bird was present. However, it wasn't visible from the road. I re-found the bird through the bushes and helped be sure everyone got good looks.

After everyone saw the bird, we lingered and visited for a while telling stories and meeting one another. Several kind birders offered help and were eager to tell us many places we could go to find what we had left to see.

We directed our efforts towards a recent Ross' Goose report, which Laura still needed to see for the year. I was just excited to see this goose as she was when we finally found the bird in a parking lot.

I was enjoying spending time with Laura again, and knew that soon we would go our separate ways again, unsure about where and when our paths would cross next.

The Fork-tailed Flycatcher is a great bird anywhere in North America

23

RAILS AND RICE

THE MONTH of November began in the worst way possible. I returned home to Seattle, where my Subaru had been parked for the last month. As I opened the driver's side door, the wet Pacific Northwest air rushed out of the car, carrying with it musty smell of mold and mildew. Inside, it looked as if a cloud had floated through the window and rained on the black leather interior. A green fuzzy film covered the dashboard, seat-belts, carpet, and seats. Round blue blobs sprouted from the black carpet like some sort of candy-colored fungus.

Frustrated, I began by wiping it off all surfaces with a wet paper towel, careful not to disturb it too much because tiny spores flew everywhere. I held my breath, wishing I had a hazmat suit to wear for this job. It took over an hour of creative thinking to find each patch and clean it all up. I pulled each seatbelt all the way out, exposing dots of mold on the seatbelt, hidden from view but now exposed and expunged. Using Q-Tips I wiped every nook and cranny, before wiping everything down again, then vacuuming to be sure not a spore remained. Perhaps in a drier climate it is worth leaving the windows cracked for ventilation—not in the Pacific Northwest. I sure won't be making that mistake again.

The Black Rail and Yellow Rail are among the hardest birds to spot in North America, and a glimpse good enough to identify either species is highly coveted by birders everywhere. No larger than an outstretched hand, these secretive marsh birds are mostly nocturnal, and when disturbed prefer to run through the grass instead of flush. Both species are more often heard than seen.

I'd looked all over the country specifically for the Black Rail. In February on Little St. Simons Island, I explored the marshes at night, hoping to hear this elusive bird. I wasn't surprised to not hear them, as their population along the Atlantic coast has plummeted nearly 90% in recent decades. Rising sea levels and tidal flooding has nearly swamped this bird out of existence across the entire eastern coastline of North America.

Birding in Florida in February had renewed my hopes of seeing a Black Rail. Olaf and I waded through a sea of grass and swarms of mosquitoes in the Everglades. We lucked out, and heard Black Rails calling nearly underfoot, yet through the thick grasses they were impossible to see—no matter how close to us they came.

Fixed on laying eyes on a Black Rail, I tried again in July—and heard the distinct clicking of Black Rails at midnight in a Kansas field as severe thunderstorms rolled in across the surrounding grassland. I stood along roadside at the edge of a military base along the Arizona-California border later in July, yet the mouse-like bird eluded me.

Although this was frustrating, I was content recording these encounters and knowing that I would have the chance to pursue these secretive birds again in my birding career. Fortunately, that chance came in 2018 in Colorado, when I finally saw a Black Rail for the first time.

A Yellow Rail flushes in a Louisiana rice field

During my Big Year, my luck was slightly better with Yellow Rails. Each November there is a Rails and Rice festival in Louisiana, where birders can gain special access to the rice fields during harvest time, when combines often flush several species of rails and other marsh birds out of the rice as its being harvested. Laura had described this experience and showed me her photos from this trip, and I realized it was something I couldn't miss. Unfortunately, the festival had happened while I was in Alaska, but arrangements were made for a "make up" visit which blew my expectations out of the water.

I stood at the edge of Louisiana's inland sea of waist-high grass, sinking slowly into the saturated soil. Puddles formed over the tops of my ankles which were already buried in the wet muck. I second-guessed my decision to leave the safety of the dirt road, optimistic that if I disturbed the edge habitat of the rice fields that I might just get lucky and flush out a secretive marsh bird. I was early—it was an important day in my Big Year, one I'd driven hundreds of miles out of the way to find a Yellow Rail.

To kill time, I sat on my tailgate—absorbed in my search through eBird records for a location in Kansas I could bird tomorrow to find a Smith's Longspur. I inevitably ended up on Facebook, and before long my scrolling was interrupted by a growing roar of a huge machine. The International Harvester pulled up to the field's edge, and I knew I was in the right spot. This apple-red combine was a state-of-the-art piece of machinery, with a $199,000 price tag. I climbed aboard. As the cab door opened I was greeted by the overwhelming odor of cigarette smoke. Despite my typical aversion to secondhand smoke, surely I could tolerate it for a few hours if it would give me the chance to see a Yellow Rail.

It took only a glance to see that Dustin was a born and bred farmer. He looked about my age, with chestnut-brown hair spilling out from under a ball cap, and a healthy-looking beard. He wore a t-shirt and dark jeans tucked into a pair of well-worn cowboy boots. Dustin's passion for farming was contagious. He'd been driving farm equipment since he was heavy enough to trigger the seat sensor on his dad's tractor. In a flurry of quick movements, he flipped a few switches and maneuvered the joysticks, and we spun a 180 and drove into the field and began harvesting rice.

As the knobbed tires below us sank into the swampy soil, effortlessly pushing us forward, the machine head cut rice plants and spinning wheels knocked it under the behemoth and the machine did its thing. Dustin explained to me how it all worked with intricate detail, making the complex process sound utterly simple. It hadn't even been five minutes and the cigarette smoke was more than I could bear. I opted to sit outside the cab on a special wooden board across the rails outside the cab.

As we began to cut a new row on the edge of the field, mowed into uncut rice, birds began to flush continuously. First a Killdeer, and then various species of small brown sparrows. Next, Sedge Wrens, and finally the bird I'd driven here for. The first Yellow Rail to flush was unmistakable. The white trailing edge on the wings flashed as it took flight straight up and away from the combine, before banking left and dumping back into the tall vegetation. Less than a minute later, another flushed, followed by another. I began a tally on my eBird app. By the day's end I would count exactly 54 Yellow Rails.

Perhaps the cut fields around us had concentrated birds into this particular field, but the concentration of birds here was incredible! Overhead, a mixture of Red-tailed Hawks rode the breeze, with a couple of late migrating juvenile Swainson's hawks mixed in. The raptors were also taking advantage of the harvest, hovering overhead then dropping into the low stubble, on disoriented (or crushed) rodents. I watched a female Merlin climb high into the sky, until I lost her in the sun; moments later she came rocketing past, in hot pursuit of the sparrows flushing out in front of the machinery.

In a flurry of white-edged wings, a Yellow Rail took flight in front of me. I didn't need binoculars, it was so close. I could clearly see the dark eye, and beautiful golden streaks on a dark back. The bird angled away from me, and suddenly—out of nowhere, a Red-tailed Hawk opened its wings, coming out of what surely was an incredible stoop—and plucked the Yellow Rail out of the air. Somehow I managed to photograph the end of this spectacle, which surely was one of the greatest predation events I witnessed during the entire year.

Gangs of Great Egrets strategically stayed ahead of the spinning headers, snatching up anything that moved in front of the combine. I watched the egrets snatch mice, rats, bullfrogs, and even what looked like a small muskrat! Several times the egrets would become so absorbed in catching the fleeing mammal that they almost got turned into rice themselves. Dustin continually honked the high-pitched horn to keep the birds clear of the spinning header.

We stopped for a break midway through the afternoon. Dustin noticed that the feeder belts were getting clogged up, and we both rolled up our sleeves, grabbed some wrenches, and got to work unblocking the belts. I helped him take apart and clean the belts, which only deepened my mechanical knowledge and enhanced my experience for the day.

The rest of the day passed quickly, and before long it was time for me to hop off, as Dustin unloaded the harvested rice into the back of a parked semi. I thanked him for teaching me and helping me get this secretive bird in such an unusual way. I had no idea the sheer numbers of rails we would see- and this was just one rice field! I estimated that there might be hundreds in the surrounding fields.

Energized by such a cool experience, I drove for hours until well-past nightfall, until I reached the tallgrass prairies of western Missouri and Kansas. Between small towns, I easily spotted the bright lights of a Walmart parking lot, and turned in for the night. Somewhere in the middle of making a mental list of what I was grateful for from the day, I fell asleep.

24

CHRISTMAS GEESE

Before I knew it, November had passed and the calendar now flipped over to December. Like Christmas, which seems to arrive earlier year after year, the final month of 2016 had arrived sooner than expected.

I awoke in a hotel bed, rested and refreshed. Acclimated to sleeping in my car, I'll admit spending the night in a hotel in downtown Boston felt amazing. I had a huge queen bed all to myself, and it was free! I had met up with my high school birding mentor Brad to search for the Pink-footed Goose together in December. He used his reward points to book our hotel, and I was incredibly grateful for his generosity.

Brad and I stayed up late, catching up on my year. In high school, I loved asking Brad questions about his birding adventures all over the world. Now, it was him asking me all of the questions—where I saw each different species of bird, when I went to Alaska, and how I persevered through the different challenges of doing a Big Year on a budget. I told him all about the hotel showers, eating ramen, and sleeping in car.

With our combined experience, we thought it best to take

the "Skua" approach to finding the Pink-footed Goose. Many people would be out scanning the farm fields, lakes, and suburban parks for the Pink-footed Goose. This early in the morning, we would let them do the first scan of all the surrounding areas and swoop in and spot the bird after it had been found. While they were looking, we went to the coast to find some birds Brad wanted to see.

The smell of salty air along Massachusetts rocky coast reminded me of Hog Island. Brad and I carefully scanned the dark rocks for Purple Sandpiper, which we found busily feeding along the water line, hastily retreating up the algae-covered rocks right before a big swell broke over the rocks.

I marveled at the colorful Harlequin Ducks bathing in the surf, as the sun glanced off the males' reflective blue-gray feathers. I carefully picked a King Eider from a large flock of Common Eiders. Full of hope, I scanned the ocean for any small seabirds, looking for Dovekie. No luck. Several shearwaters glided by on long wings, tempting us to stay longer— but it was time to move on.

We shifted our birding focus into "Goose Mode" and drove around the areas it had been seen. We walked, hiked, and talked as we searched diligently through flocks of hundreds of Canada Geese, but could not find any odd ones.

Another birder gave us a tip—a Snowy Owl was nearby at Crane Beach. This wasn't far from where we were searching for the goose, and was a welcome distraction from our unproductive wild goose chase. I couldn't help but think of the last-minute Snowy Owl in *The Big Year* film as we hiked along the dune trails. Around the first sand dune, Brad spotted it—the Snowy Owl. We quietly set up my spotting scope and got the bird in it. It looked like a female, eyes closed, just resting on top of a dune in plain sight.

After watching it snooze for several minutes, we both

agreed we could continue along the trail, which happened to bring us closer to the bird. We stopped again, a couple hundred meters away, to give the bird a respectful distance. I wanted to take a few photos from a different angle, and upon moving I noticed that at the base of the dune the owl sat on, was a photographer only a stone's throw away! The owl didn't care, it kept napping as this photographer quietly took photos of it.

Feeling emboldened by the birds behavior, I ventured a little closer and also got some amazing shots before I backed off. The bird opened one eye, checking us out- and deeming us suitable to play in the sand nearby, it shut its eye and resumed its snooze. Brad and I left quite content and happy with our Snowy Owl sighting.

Nobody had reported the Pink-footed Goose yet, and the odds of two out-of-town birders finding it seemed rather unlikely. Regardless, we headed back to the epicenter of the Canada Goose flocks. From the road, we could see geese out in the pasture of a private horse facility with stables. I realized that if we got permission to go out into their fields, maybe we could get a different vantage point on the flock and spot the goose.

Knocking on doors and asking permission is part of the Big Year game—some people do it, and others don't. The latter either trespass or miss the bird because they're too timid to ask. However, I've heard so many "no's" this year that one more couldn't hurt, so I politely asked around until I found the stable owner. I introduced myself, showed her pictures of the bird and explained the magnitude of this bird showing up in her backyard, literally.

She agreed to let us walk around, and took us out herself to show where we could and couldn't go, and introduced us to the dozen horses that were meandering around the pastures with the geese.

Within minutes of setting up the scope from a good vantage point, Brad had spotted the Pink-footed Goose, hidden behind the slightly larger Canada Geese, feeding in a horse pasture, out of sight from the road. We enjoyed a few minutes of watching the goose, as it meandered around and did what geese do best: eat grass and poop.

I saw some other intrepid birders walking along the road and waved them over so they could have a look— and then followed up with the stable owner and thanked her for allowing us to bird on her property. Although she was in the middle of the lesson, she asked me to email her photos and thanked me for sharing the bird with her. This wasn't a snow-covered hot spring on top of a mountain in Colorado, but it sure was a memorable bird to share with a mentor and friend.

The Pink-footed Goose is becoming a regular winter visitor along the East Coast

As I stood near the tip of Cape Cod, my spotting scope lurched forward as the front-facing tripod leg sank fast in the wet sand. The incoming tide was now at my boots. I hadn't noticed the impending approach of the waves as I stared through the scope out into the dizzying swells of the Atlantic. Long lines of birds streamed by offshore, over the churning slate-gray waves. The small black dots whizzing by seemed to be teasing me, passing just far enough away that their identification remained a mystery.

Collectively, these dapper black and white birds are called Alcids, the bird family that includes murres, auklets, guillemots, and most famously, puffins. Built for an aquatic existence, alcids have short legs and wings and spend the majority of their lives at sea, diving deep underwater to forage on plankton (free-floating crustaceans, copepods, and invertebrates) as well as fish. I'd seen every type of Alcid in North America this year, except one: the Dovekie.

The Dovekie is the smallest of all the Atlantic seabirds, earning the name of 'Little Auk' from European birdwatchers. Dovekies are noticeably smaller than other Alcids, and weigh in at half the size of the Atlantic Puffin. Like many other species this year, I had never seen a Dovekie before in real life. I'd never really put myself in the right place at the right time to see one, and so this was a new opportunity for me. I had come close; there is a small breeding population of Dovekie on St. Lawrence Island north of Gambell, however I arrived after the summer breeding season and the birds had already departed.

Being a budget-conscious birder, I lumped the Dovekie in with other Northeastern "winter" birds- that I hoped (unrealistically?) to see all in the same trip. Both the Pink-footed and Barnacle Goose have become annual winter vagrants to the Northeast, and I assumed those would be an easy pickup on the same trip as searching for Dovekie.

A Barnacle Goose hides among a flock of Canada Geese

The majority of Dovekie sightings were from Race Point, Massachusetts, the tip of Cape Cod just beyond Provincetown. Famous as the landing place of the Mayflower in 1620, this seaside town is steeped in rich colonial history. Currently P-town is a summer destination for whale-watching trips, offering visitors the chance to see fin, humpback, and the endangered North Atlantic right whales- of which there are fewer than 500 individuals remaining. Historically, whale oil was used as fuel for lighting (whale oil lamps) and served as a major lubricant for mechanical gears during the Industrial Revolution.

Although I was searching for Dovekie, I was also on the lookout for gulls. This was a good spot to see Little Gull, and after a few hours of looking through thousands of similarly-plumaged Bonaparte's Gulls I picked up on the dark under-wing of a distant Little Gull. It disappeared in and out of the flock of "Bonies" and I managed to take a few photos as it cruised closer to the beach a while later. With that bird under my belt, the Dovekie search was on.

Several small alcids whizzed by the beach, obscured by the large swells. It was difficult to tell if they were Dovekie or not, and of course I wouldn't count them until I was 100% sure on the I.D. It would be no fun if I doubted myself, and continued my life post-2016 wondering if my "Dovekie" was actually a Murre, or a Razorbill, or a wave.

I was grateful for the help of a local birder, Steve Arena who came out and joined me. During the hours we scanned the ocean from the beach through our scopes, he spotted several Dovekie, one which managed to dive right before I peeked in his scope, and the other bird I saw, but couldn't make sense of. It was tiny, and looked like half of a Murre. The bird was black and white but I couldn't tell which direction it was facing, or even make out an eye and a beak. This far-away splotch of black and white, although confirmed by another as a Dovekie, remained an enigma to my still-developing eye.

One December afternoon, after searching all morning for a Dovekie, I decided to check out the Bird Watcher's General Store, which I'd heard about from other folks on the Cape. It was deemed "A Cape Cod Destination Icon for Over 30 Years"—and I figured it would be worth checking out. The store was filled with all things bird: feeders, seed, field guides, hats, bird houses—if you could name it, they probably had it —seriously.

"Have you heard of any recent Dovekie sightings around here?" I asked the man at the counter (I later found out was the owner) I figured he had some customers or local intel that maybe I could benefit from.

"You want to see a Dovekie?" he asked.

"More than anything!" I replied, the desperation audible in my voice. This bird was beginning to get to me. Leaving the front counter, he walked back into his store and disappeared. A couple of minutes later he reappeared. He approached me holding out his outstretched arm. In his hand was A DOVEKIE!

I carefully held the bird, which easily fit in the palm of my hand. I was too excited to feel the chill from the stiff, lifeless body in my hand- the bird had been stored in a freezer to preserve the specimen before it was sent along to an educational institution where it would be preserved as a study skin for a scientific collection.

Although I couldn't count it (ABA rules state the bird must be alive and unrestrained) seeing this small Alcid close up made for a fun plot twist, and a good close study. I returned the frozen birdsicle to the store owner, who flashed a coy smile.

I spent nearly 10 days of December on Race Point, watching the ocean through a spotting scope looking for a Dovekie. My efforts went unrewarded with not even an identifiable look at the small alcid. This was birding. The most one can do is put themselves in the right place at the right time, and let nature take care of the rest. That's why it's called birding.

Birds have wings, and can sometimes be right where they are supposed to be, and sometimes they aren't. However, the lesson I learned from searching for the Dovekie is that when you give your best effort—playing all the cards right, controlling every variable one has control over—the odds still may not be in your favor. And that's life. In fact, that's how my year began.

I thought I was doing everything right to have my desired career as a wildlife cameraman, but that course changed quickly. It dawned on me how directly the obstacles I faced throughout the year had translated directly into broader life lessons.

Despite being one of the most common owl species in North America, the Northern Saw-whet Owl is rarely encountered by people. Between its small size and nocturnal hunting habits, this owl evades detection of even the most keen-eyed birders. However, those lucky to see one will agree that it is a strong candidate for the "cutest owl of North America" award. Although it is fairly widespread, this pint-sized owl can be extremely difficult to find throughout its range. Well-aware of its abundance and distribution, I had saved this species for December, knowing that it could be easily heard in my Washington backyard around Christmas.

Mid-way through the month of December, after spotting a Little Gull in Massachusetts, my count for the year (including two provisional birds) was 749 species. Seeing or hearing one more bird would be record-breaking. The other three Big Year birders had already passed 750— hoping I would join them too making this the first year that four birders broke the 700 mark and the old record!

I thought back to January 1st when I had whistled into the darkness, hoping to hear a Northern Saw-whet Owl in Washington state. What sounded back from the darkness was not a call I was familiar with—and I hadn't seen or heard anything that sounded like the tiny owl since.

Intent on reaching 750 species, I decided to drive around some back roads on Cape Cod searching for this elusive owl. I was genuinely surprised to get out of the car at my first stop, and whistle a series of monotone toots—and have a Saw-whet answer nearby. Then another called from further away. I located several by their call that night, and was able to get a brief glimpse at one in my spotlight as it flew off. It was unsatisfactory to only hear a bird that might be written about in a future *Milestones* blurb in *Birding* magazine. If was wanting to actually lay eyes on this bird, I needed a Christmas miracle.

Sulli and I had been friends for a while, introduced by our mutual friend Dick, a birder from Sulli's home state of Illinois. Our paths previously crossed in June on the North Dakota prairies, during my marathon drive from Seattle to Maine. The circumstances didn't allow us to bird together then, but I wanted to. We both met in Ida Grove, Iowa, where eBird had been showing consistent sightings of Northern Saw-whet Owl. The key figure at the center of our owl expedition was a figurehead of birding around the town of Ida Grove.

Nearly 30 years ago, Don Poggensee was supervising children on Moorehead Park's sledding hill when he casually glanced into a pine tree and noticed his first Northern Saw-whet Owl. This soda-can-sized owl captivated the attention of the jolly Iowan, who spent the next three decades showing Saw-whet Owls to visitors with just as much excitement as the first time he saw it.

This infectious enthusiasm and accumulated knowledge about the owls earned Don a reputation in some Midwestern birding circles, and it didn't take long before I heard his name. Followers of my blog contacted me with advice and encouragement to contact Don to see "his" owls. *It's a guaranteed sighting* —they wrote.

I called Don pretty early in the morning, after Sulli and I had spent over an hour in the cold, walking through neat rows of tall pines, searching for Long-eared Owls at a nearby park. The secret ingredient to finding owls is effort. Sometimes, luck is an equally important but that is no secret.

As I listened to the phone ringing on the other end, I pictured Don sleepily answering the phone at home—after all, I was calling pretty early in the morning. After almost one too many rings, the phone was answered by a chipper *Hello!* followed by slightly labored breath, and a background of crunching snow and branches whisking off coat fabric. Don was wide awake, and already out in the field searching for Saw-whets!

I was in disbelief as he gave me directions to Moorhead Pioneer Park, where he was already afield.

"After you pass the depot, you'll round the corner and see my red truck parked on the right..." and he interrupted himself to say, "I just found a Saw-whet at eye level—why don't you drive on over here now and see it?" I couldn't believe it. *Was this real life?*

We met Don at a parking lot near the outdoor bathrooms he'd described to me over the phone. We walked across the crusty patches of snow through scattered Cedar and Pine trees, following Don up the hill. I carefully stepped through straw colored brome grass, already matted down in clumps across the hillside from prior owl excursions.

As we walked through the trees, Don pointed out different branches owls had occupied in the past. He referred to them by name, such as "Faithful" who always sat in the same spot. Just as a tour guide would, Don excitedly explained different ecological aspects of Moorehead Pioneer Park. The reason these owls are attracted to this spot is the abundance of food. Many mice eat the seeds from the brome grass and owls take advantage of such a high concentration of food at this location.

Every night after hunting the owls take a different roost, often close to where they caught and consumed prey the night before. Sometimes it's easy to find them if you know the preferred perches, and sometimes it's a hunt. Don has spent decades in these hills locating Saw-whets, and he seems to have it down to a science.

A Northern Saw-whet Owl perched among the pines

As we walked together through the evergreen trees, Don paused mid-sentence and looked at us with a twinkle in his eye. I looked past him into a short pine tree, and spotted the owl he'd found earlier in the morning. He smiled, building the dramatic effect for others who had not yet spotted the bird behind him. To my surprise, Don walked directly underneath the bird, pointing it out to the group and began talking to it as if the bird were an old friend.

Don waved us closer too, and I realized I had stopped several meters away at the edge of my comfort zone. It was clear that he knew these birds and respected them, yet this owl seemed unfazed by our presence. After initially checking us out, he closed his eyes and went back to sleep, unbothered by our presence. After we took all the pictures our hearts desired, we left the owl in the same spot, eyes slitted and snoozing away.

Afterwards, Don took us to the new Nature Education Center, which was a beautiful building with educational displays, bird feeders, and friendly and knowledgeable staff. I sat down and interviewed Don for The Birding Project, learning more about his military service, conservation work, and development of Ida Grove's unofficial owl tourism industry.

I couldn't have had a better day and experience finding Saw-whet Owls. I affectionately dubbed Don Poggensee the "Saw-whet Santa" who gave me an incredible experience, which was more than just a check on my list. I drove away from Moorehead Pioneer Park with a deeper understanding of the park's history, and a glimpse into the secret lives of Saw-whets.

Some days are memorable because of the birds seen, or the people you're birding with. This was one of those days where everything just worked out perfectly. Following our Saw-whet Owl adventure, Sulli and I crossed the border and drove into South Dakota, which was my 49th state this year. It was neat to enjoy his company, and would become the first of many trips together in the future.

25

THE YEAR'S END

WHEN ALASKA AIRLINES Flight 713 touched down in Seattle on Christmas Day, I realized this might be my last flight of the year. It had been 360 days since I started this adventure, and now I was ending nearly where it had began. More importantly, I wasn't ending the year alone.

Teresa sat by my side smiling at me. *Welcome to Seattle.* She held my hand tightly, giving it a squeeze. I could tell she was happy to be here with me. We both returned home to my family to celebrate Christmas together. I'd never missed spending a Christmas with family, and I wasn't going to make this year the first.

A sense of déjà vu washed over me as I drove down the narrow winding road to my grandparent's house to celebrate Christmas with the entire family. We drove under the same old-growth trees I had driven under as a child, the same towering trees my mom had looked up at since her early years. I learned how to drive on this road, sitting on my dads lap and steering the car as he worked the pedals. (*This was at an age I probably shouldn't put into print*) This same road whereI started this whole adventure on in the wee hours of January 1st on my way to the ferry in Port Angeles.

Following the festivities, the hours passed without notice as I sat relaxing on the couches in front of the crackling fire. It was nice to be focused in the present, surrounded by family. In lieu of giving gifts, the adults in the family each shared a charity they had selected that is important to them. We put the charity names in a hat, and one of the kids draws the lucky winner. This tradition replaced our gift exchange of years past, and I was immensely grateful for a loving and supportive family who understood that this year itself was a huge gift for me.

After dessert disappeared by the platefuls from the kitchen counter, it was time to hug everyone one last time before driving home. When we arrived, our cats greeted us as if we'd been gone since Thanksgiving—which I realized I practically had been absent that long!

Tired and full, we sat down on the couch for some family time. While everyone was changing into their comfy clothes, I checked Facebook and caught the latest bird news on the top of my news feed: RED-FLANKED BLUETAIL in Idaho! I re-read the details of the report. After all the driving I'd done over the year, Idaho was only a short drive away!

This was the same species I'd passed on the opportunity to chase nearly a year ago on January 2nd when a single Red-flanked Bluetail was reported on an Oregon farm. I had immediately taken a screenshot of the spot before the observer quickly changed the location to a more general point, to avoid the madness that ensues when a Code 4 bird is reported. To honor the landowner's request for no visitors, I didn't stop on my drive through Oregon on January 2nd.

This sighting—at a public location—was too good to pass up. I looked at Teresa, and she knew right away that a plan was brewing in my head. Already half-expecting me to get on a plane and go somewhere, she asked me what I was thinking of. *Well, there's this bird...*

Before 7:00 am the next morning my dad's 1997 Jeep Cherokee sat running in the driveway, packed with everything needed for a rare bird chase. With Teresa as my copilot, we drove from the wet Seattle weather up and over Snoqualmie Pass into a wall of snow, barely sliding through the drifts that had forced multiple 18-wheelers off the road into the white abyss beyond. As the miles passed, my excitement level increased—for me. Teresa slept most of the way. I draped my winter parka over her to keep her warm as the temperature dropped as we crossed eastern Washington and entered Idaho.

By quarter to three we reached Hell's Gate State Park, and paid the entry fee which on top of gas for the trip was still under $100. I remembered my rough calculations in January for how expensive each new bird would become in December, and this one came in way under my calculations. This was a very reasonable cost for a chance at a life bird—one bird most people have to go to remote islands in Alaska to hope to see.

The bluetail hadn't been seen for a while when we arrived. I anxiously walked laps around the area it had last been seen, doing a double-take of each individual robin and junco. The sun was setting, and we had searched the park thoroughly. My desire for Teresa to see this bird nearly outweighed the importance of seeing it myself. It was just one more check on an already impressive year-long tally for me; for Teresa this was her first "real" rarity chase, and I felt the pressure of not seeing the bird may crush her enthusiasm for doing this again in the future.

"We have the bird!" An excited voice shouted just upriver as one of the other birders motioned to us. After a short jog to where they stood, I looked into a tangle of Russian Olives, and there it was in all of its subtle glory flicking its blue tail. I handed my binoculars to Teresa, who smiled as it flicked its tail for her too.

We high-fived under the sunset, both relieved that the drive across the mountains and hiking around in the cold wasn't in vain. This was a true milestone- bird number 752 for the year, a life bird for Teresa, and one of only several truly rare birds we had seen together.

A beautiful sunset was forming above the steep canyon walls, and it was starting to get dark. It was time to start the seven hour drive home. Making it there and back in a day was just another day birding for me, using a birding muscle that had been conditioned all year long for a marathon day like today.

The drive back gave me a long time to think. Was this how I wanted my year to end? If I stopped now, what was I leaving on the table? There were still four days left officially, until the "Big Year" ended at midnight on December 31st. I wasn't thinking about anyone else's total, or even my own. There was one thing nagging at me- my mind was hooked on the tip of Cape Cod, and I knew that if I ended now, I'd miss my final chance in 2016 to see a Dovekie.

A Red-flanked Bluetail made a surprising visit to Idaho

The next morning, I said goodbye to Teresa and used my last standby pass to fly from Seattle to Boston on the first available flight. If you want an example of a classy birder and a real gentleman, look no further than Boston's own Neil Hayward. He graciously loaned me his car, which provided the opportunity to return to Race Point in a final play to spot a Dovekie. This act also positioned me to eclipse his big year total. (excluding the two provisional birds I had seen already)

Speaking of provisional birds, the continuing Graylag Goose reported in Rhode Island wasn't too far off my route, and I decided along the drive that I would chase it. I would hate to be so close and not make the effort to see it—after all, it was a Graylag Goose no matter where the state records committee decided it came from.

After combing through hundreds of geese blanketing a golf course pond, I had the controversial Graylag in my scope. The provenance was debatable, but to me, didn't matter. Deciding not to count it until the Rhode Island Committee voted on it, I didn't add it to my official count. It's always better to add a bird later than subtract one.

Nearly three hours later I stood on the beach with Steve, a diligent Cape Cod birder who had been the only one to consistently report Dovekies off Race Point in recent days. I needed a second set of sharp eyes to cover as much ocean as possible, increasing the chance of spotting a living Dovekie.

Over the next couple days, for many hours we scanned the ocean, combing through flocks of alcids, eiders, and scoters. Thousands of birds floated just offshore, and Steve and I talked about life, birding, and my Big Year as we scanned through as many of these birds as we could.

Minutes of mutual silence was broken when calmly, Steve told me he had a Dovekie in his scope. I tried not to move too quickly and risk bumping his tripod, and I peered in his scope and blinked a few times as I adjusted the focus. Hundreds of yard offshore, dozens of scoters bobbed up and down on the swells, but no Dovekie. It must have dove beneath the surface.

Then, while scanning through the scoters I spotted a small black and white alcid that appeared from the waves for a second. It looked like the butt of a bird, a black and white sandwich. I described the bird to Steve—it was black on top and white underneath, and I couldn't tell which way it was facing. As I scrutinized the shape, the bird vanished, swallowed by the sea.

"That's a Dovekie" Steve said, grinning. He assured me that was exactly the type of sighting he expected to get with these conditions. I saw it! But should I count it? Could it have been the back end of a murre or a Razorbill? I couldn't tell for sure. In the continuing spirit of my Big Year, unwavering from the standard I held for more than 750 species, I didn't add it to my list; I couldn't be 100% certain of the bird I had seen.

I drove back to Boston as the sun set, admitting my questionable Dovekie sighting to Neil when I returned his car. I didn't know if the feeling of defeat was due to the undesirable looks I had at the Dovekie, or if reality was settling in: the year was drawing to an end.

To the throngs of post-holiday travelers, 10pm meant nothing as they moved through the airport like lines of ants. I stood among a crowd of people at Boston Logan International Airport, feeling slightly lost. I didn't have a ticket booked, or a plan of where to go from there, but after returning Neil's car and being dropped off at the airport, I didn't really have anywhere else to go.

I laid down behind a car display near the check-in counters in Terminal 3. I had friends in the area, but didn't want to impose on their New Year's Eve plans, so the texts I composed in my head remained unsent. Sleeping in the airport was free, and I was able to think and reflect on the conclusion of my year. I'd been going nonstop since I'd left Seattle, only getting a precious few hours of sleep before birding Race Point all day. I scrolled through my phone, looking at photos of all the places I'd been.

44 years ago, California birding legend Richard Stallcup told a young Kenn Kaufman:

"The list total isn't important, but the birds themselves are important. Every bird you see. So the list is just a frivolous incentive for birding, but the birding itself is worthwhile. It's like a trip where the destination doesn't have any significance except for the fact that it makes you travel. The journey is what counts."

This gold nugget of birding wisdom is hidden within the pages of Kingbird Highway, and I thought about these words often during my Big Year. While so many people judge the success of modern-day big years based on the numbers, very few people understand that it is more so about the journey.

For much of the year, my destination was always a moving target: *the next bird*. This took me to many amazing places, and introduced me to some incredible people, who were full of wisdom, advice, and humor.

Looking back, I realized I had traveled both literally and figuratively on an amazing journey. This year had most certainly been worthwhile. I had become a better birder, through learning both from the birds and those who watched them. I became more patient with myself and others. I learned how to overcome fear, by choosing love, and chasing my passion. In the end, I better understood the avian biodiversity of an entire continent. The birds were indeed important. Each bird took me someplace new, both geographically and in my understanding of the bird and its relationship to our world.

I was fortunate to recognize early-on in the year that I was not motivated solely by a number on a list. My personal goal of seeing 700 species during the year never took precedence for me over other more important aspects of my journey.

Thinking back, I remembered experiencing birds *with* people, and that was truly memorable. I'd taken a year and learned not only a lot about myself, but about the birding community as a whole. I now knew what birds sparked people's interest, heard from hundreds of birders exactly *why* they bird, and learned through my own experience how to overcome adversity. Many of these lessons wouldn't fit in the book I had begun to write—I new I'd have to write another.

For me, birds inspired the journey which led me across the continent, in the 21st century—aided by modern technology and a supportive community of birders.

The friendships I made deepened my experience, and gave me a focus outside of myself. Birding with Laura and John gave me time to build friendships with both of them, and share our journeys together. I met and interviewed over 365 birders, learning something new from everyone I spoke with.

Midnight came and went, and the year ended as suddenly as it had begun. After this incredible adventure, a lingering question remains: *Will I do another Big Year?*

Somewhere on a hillside in Alpine, Texas that answer is written on the desk.

A Dovekie floats somewhere off Race Point

AFTERWORD

On January 1, 2017 I woke up and went birding—the exact opposite of what many people assume one might do after completing a record-breaking Big Year.

After 366 days, my birding momentum could not be slowed. I spent the entire day along the New England coastline, hoping for a better look at a Dovekie—without success.

In February I accepted a full-time teaching position at The Link School, teaching experiential Science classes focused on Mountain Ecology, Sustainability, and Integrated Science, and traveling with students to Colombia and Peru. I loved living in the mountains, sharing my passion for birds and wild places with such an incredible group of students and staff.

I've returned to Ohio each year for the Biggest Week in American Birding festival. Standing shoulder-to-shoulder along the Magee Marsh boardwalk with hundreds of people reminds me that birds really do bring people together. There's certainly less-crowded places to ponder that fact—but I find great joy in the diversity, inclusiveness, and love that is shared by the birding community at this special event.

Birds continue to be a motivation and inspiration for me. After fulfilling one of my lifelong dreams of doing a Big Year, I am focused much less on my own experience in the field, and more on improving the experience of others. I want to make sure that all have an equal opportunity to learn the many lessons birds can teach us.

I have found joy in the common birds, noting new behavior and studying birds in a more relaxed manner than I had before. I'm grateful for the fleeting glimpses, quick fly-bys, and obscure call-notes I couldn't identify. I don't regret skipping Hawaii, although my bird list would have certainly benefitted from some tropical island air. (*The ABA later allowed the 2016 Big Year birders to include Hawaiian birds in their year lists—I was the only one who didn't go*)

The Birding Project continues, with new ideas for growth and development on the horizon. For now, it remains an educational website to share birds and birding with others.

Currently, I am now focused on pursuing opportunities to help advance birding forward, promoting conservation and helping people connect with birds. We will see what the future holds, but I am positive it will be bright.

ACKNOWLEDGMENTS

It is nearly impossible to summarize my gratitude for everyone who helped me over the course of the year.

My parents provided unflinching support and unconditional love every day of the year, regardless of the decisions I made. From providing food, airline passes, logistical support, and a home to return to—they did it all with a smile and expected only good.

My family provided places to stay, logistical support, encouragement, and love. Kevin and Paighton, you made my time in Texas more comfortable and provided incredible support during the year. The love you share inspires many, and I'm so grateful to have been part of your beautiful marriage ceremony.

My grandparents, aunts and uncles, and cousins—you all contributed in unique ways that helped ease the burdens I took on to complete this journey.

I owe a special thank you to Teresa, whose strong heart, compassion, and tireless patience made it possible for us to move forward together and share many incredible adventures in the years since.

To the guys at Maven, thank you for believing in me. Your clarity and brilliance as a team of passionate innovators shows in your optics, and the quality company you've built—keep it up!

To the team on Little St. Simons—thank you for welcoming me into the fold and allowing me to help out. There's no doubt both of our needs were met.

Thank you Bobby, Natalie, and my Link School family for allowing me to join your community of lifelong learners. I've been so fortunate to have a second home in Buena Vista, Colorado.

This story would not have been possible or happened in the way that it did, were it not for the engagement and support of the North American birding community.

I'm grateful for the opportunity to attend Hog Island Audubon Camp, and my sincerest thanks go out to the people who made this financially possible.

I'm grateful for birding role models, mentors, and exemplary human beings. Kenn Kaufman is all three and more. His support of *Falcon Freeway* means the world to me, and I'm grateful for every minute of this man's time he has spent encouraging me and helping me on my learning journey through this process.

The experts afield that help spot and identify birds can't be acknowledged enough. The pelagic guides and spotters on Debi Shearwater and Brian Patteson's trips helped teach me about seabirds and conservation, making this one of my favorite ways to enjoy birds.

The three months I spent in Alaska went smoothly and (mostly) according to plan, thanks to the assistance of John Puschock, Neil Hayward, Isaac Helmericks, Leanna Mack, and Dave Sonneborn. And most importantly, Paul Lehman's guidance and willingness to show me the ropes in Gambell helped me understand why he has returned year after year to this remote corner of Alaska. Thank you, Paul.

I owe gratitude to Joe Lill for tracking the Big Year numbers for me and all of my fellow Big Year birders. His keen eyes and dedication to this task helped to keep everyone up to speed and on the same page with the lists.

Andy Bankert's excitement and enthusiasm helped me realize I could actually do a Big Year, and his help with planning the logistics more than once was invaluable. I undoubtably saw more birds and did the "right thing" countless times because of his advice.

Tiffany Kersten—thank you for suggesting I interview birders. As a result, The Birding Project grew from this idea and these interviews reached thousands of people, inspiring and connecting a community of birders.

To anyone who posted about a rarity or eBirded at a location prior to my visit, thank you. Your observations, photographs, and information you provided made it easier (or sometimes more difficult!) to find birds. The knowledge of local birders is invaluable and under-recognized when Big Year totals are celebrated. Every bird counts!

To the birders who gave their time to speak with me and interview for The Birding Project, thank you. Your authentic and honest words of wisdom, advice, humor, and insight helped me learn more about the diverse community of people who are all connected by a shared love of birds. I hope to take your words and create something impactful in the near future.

Writing is hard work, and a very different kind of work than I'm used to. Sitting in front of a computer screen for months on end has been incredibly difficult for me. Lastly, I owe a debt of gratitude to everyone who reviewed my first, second, and third draft, and the "final" Advance Reader Copy which was actually nothing more than a fancy-looking fourth draft full of mistakes. Jessica Melfi, Libby Paine, Elizabeth Hagenlocher, Chris Hagenlocher, Bruce Beehler, Andrew Guttenberg, Teresa Vodopest, and Heather Barron—your diligence, keen eyes, and gentle suggestions helped me re-work my text into what it is today.

I owe a debt of gratitude to all of the people I have not named here, who have all played a role in supporting me in this journey. If you bought me food, drove me somewhere, donated to The Birding Project, shared a meal, opened your home, gave me advice, pointed out a bird, or encouraged me—I offer you my sincerest thanks. The list of individuals is long, and many of you reading this book know who you are. Thank you from the bottom of my heart!

BIG YEAR NUMBERS

61,442 total flying miles

54,332 driving miles in Subaru

5500 rental car miles

2857 miles- longest single flight (Anchorage to Chicago)

1162 walking miles (according to iPhone)

752 total countable ABA birds

738 birds photographed (98% of total birds recorded)

184 miles- shortest flight (Nome to Kotzebue, AK)

129 consecutive days without flying (1 Jan to May 9)

56 days spent in Alaska

49 states birded (48 states birded)

48 total flight legs

20 nights spent on boats

16 oil changes

5 trips to Alaska

4 heard-only birds: BLRA, BOOW, FLOW, NBTY

3 nights spent on airplanes

2 times getting pulled over

0 flat tires, speeding tickets, car accidents, and regrets

BIRDING "GREEN" AND BIG YEARS

I first learned about environmentalism at a young age—perhaps the Lorax is to blame? The creature who spoke on behalf of the Truffula trees raised his voice against very real environmental issues, posing important questions about sustainability, conservation, and economic development.

Birds are the real-life Lorax. They are barometers for the health of entire ecosystems—the "canary in the coal mine". Today, bird populations are declining faster than ever—across the world's grasslands, forests, oceans. Every habitat is being affected. If we refuse to acknowledge the science behind our warming planet, and turn a blind eye to the ecological requirements of the organisms we share our planet with—what will be left?

Every human on the planet consume resources and generate waste. People around the world consume resources at different rates, leaving an "ecological footprint" of varying sizes, affected by our decisions and activities.

Birders are largely an environmentally-conscious group of individuals. However, "competitive" birdwatching can be a carbon-intensive hobby. Big Years are associated with a larger-than-average carbon footprint. Increased global carbon emissions fuel climate change, which can displace and hurt the birds we love.

Not all Big Years are carbon-intensive. In 2014, Dorian Anderson biked 17,830 miles through 28 states, observing 617 species of birds and raised nearly $50,000 for bird conservation. This approach is admirable, but we're not likely to see many Big Years done exclusively by bike in the future.

Birding "green" has never truly taken off on a wide scale. As meticulous as birders can be about keeping track of when and where they recorded a particular species, nobody seems too keen on tracking how many gallons of fuel they burned to see a bird—or doing something about it. (I'm aware some birders do!)

For emissions that are impossible to reduce (for example, flying to Alaska) purchasing a carbon offset can help reduce controllable carbon emissions elsewhere in the world. There are many projects to choose to support—some retrofit landfills to capture methane, produce electricity, or help rural Kenyans install water purification systems that don't emit carbon.

Investing in a carbon offset program was not intended to assuage my guilt, nor was it a "get out of jail free" card for attempting a Big Year on a continental scale. It was intended to start a pattern of Big Year birders taking action and purchasing a carbon offset for their travel.

Inspired by what I was learning in my sustainability classes, I figured this action was a better alternative to inaction. It would be a learning experience not only for me, but those who I shared my Big Year journey with.

Although it may not be a perfect solution to the problem, it felt good to invest in projects that help reduce poverty in the developing world, and support carbon-capture projects around the US.

Purchasing carbon offsets is not an expensive endeavor relative to the travel one is offsetting. I set aside some funds monthly so on Earth Day (April 2017) I fully offset the carbon footprint for the entirety of 2016. In addition, I made a serious effort to make different lifestyle choices the following year and beyond. (such as traveling less, biking to work, etc.)

In recent years, there have been multiple Carbon Offset Birding Projects (COBP's) which encourage birders to track their carbon emissions resulting directly from their birding activities, and then contributing to an offset program that benefits birds and bird habitats. There's many to choose from, and doing a little online research can help sort through the options.

63,934 lbs: 2016 Average CO_2e Emissions of US Citizen*:

67,078 lbs: My 2016 CO_2e Emissions
    -Driving: 48,922 lbs CO_2 e
    -Public Transit: 143 lbs CO_2 e
    -Air Travel: 18,013 lbs CO_2 e
    -Home Energy: 0** lbs CO_2 e

Terrapass CO_2 Credits Purchased: 68,000 lbs offset
    Lifestraw Co_2 Credits Purchased: 2,000 lbs offset

Learn more: Boulder Audubon's Carbon Offset Bird Project
    https://www.boulderaudubon.org/carbon-offset-bird-project/
    *Source: www.terrapass.com Carbon Calculator
    **In the audit, I left this field blank because I didn't live in a single family home, rather slightly increased energy use of those I stayed with on the road. To compensate for this fact, I added approximately 3,000 lbs. of CO_2 output to my emissions total—providing a margin for error in the calculations.

TIPS FOR LIVING ON THE ROAD

Here are a few of the tips/tricks I learned living on the road:

Eating

-The key to healthy eating is balance, variety, and moderation.
-**Bring a cooler**! Bagged ice costs money, but it's free if you know where to look (Hint: check hotel ice machines, seafood markets, sometimes McDonald's)
-**Shop local** when possible. There's plenty of roadside produce stands where you can buy affordable fresh fruit, vegetables, and nuts. It costs more than Walmart, but is worth it.
-Know your wild plants. I picked strawberries, raspberries, blackberries, apples, and persimmons while birding across the US. *Caution: know your fungi before consuming mushrooms.*
-**Recycle** a plastic milk carton to store water. It's easy to refill water bottles at fast food restaurants or Starbucks. Avoid buying bottled water unless necessary.

-**Use coupons** from discarded local papers to save money on groceries!

-Costco, Trader Joe's, and several other grocery stores offer free samples. Don't be greedy, but don't pass up the opportunity for free food. You may learn you like something that looks gross.

Using technology

-**Use apps** like GasBuddy to find cheapest gas in the next town. There's also apps for tolls, navigation—everything! I can't emphasize how nice it was to occasionally drive into the next large town after a long day on the road, stop by Dominoes Pizza, and have two large, 2-topping pizzas waiting for me for only 12 bucks. One was dinner, the other lunch the next day—ordered and enjoyed online, on the road.

-Use Yelp and check in to certain restaurants, and get free food! Other restaurant apps also offer free food to reward customer loyalty when using their app.

-**Network!** Use social media to connect with a nationwide community of people who want to help you. People are willing and ready to share a meal, open their guest room, share use of their washer and dryer, and hear stories from the road. There's plenty of apps and websites for connecting people, including couchsurfing.com and birdingpal.org

Car Camping

-**Sleep in Wal-Mart parking lots**. Be sure to check first, as not all store managers or local laws allow it.

-Arrive after dark, and survey the lot. Where is the activity the greatest? Where are other cars parked?

-**Sleep with the car locked**, and don't box yourself in.

-Park under a burned out light, under a tree, or find a dark corner in the parking lot. You can also hang clothes in the windows to block the light (and use earplugs!)

-Brush teeth, wash face, and use bathroom inside Wal-Mart. If you go early in the morning and late at night the bathroom usually will be clean. It's nice to not leave your car during the night to use the bathroom.

-Always **crack the windows** to avoid waking up in the morning with a wet sleeping bag.

-Second reason to sleep with car windows open: if it's cold you'll have to scrape the ice off the inside of the windows the next morning as well as the outside

-Seek out a small, privately owned hotel during the first half of the day, to **shower in a vacant room** someone has already checked out from. This strategy worked for me multiple times —the front desk even provided towels and fresh toiletries. Be sure to leave a tip for the maid.

-Clean rivers and creeks work just as well for bathing. Use Dr. Bronner's biodegradable soap!

Spending Money

-Sign up for an airline rewards credit card. You'll spend money regardless (on fuel/food), so put it on a card and get air miles. Look for special promotions and double miles.

-**Buy the 'America the Beautiful' National Parks Pass**. ($80 for an annual pass) It pays for itself in about four visits, and is valid for discounted camping fees in National Forests.

-Buy a Duck Stamp ($25) to **support conservation**. The stamp also serves as a year-long pass into all National Wildlife Refuges across the country.

BIRD LIST

The following is a list of birds in the order they were first encountered and positively identified during the year.

1. Barn Owl Port Angeles, WA 1 Jan
2. Canada Goose Port Angeles, WA 1 Jan
3. Eurasian Wigeon Port Angeles, WA 1 Jan
4. American Wigeon Port Angeles, WA 1 Jan
5. Mallard Port Angeles, WA 1 Jan
6. Surf Scoter Port Angeles, WA 1 Jan
7. Long-tailed Duck Port Angeles, WA 1 Jan
8. Bufflehead Port Angeles, WA 1 Jan
9. Common Merganser Port Angeles, WA 1 Jan
10. Red-breasted Merganser Port Angeles, WA 1 Jan
11. Common Loon Port Angeles, WA 1 Jan
12. Horned Grebe Port Angeles, WA 1 Jan
13. Red-necked Grebe Port Angeles, WA 1 Jan
14. Double-crested Cormorant Port Angeles, WA 1 Jan
15. Pelagic Cormorant Port Angeles, WA 1 Jan
16. Mew Gull Port Angeles, WA 1 Jan

17. Glaucous-winged Gull Port Angeles, WA 1 Jan
18. Rock Pigeon Port Angeles, WA 1 Jan
19. Harlequin Duck Victoria Ferry, WA 1 Jan
20. White-winged Scoter Victoria Ferry, WA 1 Jan
21. Pacific Loon Victoria Ferry, WA 1 Jan
22. Common Murre Victoria Ferry, WA 1 Jan
23. Common Goldeneye Victoria Ferry, WA 1 Jan
24. Hooded Merganser Victoria Ferry, WA 1 Jan
25. Northwestern Crow Port Angeles, WA 1 Jan
26. Anna's Hummingbird Redwing Stakeout, BC 1 Jan
27. Bald Eagle Redwing Stakeout, BC 1 Jan
28. Green-winged Teal Redwing Stakeout, BC 1 Jan
29. Turkey Vulture Redwing Stakeout, BC 1 Jan
30. Northern Flicker Redwing Stakeout, BC 1 Jan
31. Merlin Redwing Stakeout, BC 1 Jan
32. Steller's Jay Redwing Stakeout, BC 1 Jan
33. Common Raven Redwing Stakeout, BC 1 Jan
34. Chestnut-backed Chickadee Redwing Stakeout, BC 1 Jan
35. Pacific Wren Redwing Stakeout, BC 1 Jan
36. Red-breasted Nuthatch Redwing Stakeout, BC 1 Jan
37. Bushtit Redwing Stakeout, BC 1 Jan
38. Golden-crowned Kinglet Redwing Stakeout, BC 1 Jan
39. Bewick's Wren Redwing Stakeout, BC 1 Jan
40. American Robin Redwing Stakeout, BC 1 Jan
41. Hermit Thrush Redwing Stakeout, BC 1 Jan
42. Fox Sparrow Redwing Stakeout, BC 1 Jan
43. Dark-eyed Junco Redwing Stakeout, BC 1 Jan
44. European Starling Redwing Stakeout, BC 1 Jan
45. Spotted Towhee Redwing Stakeout, BC 1 Jan
46. Golden-crowned Sparrow Redwing Stakeout, BC 1 Jan
47. Pine Siskin Redwing Stakeout, BC 1 Jan
48. House Sparrow Redwing Stakeout, BC 1 Jan
49. Great Blue Heron Victoria Ferry, BC 1 Jan

50. Redwing Redwing Stakeout, BC 1 Jan

51. Northern Shoveler Gog-Le-Hi-Te Wetlands, WA 2 Jan

52. Killdeer Tacoma, WA 2 Jan

53. Wilson's Snipe Gog-Le-Hi-Te Wetlands, WA 2 Jan

54. Ring-billed Gull Gog-Le-Hi-Te Wetlands, WA 2 Jan

55. Western Gull Gog-Le-Hi-Te Wetlands, WA 2 Jan

56. Herring Gull Gog-Le-Hi-Te Wetlands, WA 2 Jan

57. HA Gog-Le-Hi-Te Wetlands, WA 2 Jan

58. Song Sparrow Gog-Le-Hi-Te Wetlands, WA 2 Jan

59. Western Meadowlark Gog-Le-Hi-Te Wetlands, WA 2 Jan

60. Snow Goose Husted Road, CA 3 Jan

61. Greater White-fronted Goose Husted Road, CA 3 Jan

62. Eurasian Collared-Dove Husted Road, CA 3 Jan

63. Mourning Dove Husted Road, CA 3 Jan

64. Horned Lark Husted Road, CA 3 Jan

65. White-crowned Sparrow Husted Road, CA 3 Jan

66. Yellow-billed Magpie I-5 Corridor. CA 3 Jan

67. American Pipit Hahn Rd., CA 3 Jan

68. Red-winged Blackbird Hahn Rd., CA 3 Jan

69. Brown-headed Cowbird Hahn Rd., CA 3 Jan

70. Brewer's Blackbird Hahn Rd., CA 3 Jan

71. Loggerhead Shrike Modesto, CA 3 Jan

72. Canvasback Ceres WTP, CA 3 Jan

73. Lesser Scaup Ceres WTP, CA 3 Jan

74. Redhead Ceres WTP, CA 3 Jan

75. Ruddy Duck Ceres WTP, CA 3 Jan

76. Eared Grebe Ceres WTP, CA 3 Jan

77. Ring-necked Duck Ceres WTP, CA 3 Jan

78. Cooper's Hawk Ceres WTP, CA 3 Jan

79. American Coot Ceres WTP, CA 3 Jan

80. Black-necked Stilt Ceres WTP, CA 3 Jan

81. American Avocet Ceres WTP, CA 3 Jan

82. Dunlin Ceres WTP, CA 3 Jan

83. Least Sandpiper Ceres WTP, CA 3 Jan

84. Bonaparte's Gull Ceres WTP, CA 3 Jan

85. Black-headed Gull Ceres WTP, CA 3 Jan

86. American Crow Ceres WTP, CA 3 Jan

87. Western Sandpiper Ceres WTP, CA 3 Jan

88. Long-billed Dowitcher Ceres WTP, CA 3 Jan

89. California Gull Ceres WTP, CA 3 Jan

90. Nuttall's Woodpecker Ceres WTP, CA 3 Jan

91. White-throated Swift Ceres WTP, CA 3 Jan

92. Blue-winged Teal Merced NWR, CA 3 Jan

93. Cinnamon Teal Merced NWR, CA 3 Jan

94. Gadwall Merced NWR, CA 3 Jan

95. Northern Pintail Merced NWR, CA 3 Jan

96. Greater Scaup Merced NWR, CA 3 Jan

97. Pied-billed Grebe Merced NWR, CA 3 Jan

98. American White Pelican Merced NWR, CA 3 Jan

99. Great Egret Merced NWR, CA 3 Jan

100. Snowy Egret Merced NWR, CA 3 Jan

101. Black-crowned Night-Heron Merced NWR, CA 3 Jan

102. White-faced Ibis Merced NWR, CA 3 Jan

103. Northern Harrier Merced NWR, CA 3 Jan

104. Red-shouldered Hawk Merced NWR, CA 3 Jan

105. Common Gallinule Merced NWR, CA 3 Jan

106. Sandhill Crane Merced NWR, CA 3 Jan

107. Long-billed Curlew Merced NWR, CA 3 Jan

108. Great Horned Owl Merced NWR, CA 3 Jan

109. American Kestrel Merced NWR, CA 3 Jan

110. Black Phoebe Merced NWR, CA 3 Jan

111. Tree Swallow Merced NWR, CA 3 Jan

112. Marsh Wren Merced NWR, CA 3 Jan

113. Ruby-crowned Kinglet Merced NWR, CA 3 Jan

114. Yellow-rumped Warbler Merced NWR, CA 3 Jan

115. Savannah Sparrow Merced NWR, CA 3 Jan

116. Lincoln's Sparrow Merced NWR, CA 3 Jan
117. Brant San Diego River Mudflats, CA 4 Jan
118. Western Grebe San Diego River, CA 4 Jan
119. Brown Pelican San Diego River, CA 4 Jan
120. Osprey San Diego River, CA 4 Jan
121. Ridgway's Rail San Diego River, CA 4 Jan
122. Black-bellied Plover San Diego River, CA 4 Jan
123. Semipalmated Plover San Diego River, CA 4 Jan
124. Marbled Godwit San Diego River, CA 4 Jan
125. Ruddy Turnstone San Diego River, CA 4 Jan
126. Red Knot San Diego River, CA 4 Jan
127. Sanderling San Diego River, CA 4 Jan
128. Greater Yellowlegs San Diego River, CA 4 Jan
129. Willet San Diego River, CA 4 Jan
130. Heermann's Gull San Diego River, CA 4 Jan
131. Forster's Tern San Diego River, CA 4 Jan
132. Royal Tern San Diego River, CA 4 Jan
133. Black Skimmer San Diego River, CA 4 Jan
134. Belted Kingfisher San Diego River, CA 4 Jan
135. Say's Phoebe San Diego River, CA 4 Jan
136. Black-vented Shearwater San Diego, CA 4 Jan
137. Brandt's Cormorant San Diego, CA
138. Black Turnstone San Diego, CA 4 Jan
139. Surfbird San Diego, CA 4 Jan
140. Brown Booby Cabrillo Nat'l Monument, CA 4 Jan
141. California Scrub-Jay Cabrillo Nat'l Monument, CA 4 Jan
142. California Towhee Cabrillo Nat'l Monument, CA 4 Jan
143. Wrentit San Diego Safari Park, CA 4 Jan
144. Western Bluebird San Diego Safari Park, CA 4 Jan
145. Northern Mockingbird San Diego Safari Park, CA 4 Jan
146. Phainopepla San Diego Safari Park, CA 4 Jan
147. House Finch San Diego Safari Park, CA 4 Jan
148. Sharp-shinned Hawk San Diego Archael. Center, 4 Jan

149. Rock Wren San Diego Archael. Center, 4 Jan
150. Blue-gray Gnatcatcher San Diego Archael. Center, 4 Jan
151. Burrowing Owl Bono Salton Sea NWR, CA 5 Jan
152. Abert's Towhee Bono Salton Sea NWR, CA 5 Jan
153. Neotropic Cormorant Salton Sea-south end, CA 5 Jan
154. Cattle Egret Salton Sea-south end, CA 5 Jan
155. Sora Salton Sea-south end, CA 5 Jan
156. Greater Roadrunner Salton Sea-south end, CA 5 Jan
157. Peregrine Falcon Salton Sea-south end, CA 5 Jan
158. Northern Rough-winged Swallow Salton Sea CA 5 Jan
159. Barn Swallow Salton Sea-south end, CA 5 Jan
160. Caspian Tern Salton Sea-Obsidian Butte, CA 5 Jan
161. Yellow-footed Gull Salton Sea-Obsidian Butte, CA 5 Jan
162. Spotted Sandpiper Riverside Park, CA 5 Jan
163. Gila Woodpecker Riverside Park, CA 5 Jan
164. Great-tailed Grackle Brandt Rd, Calipatria, CA 5 Jan
165. Streak-backed Oriole Riverside Park, AZ 6 Jan
166. Inca Dove Yuma W. Wetlands, AZ 6 Jan
167. Ladder-backed Woodpecker Yuma West Wetlands, 6 Jan
168. Verdin Yuma West Wetlands, AZ 6 Jan
169. Crissal Thrasher Yuma West Wetlands, AZ 6 Jan
170. Orange-crowned Warbler Yuma West Wetlands, 6 Jan
171. Gambel's Quail Gilbert Water Ranch, AZ 6 Jan
172. Harris's Hawk Gilbert Water Ranch, AZ 6 Jan
173. Curve-billed Thrasher Gilbert Water Ranch, AZ 6 Jan
174. Bridled Titmouse Catalina State Park, AZ 7 Jan
175. Brown Creeper Catalina State Park, AZ 7 Jan
176. Canyon Wren Catalina State Park, AZ 7 Jan
177. Rufous-backed Robin Catalina State Park, AZ 7 Jan
178. Chipping Sparrow Catalina State Park, AZ 7 Jan
179. Canyon Towhee Catalina State Park, AZ 7 Jan
180. Northern Cardinal Catalina State Park, AZ 7 Jan
181. Pyrrhuloxia Catalina State Park, AZ 7 Jan

182. Golden Eagle Florida Canyon-lower, AZ 7 Jan
183. White-winged Dove Florida Canyon-lower, AZ 7 Jan
184. Elegant Trogon Florida Canyon-lower, AZ 7 Jan
185. Cactus Wren Florida Canyon-lower, AZ 7 Jan
186. Black-capped Gnatcatcher Florida Canyon, AZ 7 Jan
187. Painted Redstart Florida Canyon, AZ 7 Jan
188. Black-chinned Sparrow Florida Canyon, AZ 7 Jan
189. Arizona Woodpecker Huachuca Canyon, AZ 7 Jan
190. Montezuma Quail Huachuca Canyon, AZ 8 Jan
191. Acorn Woodpecker Huachuca Canyon, AZ 8 Jan
192. Hammond's Flycatcher Huachuca Canyon, AZ 8 Jan
193. Mexican Jay Huachuca Canyon, AZ 8 Jan
194. White-breasted Nuthatch Huachuca Canyon, AZ 8 Jan
195. Townsend's Warbler Huachuca Canyon, AZ 8 Jan
196. Lesser Goldfinch Huachuca Canyon, AZ 8 Jan
197. Wild Turkey Huachuca Canyon, AZ 9 Jan
198. Red-naped Sapsucker Huachuca Canyon, AZ 9 Jan
199. Sinaloa Wren Huachuca Canyon, AZ 9 Jan
200. Rufous-crowned Sparrow Huachuca Canyon, AZ 9 Jan
201. Louisiana Waterthrush San Pedro RNCA, AZ 9 Jan
202. Black-throated Sparrow San Pedro RNCA, AZ 9 Jan
203. Lark Bunting San Pedro RNCA, AZ 9 Jan
204. Vesper Sparrow San Pedro RNCA, AZ 9 Jan
205. Green-tailed Towhee San Pedro RNCA, AZ 9 Jan
206. Yellow-headed Blackbird San Pedro RNCA, AZ 9 Jan
207. Rivoli's Hummingbird Battiste Bed & Breakfast 9 Jan
208. Broad-billed Hummingbird Battiste Bed & Breakfast 9 Jan
209. Yellow-eyed Junco Battiste Bed & Breakfast 9 Jan
210. Scott's Oriole Battiste Bed & Breakfast 9 Jan
211. Western Screech-Owl Carr Canyon, AZ 9 Jan
212. Whiskered Screech-Owl Carr Canyon, AZ 9 Jan
213. Rufous-capped Warbler Florida Canyon, AZ 10 Jan
214. Black-tailed Gnatcatcher Amado WTP, AZ 10 Jan

215. Rufous-winged Sparrow Amado WTP, AZ 10 Jan

2. Ferruginous Hawk Hurley, NM 10 Jan

217. Wood Duck San Felipe Creek, TX 12 Jan

218. Ringed Kingfisher San Felipe Creek, TX 12 Jan

219. Golden-fronted Woodpecker San Felipe Creek, 12 Jan

220. Great Kiskadee San Felipe Creek, TX 12 Jan

221. Black-crested Titmouse San Felipe Creek, TX 12 Jan

222. Carolina Wren San Felipe Creek, TX 12 Jan

223. Cedar Waxwing San Felipe Creek, TX 12 Jan

224. Chihuahuan Raven Eagle Pass, TX 12 Jan

225. Crested Caracara Eagle Pass, TX 12 Jan

226. Mottled Duck Laredo, TX 12 Jan

227. Northern Bobwhite Laredo, TX 12 Jan

228. Black Vulture Laredo, TX 12 Jan

229. Gray Hawk Laredo, TX 12 Jan

230. Red-billed Pigeon Laredo, TX 12 Jan

231. Yellow-bellied Sapsucker Laredo, TX 12 Jan

232. Cave Swallow Laredo, TX 12 Jan

233. House Wren Laredo, TX 12 Jan

234. Long-billed Thrasher Laredo, TX 12 Jan

235. Morelet's Seedeater Laredo, TX 12 Jan

236. Olive Sparrow Laredo, TX 12 Jan

237. Black-bellied Whistling-Duck Weslaco, TX 13 Jan

238. Plain Chachalaca Weslaco, TX 13 Jan

239. Green Heron Weslaco, TX 13 Jan

240. White-tipped Dove Weslaco, TX 13 Jan

241. Buff-bellied Hummingbird Weslaco, TX 13 Jan

242. Green Kingfisher Frontera Audubon Center, TX 13 Jan

243. Green Parakeet Frontera Audubon Center, TX 13 Jan

244. Tropical Kingbird Frontera Audubon Center, TX 13 Jan

245. White-eyed Vireo Frontera Audubon Center, TX 13 Jan

246. Blue-headed Vireo Frontera Audubon Center, TX 13 Jan

247. Green Jay Frontera Audubon Center, TX 13 Jan

248. Clay-colored Thrush Frontera Audubon Center, 13 Jan
249. Ovenbird Frontera Audubon Center, TX 13 Jan
250. Black-and-white Warbler Frontera Audubon, TX 13 Jan
251. Tropical Parula Frontera Audubon Center, TX 13 Jan
252. Black-throated Green Warbler Weslaco, TX 13 Jan
253. Wilson's Warbler Frontera Audubon, TX 13 Jan
254. Crimson-collared Grosbeak Frontera, TX 13 Jan
255. Black-headed Grosbeak Frontera Audubon, TX 13 Jan
256. Painted Bunting Frontera Audubon Center, TX 13 Jan
257. American Goldfinch Frontera Audubon, TX 13 Jan
258. Least Grebe Santa Ana NWR, TX 13 Jan
259. Northern Jacana Santa Ana NWR, TX 13 Jan
260. Lesser Yellowlegs Santa Ana NWR, TX 13 Jan
261. Eastern Phoebe Santa Ana NWR, TX 13 Jan
262. Common Yellowthroat Santa Ana NWR, TX 13 Jan
263. Tricolored Heron Anzalduas Park, TX 13 Jan
264. White-tailed Kite Anzalduas Park, TX 13 Jan
265. White-tailed Hawk Anzalduas Park, TX 13 Jan
266. Vermilion Flycatcher Anzalduas Park, TX 13 Jan
267. Sprague's Pipit Anzalduas Park, TX 13 Jan
268. Anhinga Bentsen-Rio Grande SP, TX 14 Jan
269. Swainson's Hawk Robstown, TX 14 Jan
270. Barred Owl Lyons/Shelley Park, TX 14 Jan
271. Greater Pewee Lyons/Shelley Park, TX 14 Jan
272. Couch's Kingbird Lyons/Shelley Park, TX 14 Jan
273. Carolina Chickadee Lyons/Shelley Park, TX 14 Jan
274. Golden-crowned Warbler Lyons/Shelley Park, TX 14 Jan
275. Flame-colored Tanager Lyons/Shelley Park, TX 14 Jan
276. Roseate Spoonbill Lamar Beach Rd., TX 14 Jan
277. Whooping Crane Lamar Beach Rd., TX 14 Jan
278. Laughing Gull Lamar Beach Rd., TX 14 Jan
279. Boat-tailed Grackle Lamar Beach Rd., TX 14 Jan
280. Snowy Plover Corpus Christi, TX 14 Jan

281. Virginia Rail Hazel Bazemore Park, TX 14 Jan

282. Common Pauraque Hazel Bazemore Park, TX 14 Jan

283. Reddish Egret Mustang Island, TX 15 Jan

284. White Ibis Mustang Island, TX 15 Jan

285. Piping Plover Mustang Island, TX 15 Jan

286. Lesser Black-backed Gull Mustang Island, TX 15 Jan

287. Black Tern Mustang Island, TX 15 Jan

288. American Bittern Turnbull Birding Center, TX 15 Jan

289. Little Blue Heron Turnbull Birding Center, TX 15 Jan

290. Gray Catbird Turnbull Birding Center, TX 15 Jan

291. Common Ground-Dove Corpus Christi, TX 15 Jan

292. Lark Sparrow Corpus Christi, TX 15 Jan

293. Bronzed Cowbird Corpus Christi, TX 15 Jan

294. Blue Jay Allston St., Houston, TX 16 Jan

295. American Woodcock Houston Arboretum, TX 16 Jan

296. Red-bellied Woodpecker Houston Arboretum, TX 16 Jan

297. Tufted Titmouse Houston Arboretum, TX 16 Jan

298. Pine Warbler Houston Arboretum, TX 16 Jan

299. White-throated Sparrow Houston Arboretum, TX 16 Jan

300. Fulvous Whistling-Duck Hermann Park, TX 16 Jan

301. Egyptian Goose Hermann Park, TX 16 Jan

302. Downy Woodpecker Hermann Park, TX 16 Jan

303. American Black Duck Carlyle Lake, IL 19 Jan

304. American Tree Sparrow Carlyle Lake, IL 19 Jan

305. Cackling Goose Carlyle Lake, IL 19 Jan

306. Glaucous Gull Carlyle Lake, IL 19 Jan

307. Great Black-backed Gull Carlyle Lake, IL 19 Jan

308. Rough-legged Hawk Ferrin Rd., Carlyle, IL 19 Jan

309. Eastern Meadowlark Wortman Rd., Carlyle, IL 19 Jan

310. Rusty Blackbird Coles Creek Rd., Carlyle, IL 19 Jan

311. Common Grackle Coles Creek Rd., Carlyle, IL 19 Jan

312. Short-eared Owl Sand Ridge Rd., Carlyle, IL 19 Jan

313. Eurasian Tree Sparrow Ballwin, MO 21 Jan

314. Mute Swan Riverlands Sanctuary, MO 23 Jan

315. Trumpeter Swan Riverlands Sanctuary, MO 23 Jan

316. Tundra Swan Riverlands Sanctuary, MO 23 Jan

317. Black-capped Chickadee CBCA, MO 23 Jan

318. Eastern Bluebird Busch CA, MO 23 Jan

319. Pileated Woodpecker Busch CA, MO 24 Jan

320. Clapper Rail St. Marks NWR, FL 27 Jan

321. Swamp Sparrow St. Marks NWR, FL 27 Jan

322. Sedge Wren St. Marks NWR, FL 27 Jan

323. Yellow-throated Warbler St. Marks NWR, FL 27 Jan

324. Brown-headed Nuthatch St. Marks NWR, FL 27 Jan

325. Nelson's Sparrow St. Marks NWR, FL 27 Jan

326. Henslow's Sparrow St. Marks NWR, FL 27 Jan

327. Eastern Towhee St. Marks NWR, FL 27 Jan

328. Fish Crow Suncoast Blvd., Homosassa, FL 27 Jan

329. Magnificent Frigatebird Bunche Beach Pres., FL 28 Jan

330. American Oystercatcher Bunche Beach Pres., FL 28 Jan

331. Wilson's Plover Bunche Beach Pres., FL 28 Jan

332. Short-billed Dowitcher Bunche Beach Pres., FL 28 Jan

333. American Flamingo Bunche Beach Pres., FL 28 Jan

334. Wood Stork Florida Panther NWR, FL 28 Jan

335. Short-tailed Hawk Big Cypress Nat. Preserve, FL 28 Jan

336. Summer Tanager Markham Park, FL 28 Jan

337. Glossy Ibis Markham Park, FL 29 Jan

338. Gray-headed Swamphen Markham Park, FL 29 Jan

339. Monk Parakeet Markham Park, FL 29 Jan

340. American Redstart Markham Park, FL 29 Jan

341. Northern Parula Markham Park, FL 29 Jan

342. Palm Warbler Markham Park, FL 29 Jan

343. Prairie Warbler Markham Park, FL 29 Jan

344. Western Spindalis Markham Park, FL 29 Jan

345. Indigo Bunting Markham Park, FL 29 Jan

346. Spot-breasted Oriole Markham Park, FL 29 Jan

347. Red-whiskered Bulbul Kendallwood area, FL 29 Jan
348. White-winged Parakeet Ocean Bank, FL 29 Jan
349. Common Myna 7th Street, Miami, FL 29 Jan
350. Scaly-breasted Munia Charles Deering Estate, FL 30 Jan
351. Great Crested Flycatcher Black Point Marina, FL 30 Jan
352. Ruby-throated Hummingbird Matheson Park, FL 30 Jan
353. Yellow-throated Vireo Matheson Park, FL 30 Jan
354. Snail Kite Loxahatchee NWR, FL 30 Jan
355. Limpkin Loxahatchee NWR, FL 30 Jan
356. Smooth-billed Ani Loxahatchee NWR, FL 30 Jan
357. Muscovy Duck Boynton Beach, FL 31 Jan
358. Purple Gallinule Loxahatchee NWR, FL 31 Jan
359. Nanday Parakeet Loxahatchee NWR, FL 31 Jan
360. Grasshopper Sparrow Loxahatchee NWR, FL 31 Jan
361. Least Bittern Green Cay Wetlands, FL 31 Jan
362. Nashville Warbler Green Cay Wetlands, FL 31 Jan
363. Northern Gannet Wavecrest Ave, Indiatlantic, FL 31 Jan
364. Florida Scrub-Jay Ocala NF, FL 1 Feb
365. Eastern Screech-Owl Little St. Simons Island, GA 7 Feb
366. Saltmarsh Sparrow Little St. Simons Island, GA 12 Feb
367. Red-throated Loon Little St. Simons Island, GA 13 Feb
368. Field Sparrow Little St. Simons Island, GA 15 Feb
369. Zenaida Dove Long Key SP, FL 22 Feb
370. Black Rail Everglades NP, FL 22 Feb
371. Scissor-tailed Flycatcher Everglades NP, FL 22 Feb
372. Blue Bunting Frontera Audubon Center, TX 1 Mar
373. Hooded Oriole Frontera Audubon Center, TX 1 Mar
374. Red-crowned Parrot Indiana Ave, Weslaco, TX 1 Mar
375. Hook-billed Kite Bentsen-Rio Grande WBC, TX 2 Mar
376. Northern Beardless-Tyrannulet Mission, TX 2 Mar
377. Altamira Oriole Bentsen-Rio Grande WBC, TX 2 Mar
378. Audubon's Oriole Bentsen-Rio Grande WBC, TX 2 Mar
379. Aplomado Falcon Boca Chica, Brownsville, TX 3 Mar

380. Cassin's Sparrow Laguna Atascosa NWR, TX 3 Mar

381. Gull-billed Tern Shore Dr., Port Isabel, TX 3 Mar

382. Harris's Sparrow Kiehl River Bend Park, TX 3 Mar

383. Chestnut-collared Longspur Brownfield, TX 4 Mar

384. Winter Wren Lubbock, TX 5 Mar

385. Scaled Quail Tahoka, TX 6 Mar

386. Common Crane Brownfield, TX 6 Mar

387. Lewis's Woodpecker Buena Vista, CO 7 Mar

388. Mountain Chickadee Buena Vista, CO 7 Mar

389. Mountain Bluebird Buena Vista, CO 7 Mar

390. Pinyon Jay Buena Vista, CO 7 Mar

391. Hairy Woodpecker Buena Vista, CO 8 Mar

392. Black-billed Magpie Buena Vista, CO 8 Mar

393. Pygmy Nuthatch Buena Vista, CO 8 Mar

394. Northern Goshawk Chaffee, CO 8 Mar

395. Clark's Nutcracker Chaffee, CO 8 Mar

396. Barrow's Goldeneye Buena Vista, CO 9 Mar

397. Canada Jay Monarch Pass, CO 9 Mar

398. Cassin's Finch Buena Vista, CO 10 Mar

399. Sage Thrasher Monticello, UT 11 Mar

400. Prairie Falcon Slickhorn Canyon, UT 12 Mar

401. Woodhouse's Scrub-Jay Slickhorn Canyon, UT 12 Mar

402. Townsend's Solitaire Slickhorn Canyon, UT 12 Mar

403. Juniper Titmouse Blanding, UT 14 Mar

404. Williamson's Sapsucker San Isabel NF, CO 18 Mar

405. Long-eared Owl Barr Lake SP, CO 19 Mar

406. Pine Grosbeak State Forest SP, CO 19 Mar

407. Gray-crowned Rosy-Finch Walden, CO 20 Mar

408. Evening Grosbeak Hogadon Rd., Casper, WY 21 Mar

409. Greater Sage-Grouse WY 22 Mar

410. Northern Shrike Shoshone NF, WY 22 Mar

411. American Dipper Sinks Canyon SP, WY 22 Mar

412. Chukar Timberline Trail, Lander, WY 23 Mar

413. Ring-necked Pheasant Lander, WY 23 Mar
414. Black Rosy-Finch Lander, WY 23 Mar
415. Sagebrush Sparrow Hudson, WY 26 Mar
416. Brown-capped Rosy-Finch Mesa, CO 27 Mar
417. Red Crossbill Grand Mesa, CO 27 Mar
418. Gunnison Sage-Grouse Waunita Lek, CO 28 Mar
419. Boreal Owl Grand Mesa, CO 28 Mar
420. Common Poorwill Roswell, NM 29 Mar
421. Rose-throated Becard Cluff Ranch, AZ 29 Mar
422. Bell's Vireo Cluff Ranch, AZ 29 Mar
423. Yellow Warbler Cluff Ranch, AZ 29 Mar
424. Cliff Swallow Safford, AZ 29 Mar
425. Lesser Prairie-Chicken Roswell Area, NM 30 Mar
426. Brewer's Sparrow Roswell, NM 30 Mar
427. Black-chinned Hummingbird Junction, TX 30 Mar
428. Golden-cheeked Warbler Junction, TX 30 Mar
429. Black-capped Vireo South Llano River SP, TX 31 Mar
430. Yellow-breasted Vireo South Llano River SP, TX 31 Mar
431. Broad-winged Hawk Houston, TX 1 Apr
432. Purple Martin Houston, TX 1 Apr
433. Chimney Swift W.G. Jones SF, TX 2 Apr
434. Red-cockaded Woodpecker W.G. Jones SF, TX 2 Apr
435. Upland Sandpiper Attwater P. Chicken NWR, TX 4 Apr
436. American Golden-Plover Bolivar Flats, TX 6 Apr
437. Semipalmated Sandpiper Bolivar Flats, TX 6 Apr
438. Least Tern Bolivar Flats, TX 6 Apr
439. Common Tern Galveston Seawall, TX 6 Apr
440. Sandwich Tern Galveston Seawall, TX 6 Apr
441. Chuck-will's-widow High Island, TX 7 Apr
442. Swainson's Thrush High Is.-Boy Scout Woods, TX 7 Apr
443. Brown Thrasher High Is.-Boy Scout Woods, TX 7 Apr
444. Worm-eating Warbler High Island, TX 7 Apr
445. Prothonotary Warbler High Island, TX 7 Apr

446. Tennessee Warbler High Is.-Boy Scout Woods, TX 7 Apr

447. Hooded Warbler High Is.-Boy Scout Woods, TX 7 Apr

448. King Rail Anahuac NWR, TX 7 Apr

449. Yellow-crowned Night-Heron Anahuac NWR, TX 7 Apr

450. Eastern Kingbird Anahuac NWR, TX 7 Apr

451. Seaside Sparrow Anahuac NWR, TX 7 Apr

452. Orchard Oriole Anahuac NWR, TX 7 Apr

453. Whimbrel Anahuac NWR, TX 7 Apr

454. Pectoral Sandpiper Anahuac NWR, TX 7 Apr

455. Swallow-tailed Kite Grosse Tete, LA 8 Apr

456. Acadian Flycatcher Sherburne WMA, LA 8 Apr

457. Red-eyed Vireo Sherburne WMA, LA 8 Apr

458. Wood Thrush Sherburne WMA, LA 8 Apr

459. Swainson's Warbler Sherburne WMA, LA 8 Apr

460. Kentucky Warbler Sherburne WMA, LA 8 Apr

461. Red-headed Woodpecker Olustee Bfld SP, FL 9 Apr

462. Purple Sandpiper Lighthouse Point Park, FL 9 Apr

463. Bachman's Sparrow Torreya SP, FL 9 Apr

464. White-crowned Pigeon Bill Baggs SP, FL 11 Apr

465. Northern Waterthrush Bill Baggs SP, FL 11 Apr

466. Blackpoll Warbler Bill Baggs SP, FL 11 Apr

467. Black-throated Blue Warbler Bill Baggs SP, FL 11 Apr

468. Mangrove Cuckoo Black Point Marina, FL 11 Apr

469. Common Nighthawk Everglades NP, FL 12 Apr

470. Western Kingbird 392nd St., Homestead, FL 12 Apr

471. Gray Kingbird 392nd St., Homestead, FL 12 Apr

472. Baltimore Oriole 320th St., Homestead, FL 12 Apr

473. Shiny Cowbird 320th St., Homestead, FL 12 Apr

474. Black-whiskered Vireo Carysfort Circle, FL 13 Apr

475. Cape May Warbler Carysfort Circle, FL 13 Apr

476. Masked Booby Hospital Key, FL 15 Apr

477. Brown Noddy Fort Jefferson, FL 15 Apr

478. Black Noddy Fort Jefferson, FL 15 Apr

479. Sooty Tern Fort Jefferson, FL 15 Apr
480. Bank Swallow Fort Jefferson, FL 17 Apr
481. Yellow-billed Cuckoo Fort Jefferson, FL 15 Apr
482. Rose-breasted Grosbeak Fort Jefferson, FL 17 Apr
483. Magnolia Warbler Mizell-Johnson SP, FL 18 Apr
484. Antillean Nighthawk Big Pine Key, FL 19 Apr
485. Cuban Vireo Ft. Zachary Taylor SP, FL 19 Apr
486. Solitary Sandpiper J. Davis Parish Landfill, LA 21 Apr
487. Dickcissel J. Davis Parish Landfill, LA 21 Apr
488. Mississippi Kite Grosse Tete, LA 21 Apr
489. Eastern Wood-Pewee Peveto Woods, LA 21 Apr
490. Golden-winged Warbler Peveto Woods, LA 21 Apr
491. Scarlet Tanager Peveto Woods, LA 21 Apr
492. Blue Grosbeak Peveto Woods, LA 21 Apr
493. Warbling Vireo Sabine Woods, TX 22 Apr
494. Veery Sabine Woods, TX 22 Apr
495. Willow Flycatcher Sabine Woods, TX 22 Apr
496. Gray-checked Thrush Sabine Woods, TX 22 Apr
497. Blackburnian Warbler Sabine Woods, TX 22 Apr
498. Stilt Sandpiper Texas Point NWR, TX 22 Apr
499. Wilson's Phalarope Texas Point NWR, TX 22 Apr
500. Hudsonian Godwit Winnie, TX 22 Apr
501. Cerulean Warbler Smith Oaks Sanctuary, TX 22 Apr
502. Chestnut-sided Warbler Smith Oaks Sanct. TX 22 Apr
503. Baird's Sandpiper Pattison, TX 23 Apr
504. Buff-breasted Sandpiper Pattison, TX 23 Apr
505. Brown-crested Flycatcher Junction, TX 24 Apr
506. Clay-colored Sparrow Junction, TX 24 Apr
507. Gray Vireo Ft. Lancaster Overlook, TX 24 Apr
508. Common Black Hawk Big Bend NP, TX 24 Apr
509. Lesser Nighthawk Big Bend NP, TX 24 Apr
510. Elf Owl Big Bend NP, TX 24 Apr
511. Mexican Whip-poor-will Big Bend NP, TX 25 Apr

512. Flammulated Owl Big Bend NP, TX 25 Apr
513. Blue-throated Hummingbird Big Bend NP, TX 25 Apr
514. Broad-tailed Hummingbird Big Bend NP, TX 25 Apr
515. Cordilleran Flycatcher Big Bend NP, TX 25 Apr
516. Colima Warbler Big Bend NP, TX 25 Apr
517. Hepatic Tanager Big Bend NP, TX 25 Apr
518. Western Tanager Big Bend NP, TX 25 Apr
519. Clark's Grebe McNary Reservoir, TX 25 Apr
520. Lucifer Hummingbird Ash Canyon B&B, AZ 26 Apr
521. Costa's Hummingbird Ash Canyon B&B, AZ 26 Apr
522. Rufous Hummingbird Ash Canyon B&B, AZ 26 Apr
523. Spotted Owl Miller Canyon, AZ 26 Apr
524. Cassin's Kingbird Miller Canyon, AZ 26 Apr
525. Plumbeous Vireo Onion Saddle, AZ 26 Apr
526. Violet-green Swallow Stateline Rd., AZ 26 Apr
527. Mexican Chickadee Barfoot Park, AZ 26 Apr
528. Grace's Warbler Silver Creek, AZ 26 Apr
529. Tufted Flycatcher Ramsey Canyon, AZ 27 Apr
530. Cassin's Vireo Ramsey Canyon, AZ 27 Apr
531. Black-throated Gray Warbler Ramsey Cyn, AZ 27 Apr
532. Red-faced Warbler Ramsey Canyon, AZ 27 Apr
533. Olive-sided Flycatcher Patagonia Rest Area, AZ 27 Apr
534. Thick-billed Kingbird Patagonia Rest Area, AZ 27 Apr
535. Dusky Flycatcher Carr Canyon, AZ 27 Apr
536. Buff-breasted Flycatcher Carr Canyon, AZ 27 Apr
537. Dusky-capped Flycatcher Carr Canyon, AZ 27 Apr
538. Ash-throated Flycatcher Paton Center, AZ 27 Apr
539. Botteri's Sparrow Circulo Montana, Nogales, AZ 27 Apr
540. Band-tailed Pigeon Patagonia, AZ 28 Apr
541. Violet-crowned Hummingbird Patagonia, AZ 28 Apr
542. Pacific-slope Flycatcher Patagonia, AZ 28 Apr
543. Lucy's Warbler Patagonia, AZ 28 Apr
544. Buff-collared Nightjar California Gulch, AZ 28 Apr

545. Virginia's Warbler California Gulch, AZ 28 Apr

546. Vaux's Swift Patagonia Highway, AZ 28 Apr

547. Five-striped Sparrow California Gulch, AZ 29 Apr

548. Zone-tailed Hawk Sycamore Canyon, AZ 29 Apr

549. Gilded Flicker Saguaro NP, AZ 29 Apr

550. Bullock's Oriole Saguaro NP, AZ 29 Apr

551. Bendire's Thrasher Baseline Rd., AZ 29 Apr

552. Rosy-faced Lovebird Scottsdale, AZ 29 Apr

553. Lazuli Bunting Grand Canyon NP, AZ 1 May

554. Ross's Goose Apollo Park, CA 2 May

555. Bell's Sparrow Avenue C, Lancaster, CA 2 May

556. California Quail Avenue B, Rosamond, CA 2 May

557. LeConte's Thrasher Avenue B, Rosamond, CA 2 May

558. Tricolored Blackbird Holiday Lake, CA 2 May

559. California Thrasher, CA 2 May

560. Lawrence's Goldfinch , CA 2 May

561. Oak Titmouse Angeles NF, CA 2 May

562. Allen's Hummingbird Rancho Palos Verde, CA 2 May

563. California Gnatcatcher Rancho Palos Verde, CA 2 May

564. Spotted Dove Virginia St., Lynwood, CA 2 May

565. Black Scoter Ballona Creek, CA 2 May

566. Elegant Tern Ballona Creek, CA 2 May

567. Wandering Tattler Ballona Creek, CA 2 May

568. Mountain Quail Los Angeles NF, CA 2 May

569. Red-breasted Sapsucker Angeles Crest Hwy., CA 3 May

570. White-headed Woodpecker Angeles NF, CA 3 May

571. Western Wood-Pewee Angeles NF, CA 3 May

572. Hutton's Vireo Angeles NF, CA 3 May

573. Hermit Warbler Angeles NF, CA 3 May

574. Purple Finch Angeles NF, CA 3 May

575. Black Oystercatcher Los Angeles, CA 3 May

576. Parasitic Jaeger San Pedro Channel, CA 3 May

577. Sooty Shearwater San Pedro Channel, CA 3 May

578. Cassin's Auklet North Pacific Ocean, CA 3 May

579. Pink-footed Shearwater North Pacific Ocean, CA 3 May

580. Red-necked Phalarope Pacific Ocean Pelagic, CA 4 May

581. Red Phalarope Pacific Ocean Pelagic, CA 4 May

582. South Polar Skua Pacific Ocean Pelagic, CA 4 May

583. Pomarine Jaeger Pacific Ocean Pelagic, CA 4 May

584. Rhinoceros Auklet Pacific Ocean Pelagic, CA 4 May

585. Sabine's Gull Pacific Ocean Pelagic, CA 4 May

586. Laysan Albatross Pacific Ocean Pelagic, CA 4 May

587. Black-footed Albatross Pacific Ocean Pelagic, CA 4 May

588. Leach's Storm-Petrel Pacific Ocean Pelagic, CA 4 May

589. Ashy Storm-Petrel Pacific Ocean Pelagic, CA 4 May

590. Northern Fulmar Pacific Ocean Pelagic, CA 4 May

591. Murphy's Petrel Pacific Ocean Pelagic, CA 4 May

592. Hawaiian Petrel Pacific Ocean Pelagic, CA 4 May

593. Cook's Petrel Pacific Ocean Pelagic, CA 4 May

594. Parakeet Auklet Pacific Ocean Pelagic, OR 5 May

595. Arctic Tern Pacific Ocean Pelagic, OR 5 May

596. Fork-tailed Storm-Petrel Pacific Ocean Pelagic, OR 5 May

597. Pigeon Guillemot Strait of Juan de Fuca, WA 6 May

598. Marbled Murrelet Strait of Juan de Fuca, WA 6 May

599. Pacific Golden-Plover Panama Flats, Victoria, BC 6 May

600. Eurasian Skylark Victoria Airport, BC 6 May

601. Yellow-billed Loon Port Angeles, WA 6 May

602. Bay-breasted Warbler Magee Marsh, OH 10 May

603. Canada Warbler Ottawa NWR, OH 10 May

604. Black-billed Cuckoo Magee Marsh, OH 11 May

605. Curlew Sandpiper Raab Rd., Holland, OH 12 May

606. Least Flycatcher Magee Marsh, OH 12 May

607. Kirtland's Warbler Magee Marsh, OH 12 May

608. Blue-winged Warbler Irwin Prairie State NP, OH 12 May

609. Tufted Duck Marsh, Adak, AK 15 May

610. Lapland Longspur Marsh, Adak, AK 15 May

611. Smew Airport Runway, AK May
612. Rock Ptarmigan Adak Airport, Adak, AK May
613. Ruff Adak Airport, Adak,AK May
614. Common Snipe Adak Airport, Adak, AK May
615. Gyrfalcon Adak Airport, Adak, AK May
6. Common Eider Adak Island, AK May
617. Kittlitz's Murrelet Adak Island, AK May
618. Bar-tailed Godwit Adak Airport, Adak, AK May
619. Short-tailed Albatross Attu Island, AK 17 May
620. Short-tailed Shearwater Attu Island, AK 17 May
621. Thick-billed Murre Attu Island, AK 17 May
622. Ancient Murrelet Attu Island, AK 17 May
623. Least Auklet Attu Island, AK 17 May
624. Tufted Puffin Attu Island, AK 17 May
625. Black-legged Kittiwake Attu Island, AK 17 May
626. Red-legged Kittiwake Attu Island, AK 17 May
627. Crested Auklet Attu Island, AK 18 May
628. Slaty-backed Gull Kiska Island, AK 18 May
629. Red-faced Cormorant Attu Island, AK 19 May
630. Snow Bunting Attu Island, AK 19 May
631. Brambling Attu Island, AK 19 May
632. Long-toed Stint Attu Island, AK 20 May
633. Rock Sandpiper Attu Island, AK 20 May
634. Wood Sandpiper Attu Island, AK 20 May
635. Snowy Owl Attu Island, AK 20 May
636. Rustic Bunting Attu Island, AK 20 May
637. Horned Puffin Attu Island, AK 21 May
638. Emperor Goose Attu Island, AK 21 May
639. Aleutian Tern Attu Island, AK 25 May
640. Eyebrowed Thrush Attu Island, AK 25 May
641. White Wagtail Attu Island, AK 26 May
642. Terek Sandpiper Attu Island, AK 26 May
643. Common Sandpiper Attu Island, AK 26 May

644. Gray-tailed Tattler Attu Island, AK 26 May
645. Mottled Petrel Puk-uk Pelagic, AK 27 May
646. Whiskered Auklet Adak Island, AK 29 May
647. Far Eastern Curlew Adak Island, AK 29 May
648. Boreal Chickadee Chugach SP, Anchorage, AK 30 May
649. Varied Thrush Far North Bicentennial Park, AK 30 May
650. Bohemian Waxwing Glenn Hwy., Palmer, AK 30 May
651. Common Redpoll Hillside Park, AK 31 May
652. Pine Flycatcher Aliso Spring, AZ 1 Jun
653. Northern Pygmy-Owl Madera Canyon, AZ 2 Jun
654. Sulphur-bellied Flycatcher Madera Canyon, AZ 2 Jun
655. Varied Bunting Madera Canyon, AZ 2 Jun
656. Slate-throated Redstart Pinery Canyon, AZ 3 Jun
657. Olive Warbler Mt. Lemmon, AZ 5 Jun
658. Sharp-tailed Grouse Sentinel Butte, ND 10 Jun
659. Bobolink Little Missouri Nat. Grass., ND 10 Jun
660. Baird's Sparrow Talkington Dam, ND 10 Jun
661. Franklin's Gull Dewald Slough, ND 10 Jun
662. White-rumped Sandpiper Dewald Slough, ND 10 Jun
663. Yellow-bellied Flycatcher McDavitt, MN 11 Jun
664. Alder Flycatcher McDavitt, MN 11 Jun
665. Connecticut Warbler McDavitt, MN 11 Jun
666. Mourning Warbler McDavitt, MN 11 Jun
667. LeConte's Sparrow McDavitt, MN 11 Jun
668. Manx Shearwater Revere Beach, MA Jun
669. Great Cormorant Nahant, MA Jun
670. Bicknell's Thrush Mount Holly, VT 17 Jun
671. Little Egret Tidewater Farm, Falmouth, ME 19 Jun
672. Black Guillemot Harpswell, ME 19 Jun
673. Atlantic Puffin Eastern Egg Rock, ME 21 Jun
674. Roseate Tern Eastern Egg Rock, ME 21 Jun
675. Razorbill Eastern Egg Rock, ME 22 Jun
676. Philadelphia Vireo Mt. Washington Auto Rd., NH 23 Jun

677. Eastern Whip-poor-will Illinois Beach SP, IL 26 Jun
678. Long-tailed Jaeger Nome River mouth, AK 28 Jun
679. Eastern Yellow Wagtail Nome River mouth, AK 28 Jun
680. Hoary Redpoll Nome River mouth, AK 28 Jun
681. Willow Ptarmigan Nome-Kougarok Rd., AK 29 Jun
682. Arctic Loon Nome-Kougarok Rd., AK 29 Jun
683. Bristle-thighed Curlew Nome-Kougarok Rd., AK 29 Jun
684. Arctic Warbler Nome-Kougarok Rd., AK 29 Jun
685. Northern Wheatear Nome-Council Rd., AK 30 Jun
686. Common Ringed-Plover Teller, AK 1 Jul
687. Spectacled Eider Safety Sound, Nome, AK 2 Jul
688. Bluethroat Nome-Kougarok Rd., AK 2 Jul
689. King Eider Safety Sound, Nome, AK 2 Jul
690. Gray Flycatcher Cedro Creek, NM 7 Jul
691. Groove-billed Ani Mitchell Lk. Audubon Cen., TX 11 Jul
692. Mexican Violetear Rio Medina, TX 11 Jul
693. Plain-capped Starthroat Santa Rita Lodge, AZ 13 Jul
694. Berylline Hummingbird Beatty's Guest Ranch, AZ 15 Jul
695. Nutting's Flycatcher Bill Williams R. NWR, AZ 20 Jul
696. Black Storm-Petrel North Pacific Ocean, CA 21 Jul
697. Island Scrub-Jay Santa Cruz Island, CA 22 Jul
698. Black Swift Andrew Molera SP, CA 23 Jul
699. California Condor Highway 1, Big Sur, CA 23 Jul
700. Himalayan Snowcock Island Lake, NV 25 Jul
701. Great Gray Owl Teton, WY 27 Jul
702. Dusky Grouse Glacier NP-Logan Pass, MT 29 Jul
703. Am. Three-toed Woodpecker Glacier NP, MT 29 Jul
704. White-winged Crossbill Glacier NP, MT 29 Jul
705. MacGillivray's Warbler Glacier NP, MT 29 Jul
706. Spruce Grouse North Fork Rd., Polebridge, MT 30 Jul
707. Calliope Hummingbird Flathead NF, MT 30 Jul
708. Black-backed Woodpecker Glacier NP, MT 31 Jul
709. Gray Partridge US 89, Choteau, MT 31 Jul

710. McCown's Longspur Bellview Rd., MT 31 Jul

711. Scripp's Murrelet Shearwater Journeys, CA 13 Aug

712. Craveri's Murrelet Shearwater Journeys, CA 13 Aug

713. Wilson's Storm-Petrel Shearwater Journeys, CA 13 Aug

714. Cory's Shearwater Hatteras Pelagic, NC 26 Aug

715. Audubon's Shearwater Hatteras Pelagic, NC 26 Aug

716. Bridled Tern Hatteras Pelagic, NC 26 Aug

717. Black-capped Petrel Hatteras Pelagic, NC 26 Aug

718. Great Shearwater Hatteras Pelagic, NC 26 Aug

719. Band-rumped Storm-Petrel Hatteras Pelagic, NC 26 Aug

720. White-tailed Tropicbird Hatteras Pelagic, NC 26 Aug

721. Sharp-tailed Sandpiper Gambell, AK 30 Aug

722. Red-throated Pipit Gambell, AK 30 Aug

723. Siberian Accentor Gambell, AK 7 Sept

724. Iceland Gull Gambell, AK 11 Sept

725. Thayer's Gull Gambell, AK 11 Sept

726. Steller's Eider Gambell, AK 12 Sept

727. McKay's Bunting Gambell, AK 18 Sept

728. Northern Hawk-Owl Glenn Hwy., Palmer, AK 26 Sept

729. Variegated Flycatcher South Padre Island, TX 2 Oct

730. Sooty Grouse Mt. Rainier NP, WA 9 Oct

731. Ruffed Grouse Mt. Rainier NP, WA 10 Oct

732. White-tailed Ptarmigan Mt. Rainier NP, WA 10 Oct

733. Little Stint San Jacinto Wildlife Area, CA 12 Oct

734. Blue-footed Booby Sugarloaf Is., Offshore, CA 17 Oct

735. Buller's Shearwater Offshore, CA 17 Oct

736. Lesser Sand-Plover Point Reyes Ntl. Seashore, CA 19 Oct

737. Least Storm-Petrel Thirty Mile Bank, CA 21 Oct

738. Great Skua, Offshore MA 26 Oct

739. Yellow-legged Gull St. John's, NF 28 Oct

740. Fork-tailed Flycatcher M-35, MI 8 Nov

741. Common Scoter Siletz Bay, OR 13 Nov

742. Mountain Plover Avenue 3E, Yuma, AZ Nov

743. Ruddy Ground-Dove Roll, AZ Nov
744. Amazon Kingfisher Zacate Creek, Laredo, TX 18 Nov
745. Yellow Rail Thornwell Rice Fields, LA 21 Nov
746. Smith's Longspur Penn-Sylvania Prairie, MO 22 Nov
747. Greater Prairie-Chicken Shawnee SFL, KS 25 Nov
748. Pink-footed Goose Ipswich, MA 4 Dec
749. Little Gull Race Point, MA 6 Dec
750. Northern Saw-whet Owl Wellfleet, MA 7 Dec
751. Barnacle Goose St. Charles Cemetery, NY 12 Dec
752. Red-flanked Bluetail Hells Gate SP, ID 27 Dec

Abbreviations Used:
WTP: *Wastewater Treatment Plant*
NWR: *National Wildlife Refuge*
Natl: *National*
WBC: *World Birding Center*
NP: *National Park*
SP: *State Park*
Is: *Island*
Bfld: *Battlefield*
WMA: *Wildlife Management Area*
SFL: *State Fishing Lake*

The paragraph break image is a Peregrine Falcon tail feather
from Stuart, the author's "spark" bird

ABOUT THE AUTHOR

Following his 2016 Big Year, Christian has continued teaching and leading birding tours. His passion for teaching and learning has driven him to constantly seek new opportunities to share his love for nature with others, including instructing at Hog Island Audubon Camp and ABA Young Birder programs in Colorado. When he isn't birding, he enjoys spending time with family and friends, traveling, skiing, climbing, and practicing falconry. Christian Hagenlocher is an emerging author in the field of natural history writing. This is his first book.

ABOUT THE ILLUSTRATOR

Andrew Guttenberg drew his first recognizable bird—a Pileated Woodpecker, before his 2nd birthday. While his skills have increased significantly since then, Andrew still pursues birds with childlike wonder and boundless curiosity. Equally at home in the field or at the drawing table, Andrew does freelance illustration mostly in colored pencil, Micron pen, and gouache. His work has been published in *Birding* Magazine and *Montana Bird Distribution* and can be found online at www.andrewguttenberg.com. When he's not chasing hummingbirds around the neotropics, Andrew can be found in beautiful western Montana, with his wife, Ana Clara.